The Life of
SAINT
CLEOPA

This book, including its English edition preface, is published with
the blessing of His Eminence Teofan, Metropolitan of Moldavia and
Bukovina.
Translated by Reverend Dr. John Downie
Co-Translator: Sorina Chiper, PhD
Book layout and cover design by Archdeacon Alin V. Goga

Patristic Nectar
www.patristicnectar.org
info@patristicnectar.org

The Life of
SAINT CLEOPA

—————— *by* ——————

Archimandrite Ioanichie Bălan

PATRISTIC
NECTAR

Icon of the Pious Saints Cleopa and Paisie from Sihăstria.

Table of Contents

Foreword

In the Gospel of John, after the Lord assures the disciples that the Father "shall give you another Comforter," the "Spirit of truth" (cf. John 14:16-17), he reinforces this promise by adding: "I will not leave you comfortless; I will come to you" (John 14:18). This presence of the Savior in the bimillennial life of the Church most often takes the form of spiritual guides who lead a holy life. When you see the word of the Holy Scriptures embodied in a concrete person, whose spirit gives you rest in the Spirit, indeed you are no longer comfortless, but rather feel like a child in the presence of a caring parent.

Thousands of pilgrims or disciples, clerics or believers, who have had the blessed opportunity to meet Fr. Cleopa Ilie, bear witness to such a life. His life itself, skillfully recounted in these pages by Fr. Ioanichie Bălan, is a source of inspiration and hope for all Christians, regardless of their condition.

The child Constantin Ilie (future monk Cleopa) was born into a large family, without material means, but which gave him the greatest wealth: faith. He was an uneducated man, without theological studies, but a self-taught man who eventually theologized by watering his audience from the renewed wellspring of the texts of the Holy Fathers. He always sought tranquility and humble work, being a shepherd of sheep at the beginning of his monastic life. He accepted, however, out of obedience, to be a preacher and a confessor before the whole world, becoming an unfailing shepherd of souls. He always saw himself as lacking in virtue, as one who felt encouraged by seeing spiritual gifts in those around him. And the Lord even more adorned his soul with the grace and the undeniable sweetness of His presence.

During his lifetime, his steadfast zeal, his embrace of all with an open heart, his words that struck like thunder, his wisdom built on humble obedience—they all brought him quick fame not only throughout the whole country, but also beyond its borders. Especially in the last part of his life, simple people and prominent scholars, believers seeking blessing, people of other confessions and atheists, souls thirsting for a word "of much power," or even journalists eager to have a live experience of the "Cleopa phenomenon," they all gathered on the veranda of his cell in Sihăstria Monastery.

His words were simple, understandable to all, but of great depth. Through humble speech, often condemning himself, he placed himself lower than all, while reorienting all to the higher order of things. A skillful orator, he knew how to attract attention with unexpected phrases such as: *May heaven consume you!* But none of this was thought out in advance or as part of a specific plan. It was all spontaneous, vivid, authentic, as the Spirit inspired him to speak.

A son of the Romanian nation, of this land from which, since ancient times, many guiding stars have risen to the heaven of holiness, Elder Cleopa Ilie is also a living icon of the universality of Orthodoxy. The pages of this book contain, in the last part, an edifying selection, a synthesis of patristic thought, as if specifically made for the contemporary man, who is always in a hurry and lacks the patience to read books in their entirety. Then follows a series of his own words, teachings and spiritual counsel given on various specific occasions.

For example, as we can read in these Synaxarion pages prefaced here, *sometimes, while he was doing his rule of prayers and prostrations, the Elder was sought out persistently by the faithful. Occasionally, he would go out and speak with them for a while, then he would say: "God will tell me, 'You, monk, you have worked in other people's fields but in your own field thorns, thistle and weeds have grown. Do you work My field?' That is why I must work my own field." Then he would return to his cell and continue his rule of prayers.*

Or, in other situations, Father Cleopa used to say, *Don't turn too widely when you're ploughing, 'cause much soil won't be good for sowing,* meaning everything is to be done in moderation. Let's not hurry to embark upon great things that are beyond our inner settlement.

Even though his language is inspired by agricultural works— as we find in many of the Lord's words—the teaching is perfectly applicable in this age of increasingly advanced technology. Those who are engaged in teaching today—especially through the internet and other means of communication—can only do so with great profit if they do not forget their own asceticism, their own self-denial. Words are edifying only if they spring from a contrite heart and self-condemnation.

Here is the wisdom of a *Paterikon*-like Avva, who translates in his life what St. Paul the Apostle teaches us: "Take heed unto thyself, and unto the doctrine; continue in them: for in doing this thou shalt both save thyself, and them that hear thee" (I Timothy 4:16). In an age in which theological schools have multiplied, libraries are filled with spiritual books, and the internet overflows with words of help, we need to pause for a moment and focus our attention on the true work of Christians, that of unceasing repentance and blessed asceticism. Elder Cleopa is the voice that cries out in the desert of words that are not backed up by deeds or of deeds not accomplished for the glory of God.

This volume is published in English in the very year of the proclamation of the canonization of Elder Cleopa Ilie, together with that of his spiritual father, Elder Paisie Olaru. The Holy Synod of the Romanian Orthodox Church approved his canonization, along with that of fifteen other confessor priests, under the title "Pious Saint Cleopa of Sihăstria," who is commemorated on December 2 each year.

We bless this work, its editors and readers, with the hope that the encounter with Pious Saint Cleopa will strengthen their faith and instill in them a longing for God and for the divine life to which He calls us all.

† Teofan
Metropolitan of Moldavia
and Bukovina

Father Josiah
with His Eminence,
Metropolitan Teofan, 2024

Introduction*

Since, in recent years, pilgrimages to Elder Cleopa's tomb have increased, to the joy of us all, we found it appropriate to republish *The Life of Elder Cleopa* in an updated edition, significantly improved with biographical data and numerous original photographs.

The images, which have not been used so far, enrich the text, and will considerably contribute to the success of this long-awaited work.

We cannot forget Saint Cleopa's asceticism,** his love for Christ and for the poor, and the joy with which he greeted any of his spiritual children who would come to him for comfort and words of spiritual benefit.

---

* This is the Introduction to the second edition in Romanian.
** The Romanian term 'nevoință' literally means cutting off one's own will. Generally, it can be translated as 'asceticism', but also involves the whole range of spiritual life: obedience, love, forgiveness, humility, prayer and fasting, self-denial, etc. (*translator's note*, henceforth *t.n.*).

We cannot forget his sacrificial offering of more than 70 years of an ascetic life spent in fasting and prayer. Nor can we forget his kindness, gentleness, and the love with which he would embrace all of his spiritual children and draw us closer to Christ. That is precisely why we love him so much, for his teachings always guide us along the path of salvation.

May Christ, the Savior of the world, rest Elder Cleopa among the host of saints, where there is no pain, no sorrow, nor suffering, but life everlasting.

Archimandrite Ioanichie Balăn

The Nativity of the Theotokos,
8 September, 2001

Part One

His Childhood Home

Archimandrite Cleopa Ilie of blessed memory, our spiritual father, was born in the village of Suliţa in the county of Botoşani,[1] in Romania, on April 10, the year of our Lord 1912.

His parents, Alexandru and Ana Ilie, were living examples of Christian behavior, as they loved God, the church, and their children. They were never absent from the holy services, gave alms and often prayed together with their children, leading a life that was pure and well-pleasing to Christ.

Their house was like a church. As Saint Cleopa would say, "We had a room full of icons only. It was a kind of chapel. We would pray there. In the middle of the night we would wake up, read the Psalter, and make hundreds of prostrations. Then we would go back to sleep."

---

[1] Botoşani is a county, and a town, in the Eastern part of Romania, in the Moldavia region *(t.n.)*.

Father Cleopa's childhood home.

There were no arguments heard in their home, nor inappropriate words, nor other things displeasing to God, but their day-to-day life would flow smoothly like fresh water from a spring, for that was what they had inherited from their forefathers, and such was the Christian tradition of that area.

It was not by coincidence that he was born in that area but through God's providence. Many great people, among whom there were quite a few monks, priests, remarkable and pious Hierarchs, such as Saint John the New of Suceava (1300-1340),[2] came from the same region. We would make no mistake if we were to consider venerable Archimandrite Cleopa Ilie, our spiritual father of blessed memory, as well as his own spiritual father, Hieroschemamonk Paisie Olaru, among their ranks.

---

[2] Saint John the New was a Romanian martyr of the Ottoman Yoke. Born in 1300, he preached the gospel and so was killed in the town of Cetatea Albă, currently Bilhorod of Ukraine. His feast day is celebrated on June 2nd (the day of his martyrdom) and June 24th (the translation of his relics) *(t.n.)*.

Elder Cleopa was chosen by God since his birth to spiritually advise and comfort monastics, priests, and the multitude of the faithful. This reverent priest was the spiritual father and advisor of all those who would ask for his prayers and wanted to follow Christ. He was a blessing from God for our entire country.

The childhood home in which Archimandrite Cleopa Ilie was born was like a living church, but it did not replace the church in the village where the renowned priest of the time, Gheorghe Chiriac, began to serve in 1877. For, as His Reverence himself would say, the inhabitants of Sulița village obeyed their priest like Christ Himself and did nothing without his advice and blessing. For this reason, day-to-day life was peaceful, the church was full of believers and the children, in large numbers, would be the adornment of the village.

This is how Romanian villages were like in the first decades of the 20th century! As such, his parents were blessed by God with ten children, of whom two died at an early age, but eight children—four boys and four girls—survived.

Priest Gheorghe Chiriac,
who baptized
Father Cleopa.

The church in Sulița,
dedicated to Holy Hierarch Nicholas,
where Elder Cleopa's family would go.

His Parents

His Father

According to tradition, his father's ancestors were famous shepherds, originally from the Săliştea Sibiului commune[3] and, due to the religious persecution in the 18th century, they had to leave Ardeal[4] and move to Moldavia, settling down in Botoşani County. This memory has been passed down in the family, from the older generations, that the three maternal brothers, whose surname was Ilie, crossed the Carpathian Mountains into Moldavia. One of them settled in Botoşani County, becoming Saint Cleopa's ancestor.

The second brother, likewise a great sheep herder, settled down in Pipirig-Neamţ commune. Grigore Ilie was his last descendant, who not long ago reposed in the Lord. The third brother became a hermit in Mount Athos, where he reposed.

Alexandru Ilie, Saint Cleopa's father, was born in 1871, on September 12, in Suliţa village, Botoşani county. He was a tall, quiet man and a good householder. In 1902 he married Ana Bercea, originally from Dracşani, a neighboring village. They were married at the local church by the worthy Priest Gheorghe Chiriac, who later also baptized their ten children.

Alexandru was mainly engaged in agriculture, raising livestock and trading animals, and was one of the leading

---

[3] An administrative unit in rural areas that includes several villages *(t.n.)*.

[4] Ardeal is another term for Transylvania, the historical Romanian province which in the 18th century was part of the Austrian empire. In 1698, the Synod of Alba Iulia decided that the local Orthodox Church should be united with the Church of Rome. However, this decision was contested by some Romanian communities which refused the union with the Catholic Church. The persecution mentioned in the text was against the Orthodox Romanians who resisted this union *(t.n.)*.

householders in the village. His family owned 150 sheep, more than 20 large cattle, and 30 hectares of land.[5]

Elder Cleopa used to say the following about his father:

"May God forgive my father. He was a tall man, bald, with a big white beard, and very faithful. Every feast day he would go to church with his children and help the poor. No one ever saw him drunk or cursing or smoking or doing anything else of the kind.

I remember that my father had some boots once. One Sunday, my mother told him, 'Alexandru, wear your boots when you go to church, don't put on your *opinci*.'[6] But my father answered her, 'Woman, have you ever seen a saint painted in the church with boots on? They all wear *opinci*; I will put on *opinci*, too!'

In the morning when we were about to leave for school, our mom would tell us to eat something or to take some food in our knapsack. But Dad would say, 'No! Woman, leave' em alone, they aren't going to die!' My brothers, especially Mihai, would not eat anything until they finished reading the Psalter.

They did not give us any food before we prayed for an hour. Even when it was not during a fasting period, my father would say, 'It's not mealtime for us. When you come from school, in the afternoon. You are not a pig to eat since early in the morning.'

My father could not read, but he feared God. Would any of us fall asleep at night without saying the prayers? Or sit at the table without saying 'Our Father'? Or skip the church service on Sundays? Or would he tolerate it if he were to learn that one of us had cursed, smoked or stolen something? He would never

---

[5] Roughly 74 acres. *(t.n.)*.
[6] Handmade leather wrap shoes that Romanian peasants used to wear, tied-up with a lace around the calf, on top of high woolen socks.

ever be seen doing anything of the kind. He had a belt hanging from a nail on the wall, that he named 'Saint Nicholas.' If he were to catch us doing something bad, heaven forbid! He would say, 'Look here, "Saint Nicholas"! Go and pray! I made you with two eyes, you know how to read, read the Psalter and the prayers from the book!'

Once, when I was coming home from school, I found a harness on the road. I picked it up joyfully and brought it home. When Dad saw me, he asked me where I had stolen it from. And I said, 'I found it and thought it may be useful for us.' But Dad told me firmly, 'Go and take it back and put it right where you took it from, 'cause it wasn't you who put it there.' Then I went back and searched for traces in the dust, to find the spot where I had picked that harness from, since my father was not a man to be trifled with.

"He was the candleholder of the house. He was the master of the family."

Having attained the age of 72, Alexandru Ilie gave up his soul into the hands of Christ on February 23, 1943.

His Mother

Ana Ilie, Saint Cleopa's mother, was born on October 10, 1876, to farmers and good Christian parents. In 1902 she married Alexandru, with whom she had ten children. Of these, five children—four boys and a girl—entered monasticism.

Ana was a simple, short and illiterate woman, with an excellent memory. She often wept, since she had the gift of tears. Her greatest sorrow was that nearly all her children had died young. The only child who survived to old age was Saint Cleopa. Three sons and one daughter reposed in the Lord in monasteries and the others, in their native village. Nevertheless, she was strengthened by God with His gifts so that she could bear the cross that was meant for her.

A widow since 1943, she was brought by Elder Cleopa to the monastery and then she was tonsured a nun at Agapia Veche Monastery in 1947, receiving the name "Agafia." After more than 20 years, in the fall of 1968, on September 15th, schemanun Agafia Ilie moved to her eternal dwelling at the age of 92.

Alexandru and Ana Ilie's Children

Maria

Maria was the oldest daughter of the Ilie family, born in 1903. Being the oldest, she took care of her younger siblings and gave them a good education. She married in her native village and gave birth to a daughter. She was widowed at a young age. Shortly after, her daughter also died.

Vasile

Vasile was born in 1905, as the family's second child. Together with two younger brothers, Gheorghe and Constantin (the future Saint Cleopa), he pastured their parents' sheep around the nearby Cozancea Skete.

Here his spiritual guide was the renowned Schemamonk Paisie Olaru, who was a hermit in Cozancea forests.

In 1929, Vasile joined the monastic community of Sihăstria Skete in Neamț, under the guidance of the great Igumen Ioanichie Moroi. After two years of asceticism and obedience as a shepherd, he departed for heaven in the summer of 1931.

Gheorghe (Monk Gherasim)

Gheorghe was born in 1907. He was very gentle, pious, and wise, yet very hard on himself. His spiritual formation took place at Cozancea Skete, under obedience to Schemamonk Paisie Olaru. Then he joined the monastic community of Sihăstria Skete towards the end of 1927, and was tonsured as "monk Gherasim." He was the most zealous ascetic among all his siblings, fasting greatly and praying unceasingly. He knew the Psalter by heart and repeated it daily, herding the skete's cattle.

After six years of monastic life, he entrusted his spirit in the hands of the Lord in the fall of 1933.

Porfira

Porfira was born in 1910 and was never married. She carried the burden of the family, working in the fields and taking care of her younger siblings.

Once, when she was hoeing in the field, feeling ill, she called her brother Constantin to read the Psalter for her. While he was reading, Porfira gave up her spirit into the hands of the Lord.

Constantin (Saint Cleopa)

Constantin was born on April 10, 1912, and was the fifth of ten children. He attended primary school for seven years in his native village. He had an extraordinary memory, similar to his mother's. For three years, together with his brothers, he lived as a spiritual disciple of Schemamonk Paisie Olaru, the hermit in Cozancea Skete.

In 1929, in early December, he joined the monastic community of Sihăstria Skete together with his older brother, Vasile. After three days of being tested at the skete's gate,[7] he was received in Sihăstria's community on the feast day of Holy Hierarch Spyridon, on December 12. This is why Elder Cleopa had great reverence not only for Holy Hierarch Nicholas, the patron saint of his native village, but also for Holy Hierarch Spyridon.

---

[7] This was a tradition established by Starets Ioanichie Moroi, to test the commitment to and inclination for monastic life of persons who had declared that they wanted to join the monastic community at Sihăstria: he would keep them waiting at the gate, asking them to do apparently nonsensical tasks. The test that Elder Cleopa went through is clarified in the next section of this book *(t.n.)*.

Constantin pastured the sheep of Sihăstria Skete with other novices until 1935, when he had to join the army in the city of Botoșani. He returned to the skete in the fall of 1936 and was tonsured a monk on August 2, 1937, receiving the name Cleopa. Then, he fulfilled his monastic obedience taking care of the skete's sheep until the summer of 1942, together with Father Galaction Ilie and Father Antonie Olaru.

In June 1942, he was brought into the skete and named locum tenens for the Igumen as Starets Ioanichie Moroi was gravely ill.

In 1944, on December 27, monk Cleopa was ordained hierodeacon, and on January 23, 1945, he was ordained hieromonk by Bishop Galaction Cordun, who was at the time Starets of the Neamț Monastery. After this date, he was officially appointed Igumen of Sihăstria Skete.

In 1947, Sihăstria Skete, which numbered over 60 inhabitants, was raised to the rank of monastery, and Protosyngel Cleopa Ilie was made Archimandrite with the approval of Patriarch Nicodim.

In 1948, being surveilled by the Secret Police at the time, he withdrew for six months into the forests around Sihăstria Monastery. In 1949, on August 30, Archimandrite Cleopa Ilie was appointed Starets of Slatina Monastery in Suceava. He moved there together with 30 monks from Sihăstria Monastery, whose transfer to Slatina Monastery had been approved by Patriarch Justinian. Protosyngel Ioil Gheorghiu was named Starets of Sihăstria Monastery in his place.

In Slatina Monastery, Most Pious Elder Cleopa established a community that grew to more than 80 members. As the Secret Police was monitoring him again, between 1952 and 1954 he withdrew to Stănișoara Mountains together with Hieromonk

Arsenie Papacioc. After more than two years of hermetic life, the two of them were brought back to Slatina Monastery by the order of Patriarch Justinian.

In 1956, Father Cleopa returned to Sihăstria Monastery, where he had been tonsured, and in the spring of 1959, he withdrew for the third time to Neamţ Mountains, where he led a life of ascetic strife for more than five years.

In the fall of 1964, he returned to Sihăstria Monastery as the spiritual father of the entire monastic community, where he guided both monastics and lay persons for 34 years, without interruption, until December 2, 1998 when he gave up his spirit into the arms of Christ.

Ecaterina

Father Cleopa's third sister, Ecaterina, was born in 1914. After she finished primary school in her native village, she entered monasticism in Agapia Veche Monastery, and became a rasophore sister. She lived in self-denial here for many years, then withdrew to Agafton Monastery in Botoşani county, and passed away at a young age.

Mihai

Mihai, Elder Cleopa's third brother, was born in 1907. Together with his brothers, he pastured sheep in the meadows of Cozancea Skete for many years. In 1934 he was received as a disciple at Durău Monastery, where he led an ascetic life for some years. Later, he withdrew to Cozancea Skete, where he gave up his spirit into the hands of the Lord in 1940.

Hareta

Hareta was born in 1920. She attended primary school in her native village and helped her parents work in their fields. Like her siblings, she went to the Lord at a tender age, in order to unceasingly rejoice with the angelic hosts.

Another Two Children

Ana Ilie gave birth to two more children whose names are not known to us. They died in infancy and are buried in their native village's cemetery.

Part Two

Life and Asceticism

How Infant Constantin Was Offered to the Theotokos

In the first two months after his birth, infant Constantin was always sick. After a while, he would hardly eat anything and cried day and night. Everyone was concerned for his life.

Not knowing what else to do, his mother Ana took her sick baby to the renowned Spiritual Father Conon Gavrilescu from Cozancea Skete, who was a prominent exorcist and healed many sick people with his holy prayers.

Hieromonk Varlaam Vântu, Elder Cleopa's uncle from Cozancea Skete, who fell asleep in the Lord on Mount Athos.

*Cozancea Skete
between 1925-1935.*

When she arrived at Father Conon's cell, in front of which there were many people waiting, she told him of her pain and wept with many tears, "What should I do, Father, for my child has stopped eating and is always crying. I am afraid he will die!"

"Do you know what to do? Offer him to the Theotokos!"

"How can I offer him to the Theotokos?"

"Here is how," he said. "Take a candle and a towel, come to the church with the baby and lay him before the icon of the Theotokos."

Then, after the mother put him in front of the icon, the Father said:

"Now repeat after me, 'Mother of God, I'm offering to you this child who is sick! Do what you want with him!'"

The mother of the child venerated, in tears, the icon of the Theotokos, did three prostrations and fell to her knees crying, "Mother of God, I'm offering to you this child of mine who is sick and always crying. Do what you know best with him!"

And she passed him beneath the holy icon three times.

*The icon in front of which
Elder Cleopa was offered to
the Theotokos.*

From that moment, when infant Constantine was healed, he never had a deadly illness in his life. Father Conon told her that this child would live the longest of all of her children. This healing was a true miracle of the Theotokos.

This is how the All-Holy Virgin shows mercy to mothers who give birth to children in the fear of God.

Childhood Years

From a young age, Elder Cleopa had a lot of reverence for the Theotokos. When he was 11 years old, he learned the Akathist Hymn of the Annunciation by heart, as he himself confessed:

"We were shucking corn on the ground and I had a prayer book hidden under the husks. Up until father came with another wagon of corn cobs, I would learn another Oikos, I would learn another Kontakion. And that's how I learned the Akathist to the Mother of God."

All his siblings loved restraint from an early age. His mother would say that she sometimes put meat in their knapsacks, as lunch, when there was no fast. Yet they would not eat it but gave it away to other people, and they would eat a little piece of bread and whatever else they had.

Elder Cleopa also used to say, "When I was little and was coming home from school, we passed through a village and seeing some boys throwing stones at a house with a red tin roof, I started throwing stones, too. Our teacher heard about it, grabbed us, and gave each of us a slap. Now I thank him because he did something good for me and I remember him in my prayers!"

Constantin's mother would say that from childhood he hated worldly things and fled from them. When he grew up and started shepherding sheep, in case there was a wedding in the village, where music played, he would not pass through but take a large detour and get home bypassing the village!

Tending Sheep at Cozancea Skete

Every summer, Alexandru Ilie, the father of the children, would make a sheep pen in the hills and meadows around Cozancea Skete, about 5 kilometers away from the village. He would then entrust the sheep to his three older sons, Vasile, Gheorghe, and Constantin, who knew these blessed places from their early childhood. The cell of hermit Paisie Olaru, their spiritual father, also lay in this region.

Saint Paisie the hermit at Cozancea Skete – Botoşani.

This Hieroschemamonk, Saint Paisie Olaru, born in 1897 in Lunca commune from Botoşani county, joined the nearby monastic community of Cozancea Skete in 1922. Here he spent 26 years of asceticism in a small hermit's cell, glorifying God day and night and comforting many souls. Because of his extreme asceticism he was sought after by many faithful whom he guided spiritually.

From early childhood, Constantin and his brothers often went to Cozancea Skete, since Saint Paisie loved them very much. They chanted during services, worked in the garden, and assisted the older Fathers with whatever they needed.

That is how God arranged it, so these boys would be spiritually formed from their youth for the great ascetical work of monasticism that awaited them. Time after time, when they had some temptation, they would run to hermit Paisie and ask for spiritual advice. And he would advise them to maintain permanent silence and to ceaselessly say the Jesus Prayer,[8] to do daily prostrations and in the evening, after milking the sheep, to read the Psalter and the Akathist Hymn to the Theotokos.

Since the brothers were obedient, they never strayed from the Elder's words. But the devil would tempt them more and more, because he could not stand being defeated by some children who would drive him away with the power of the psalms.

Once, while the three were playing together, the deceiver made it so that one of them was hit so hard that the other two thought he had died.

On another occasion the devil disturbed them at prayer time. While they were praying at night, the demons would sometimes make noises in the attic and snort like pigs. At first, being younger, Constantin would ask his brothers, "Do you hear that?" Then the eldest brother, Vasile, would tell him, "Don't worry! Don't pay any attention to him! Leave him, that's all he can do!"

The enemy, seeing that the brothers were burning him with prayer and fasting, created an even bigger temptation. Late one night, while the three of them were praying on their knees and reading the Psalter around the fire in the sheep pen, [9]they suddenly saw a strange bird like a vulture, moving between them. Constantin, being more playful, laid his Psalter aside and said, "Look what a beautiful bird this is!"

---

[8] The Jesus Prayer or the Prayer of the heart: "Lord Jesus Christ, Son of God, have mercy on me, a sinner!" *(t.n.)*.

[9] Typically, not just a fence but a small shack so the sheep could have shelter *(t.n.)*.

"Be quiet, pray and stop speaking!" Vasile, the elder brother, told him.

While Constantin was looking at that strange bird, which was actually the devil, it immediately threw itself into the fire on the hearth, making a great sound and scattering all the smoldering coals, causing the sheep pen to catch fire. As a consequence, many sheep died in the fire. With difficulty, the brothers put out the fire and gathered the frightened sheep. Afterwards, they all ran to hermit Paisie and told him what they had suffered at the hands of the devil.

The Elder sprinkled the sheep and the sheep pen with holy water, and encouraged the brothers to not be afraid, because the devil has been bound by Christ and does not have the power to kill people.

How the Three Brothers Were Saved from the Temptations of Youth

When all brothers were at home, their mother was eager to get them married. This is why she would bring young ladies at their place when they held a *clacă*,[10] to husk corn and do other work, thinking that one of them, maybe, would get married. But seeing that they were not

---

[10] *Clacă* is the term used to refer to collective voluntary work done by peasants in the home or yard of someone who was inviting them. The purpose was to finish faster, in one evening, hopefully, some work that otherwise would have taken days to complete. The host would also provide food and drinks, so that such collective, voluntary work sessions were also a way for villagers to socialize and have fun *(t.n.)*.

interested in girls, she would weep and feel very bitter. But the brothers, especially Constantin, used the opportunity to tell the young ladies' stories from the *Lives of Saints* and other Orthodox books. In this way, some of them eventually entered monastic life.

Saint Cleopa would also say that in 1925 or 1926, his parents decided to hire two musicians and have a dancing party in their home, as was the local custom. They were glad to see their children dancing, so that the whole village would praise them.

One night the youth gathered and began to sing and dance. In that moment, Gheorghe saw that the icon of the Theotokos on the wall was weeping and they understood that it was a sin. Then the three brothers, Vasile, Gheorghe, and Constantin, left the house and hid themselves. Seeing that they were missing, their mother looked for them everywhere. After finding them, she said to them, "Why are you making us a laughing stock in the village? You come and dance, too!" But Gheorghe, hiding, cut the boots he was wearing with a knife. Then he told his mother, "How can I come to dance, mother, if my boots are broken?"

That night their parents understood their boys had chosen a different path in this life and from that moment they let them serve Christ alone.

While still at home, his older brothers, Gheorghe and Vasile, were preparing for monastic life. They would wake up in the middle of the night, read the Matins, the Psalter, and fast. They were also waking up Constantin, who was groggy because they were interrupting his sleep. His elder sister, Maria, had joined the Lord's Army[11] and invited Constantin, telling him, "Come

---

[11] The Lord's Army [Oastea Domnului] is an evangelical revivalist movement within the framework of the Romanian Orthodox Church vaguely similar to the Salvation Army. It had the blessing of Orthodox Hierarchs and was concerned for the moral and generally Christian development of the Orthodox people *(t.n.)*.

and join the Lord's Army, too, because you have the gift of the gab and it's not as difficult as in the monastery." Then he agreed. The following night, when his brothers woke him up again for prayer, he said that he was not going to wake up anymore and that he was not going to enter the monastery. He went back to sleep, without any worry.

Their mother was working late into the night. As she came from the well with two water buckets, she saw a large, black dog in the room where Constantin was sleeping; it was standing on his chest and licking his cheek. Then she cried out to Vasile, "Woe, Vasile, come quickly because a dog is eating up Costică!"[12] Constantin woke up and barely saw the tail of that dog, which was vanishing. Vasile told him, "That's the devil, who rejoices that you're no longer going to join the monastery!" From that moment, Constantin never doubted joining the monastery, and he would wake up in the night to pray, lest the dog would come again.

How the Devil Tempted Brother Gheorghe

In 1927, Gheorghe, the middle brother, withdrew in Cozancea to become a disciple of hermit Paisie. He lived under obedience to the Elder there, worked the garden, chanted during services and always repeated the Jesus Prayer, eating only once a day. Sometimes he would stay at Sihăstria Skete in the Neamț Mountains.

---

[12] Diminutive for Constantine *(t.n.)*.

However, one time, the enemy tempted him and following his own mind's advice, Gheorghe left this letter on the cell's table: "Forgive me, Father Paisie, I have gone into the forest for five days to repent!"

The Elder read the letter that evening and said, "This is through the devil's temptation and it won't be useful to brother Gheorghe since he left without a blessing!" In the middle of the night someone knocked on the door of the Elder's cell: "Bless me, Father Paisie, and forgive me a sinner!"

"Who are you?" asked the Elder.

"Brother Gheorghe, the sinner!"

"How can that be? Brother Gheorghe has gone to the forest to repent for five days!"

"Forgive me, Father Paisie, I've made a mistake!"

"May the Lord forgive you, brother Gheorghe. Come inside the cell and tell me what happened to you."

"For a long time, Father Paisie, I have wanted to go by myself into the woods for a couple of days to pray. So, I took the Book of Hours, the Psalter and a few candles and matches and I hid in the forest in a pit. I began to do prostrations and pray there with tears. At midnight I heard a dreadful voice, 'What are you doing here?' I turned a bit and saw a giant Turk with a terrifying face. It was the enemy! Then I said to myself, 'Why did you leave without a blessing?' Gripped with fear, I took my books and ran! So, please, Father Paisie, forgive me the sinner and take me back!"

From that hour on, brother Gheorghe never did anything without a blessing.

How Brother Gheorghe Was Received in Sihăstria Skete

Towards the end of 1927, Gheorghe entered the community of Sihăstria Skete. Seeing him very zealous, the Igumen tested him in the following manner: he made him stay for three days at the skete's gate. There he had to carry a sack of soil on his back, while reciting Psalm 50 ten times, after which he rested and started over again. At the end of the three days the Igumen came and told him:

"Listen, brother Gheorghe, how is monasticism going? Monastic life is hard! You have to fast, pray, do whatever you're commanded, bear the toil of monasticism on your back with love until you die. Will you have the patience to live in this asceticism until the end?"

Brother Gheorghe answered, "Forgive me, a sinner. With the help of God I will fulfill, according to the little strength I have, everything ordered of me."

Then the Igumen arranged for him to do obedience with the skete's cattle.

Brother Gheorghe in the Army at Cernăuți.

Brothers Vasile and Constantin's Departure to the Monastery

In the winter of 1929, after the Holy Hierarch Nicholas' feast day, Vasile and Constantin decided to go to Sihăstria-Neamț Skete, in order to serve Christ all their life. After they prayed to God, while fasting and doing prostrations, they got the blessing of the village priest, and they shared their thoughts with their parents.

The separation was most difficult for their mother, who wept constantly. But their father told her, "Old lady, hey, let them go! Why didn't we have their good mind about it when we were their age? Look, soon we are leaving this world to go to the Lord and what use was this life to us?"

Eventually, the brothers got their bags ready. They only took two knapsacks with some clothes, the Holy Scriptures, the Lives of the Saints, the Book of Hours, the Psalter and two large hand-painted icons that they deeply loved: the icon of the Theotokos that had wept in their parent's house,[13] and an icon of Saint George.

Then, kneeling down, they prayed to God and to the Theotokos to bless their journey and to make them worthy of spiritual asceticism. Their parents, Alexandru and Ana, saw them to the edge of the village, shedding tears of natural love for their children from whom they couldn't part. Their children, though, encouraged them and spoke to them of Christ and eternal life.

Seeing that their parents could not separate from them, they kissed their hands and leaving them, the eldest brother, Vasile,

---

[13] This icon was later donated by Archimandrite Cleopa Ilie as a blessing to a family in the Borca commune from Neamț region, with whom it is to this day.

began to chant the Kontakion of the Akathist of our Savior Jesus Christ, "To You, the Champion Leader and Lord, the Vanquisher of Hades, as those who have been delivered from eternal death, we offer praises to You, Your servants and Your creation[14]..." At that moment their parents started to weep loudly. This is how the brothers left for Cozancea Skete.

At Cozancea they stayed a day with their good advisor, Schemamonk Paisie, who told them about the hermits in the Neamț Mountains. And the next day they left for Suceava taking their brother Gheorghe with them.

Their Entrance into the Monastery and Spiritual Testing

Leaving on foot for Sihăstria Skete, the brothers made their first stop at Saint John the New Monastery in Suceava. Here they venerated the saint's relics, listened to the Divine Liturgy, read the Akathist Hymn to the Theotokos, and rested overnight.

Continuing on the road to Sihăstria Skete, they made their second stop at Neamț Monastery, founded by Saint Stephen the Great, where they venerated the miracle-working icon of the Theotokos, the protectress of the monasteries of Moldavia. Then they entered the Secu Valley, worshiped at Secu Monastery, founded by Nestor Ureche, and when evening came, they arrived at Sihăstria Skete. Giving glory to God, they were pleased that

---

[14] This an adaptation of the text of the hymn, rather than a literal quote (t.n.).

the Theotokos had guided their steps towards these blessed mountains, where thousands of hermits had led an ascetic life throughout the centuries.

At the monastery they were greeted by monk Ilarion, the steward of the skete: "What do you want, brothers?" he asked.

"We want to stay in the monastery, Father, and become monks."

"Do you want to dedicate your life to Christ?"

"So be it, with the help of God, Reverend Father."

"Wait here until I speak with the Father Starets."

When the old Starets heard about the arrival of the brothers, he told the steward, "Take them to the guest house and give them some food. Beginning tomorrow morning, they can stay three days and nights, at the monastery gate, each striking tree trunks at the gate with a stick while saying the Jesus Prayer, without interruption. But don't give them food until the third day. If they have patience, we're going to receive them in the monastery."

The steward returned to the brothers and brought them to the guest house, where they rested. At midnight they went to Matins, and the next day they were led to the monastery's gate where they prayed all day striking the trunk of a pine tree with sticks. When they hit the trunk, they said the prayer, "Lord Jesus…" The monks and brothers passed by them, but no one asked them anything. In the evening the steward returned and asked them,

"Hey, brothers, did the tree say something?"

"No!" they answered him.

"Is the tree hungry?"

"No," they said.

"Look, that is how a monk must have patience in the monastery! Go to the guest house after you do your prayer rule and prostrations, rest a little, then come for Matins.

The following two days they did the same, and in the evening, Starets Ioanichie Moroi came to the monastery gate, blessed the two brothers, then led them to the church and told them to venerate the miracle-working icon of the Theotokos.

Then he heard their confessions, beginning from their childhood, they received Great Holy Water, a little bit of food, and the next day they had communion with the Most-Holy Mysteries of Christ.

Finally, brothers Vasile and Constantin were sent by the Starets to tend the sheep, and brother Gheorghe continued to herd the cattle. For three months they were not allowed to see or speak to each other.

That is how these brothers, blessed by God and by the Theotokos, were received in the monastery.

The Spiritual Personality of Starets Ioanichie Moroi

Founded in 1655 by a holy hermit, Atanasie, together with his disciples, Sihăstria Skete was dependent on Neamț Monastery until 1947, when it became a self-governed monastery. The skete was renovated in 1734 by Bishop Ghedeon of Huși[15] and renewed in 1824, after the Eteria Revolution,[16] by Metropolitan Veniamin Costache. However, after the 1861-1863 secularization of monastery properties, it was nearly deserted.

---

[15] A city in Western Moldavia (*t.n.*).
[16] The 1821 Revolution in the Balkans which aimed to free Christians from the Ottoman Empire (*t.n.*).

*Protosyngel Ioanichie Moroi
(1859-1944).*

In 1884, a lumber mill was built in the immediate proximity of the skete, so the hermits withdrew to other quieter places. Just one monk, named Ionatan, continued to stay there as a guardian of the skete's church, for 25 years. Back then, in Sihăstria, the Divine Liturgy was celebrated only once a year, on September 8, the skete's feast day.

In that period, the future Hieroschemamonk Ioanichie Moroi, after a pilgrimage to the Holy Sepulcher and then to Mount Athos, renounced family life and became a monk at one of the Romanian *kelis* in Athos. In 1900, he returned to his home country and joined the monastic community of Neamţ Monastery where his obedience was to serve as a *paraclisier*.[17]

---

[17] The Romanian term "paraclisier" covers, semantically, the duties of an acolyte, sacristan and sexton *(t.n.)*.

Sihăstria Skete, general view.

In 1909, Pimen Georgescu, metropolitan of Moldavia, decided to stop operating the lumber mill at Sihăstria and to re-establish the skete. For this purpose, schemamonk Ionachie was ordained as a hieroschemamonk and sent as Igumen in this skete. This is how Sihăstria Skete was revived, under the leadership of a very zealous Athonite Igumen. For over 20 years, he celebrated the Divine Liturgy daily, being the only serving priest. Moreover, he took care of the spiritual growth of his disciples, as well as of the skete's material needs. As word came out about his asceticism, many faithful came to Sihăstria, among whom there were many young people searching for a spiritual life, including the three brothers, Vasile, Gheorghe, and Constantin. They joined the community of this skete, as they wanted to experience the best monastic asceticism, and they had been looking since their youth for such a skilled Igumen and discerning spiritual father.

From 1909 until the end of his life, in 1944, in his capacity as Igumen of Sihăstria Skete, Protosyngel Ioanichie Moroi succeeded in making this skete a true spiritual hermitage according to the model of Mount Athos. The Holy Liturgy was served daily, the Matins service was done in the middle of the night and the other services at their appropriate times. Yet, the Elder did not give the blessing to start the service until everyone came to church. Confession was done weekly, every Friday, and Holy Communion was usually given every 30 to 40 days, according to the monks' zeal. There was one meal a day on Monday, Wednesday, and Friday, cooked without oil, at three in the afternoon, and on the other days they served two meals a day cooked with oil, and various types of cheese, according to the Monastery's *typikon*.

In their cell, each monk was obliged to do the daily canon ordered for them: 300 prostrations, 600 semi-prostrations, as well as readings from the Psalter. Monks who did not attend Matins and did not do their canon went to their obedience and did not receive food until evening. Likewise, no one was allowed to receive relatives inside their cell, to have money, or to speak about worldly things.

All the monks in the skete's community read the Psalter and said the Jesus Prayer in silence and humility. There were even five fathers who knew the entire Psalter by heart and said it daily. Everyone did their ascetic work according to their strength. Some would take food to the hermits in the forest, and others would withdraw in huts in the surrounding woods. Everything, however, was done with the blessing of the Igumen.

The skete's Igumen, Protosyngel Ioanichie, led a very harsh personal ascetic life. Elder Cleopa used to say about his Starets,

"Since he served the Divine Liturgy daily, he ate nothing from Monday through Saturday, being content only with Holy

Communion and with the prosphora[18] which the celebrating priest is entitled to have. During these five days the Igumen came to the *trapeza*[19] and read an edifying fragment from the writings of Saint Theodore the Studite. However, on Saturdays and Sundays, as well as on the other great feast days, he would sit for the meal together with the entire monastic community."

"We would confess with great care. For if I did not say all my sins, my Starets would tell them to me: 'But why don't you tell that one?' or 'Say that, too, and that sin, as well.'"

Father Cleopa used to retell a miracle that had happened with his Starets, Protosyngel Ioanichie Moroi:

In 1925, after the calendar was adjusted,[20] Sihăstria's Igumen was in great doubt. He did not know if the New Calendar was good or not. So, he locked himself in his cell and began to fast and to pray to God to give him a sign whether he should follow the Old Calendar or the New Calendar.

After about 20 days of fasting, noticing that the Igumen showed no sign of being alive, the monks were worried lest he would die because of the fast. They consulted together to break into his cell to save his life.

Hierodeacon Ghemnazie Pristav, being more courageous, took the cell's door off its hinges with a cant hook and found Igumen Ioanichie collapsed on the floor, very weak, with the Psalter next to him.

Then, after gaining some strength from the Holy Mysteries and a little food, he recovered after three days and told his spiritual sons how many heavy temptations he suffered from the

---

[18] "Prescura" is a very small round loaf of bread with the seal of Christ on it, usually about two inches in diameter, that is used during the Liturgy (*t.n.*).

[19] *Trapeza* is a monastery's refectory (*t.n.*).

[20] The adjustment refers, actually, to the adoption of the New Calendar (*t.n.*).

devils during this time of intense prayer and fasting. Sometimes they threatened to kill him. Other times, they beat him with a staff of fire. Once he saw a host of devils with red koukoulions[21] saying:

"Let's cut up this old man, since he wants to become a saint!"

Then they cried out, in anger, against him:

"Who told you that one can still become a saint nowadays?"

"Well, who said that one can no longer become a saint?" the Igumen retorted.

Another day, they threatened him:

"It's pointless fasting any longer, as you will end up falling in our hands anyway!"

But he said to them, "I have hope in the mercy of God and in the prayers of the Theotokos, that I will be saved from your hands!"

After several days of fasting, he saw above him, in the air, three saints vested like bishops, who looked like the Holy Three Hierarchs. The one in the middle said, with a voice like a trumpet:

"Ioanichie, why do you doubt and don't do obedience? Don't you know that disobedience brings about death? Or haven't you read that obedience is greater than sacrifice? So, obey your superiors, for it's not you who will be held accountable for the adjustment of the calendar!"

Then, while blessing him at the same time, the three of them ascended into heavens and he saw them no more. From that day on, the Elder no longer had any doubt about the adjustment of the calendar.

In his free time, the Starets accompanied the novices to their obedience duties, worked in the garden, visited the sick and gave advice to the faithful who came to the skete. The best advice that he would often give to his disciples was, "Hey boys,

---

[21] An Orthodox monastic's headpiece (*t.n.*).

if you want to be saved, have fear of the Lord, keep your mind pure and don't forget the Jesus Prayer!"

Protosyngel Ioanichie Moroi also had the gift of working miracles, and occasionally drove out evil spirits from people.

Once he was called to Târgu Neamţ to bless the house for a faithful family. Novice Constantin Ilie went with him. After he finished the blessing service, the faithful hosts offered him a cup of coffee with milk. However, the Elder never ate outside of the monastery. They insisted that he try it and the Starets said, "Look, I will bless this cup and if you don't see any sign, then I will taste it."

He blessed the cup with milk and immediately they all saw a snake squirming in the cup and they were all horrified, saying, "We poured milk in the cup, where did this snake come from? Please forgive us!" The Elder then said, "This is the devil of gluttony!" And blessing the cup again, the serpent disappeared. After that, the host threw out the milk.

Another time, a novice from the skete wanted to go to Târgu Neamţ to buy something for himself. He did not, however, get a blessing from the Starets. As he was walking along the path, seven devils in the form of monks, very hideous to behold, met him and beat him with staffs of fire, torturing him cruelly and chasing him through the forest. Then, arriving at the skete, being pursued by the demons, he cried out for all to hear, "Don't leave me! Seven after me! Don't leave me! Seven after me!"

Capturing him, the novices tied him up and told the Starets. He read the prayer for the absolution from curses and deliverance from all unclean spirits. Then he told the novices to untie him. But they said, "What if he runs away again?" The Starets said laughing, "Don't be frightened. If God has untied him, you shouldn't keep him tied anymore!" So, that is how, "with the Elder's prayers, the novice recovered his health completely.

Here are just a few of the miraculous deeds of pious Hieroschema monk and Starets Ioanichie Moroi, who guided Sihăstria Skete for 35 years and spiritually guided many youths, whose leader would be Archimandrite Cleopa Ilie.

Brother Constantin's Early Temptations

While novice Constantin was doing obedience with the livestock, he shared a cell with another novice named Nicolae, who liked order and cleanliness. Coming back from his obedience once, Constantin took off his *opinci* and entered the cell without shaking out his clothes. As soon as novice Nicolae saw him, he gave him a slap for not keeping things clean.

Constantin went to his older brothers, unshod and half-dressed as he was, and told them what happened. But they pricked his conscience telling him, "Brother Constantin, where are Christ's wounds on your body?"

Later Elder Cleopa told us, "See how my older brothers comforted me! As I had no shelter, brother Vasile, the beekeeper of the skete, hosted me for a while in a room where he kept the beehive frames." Elder Cleopa would also say, "When I was young, I used to come in from the stable and rest at Father Petru Ganea's until midnight. He had a cell and everyone slept on the floor, on mats, since there weren't many cells. We were four disciples: Simion, Nistor, Pavel, and me."

"Hey, Costache! Hey, Nistor! Hey, Simion! Hey, Paul! Have you heard the Archangel's voice?" That is what he would tell us when the bells were ringing at night. "Well, city lads , come for the prayer!" For if we did not go to Matins, the following day he would not give us food.

"Well, Costache, take your *opinci*!" It was winter then and I would run barefoot to the chapel, so as not to waste time lacing up my *opinci*. The woolen socks were in the cell, on the masonry stove; they were wet. The chapel was where now stands the *aghiasmatar*[22]. I stood there unshod and Father Petru said to Elder Ioanichie Moroi, "Well, Father Starets, this boy is standing in the corner behind the door and he runs barefoot through the snow. He's going to get sick!"

But Elder Ioanichie said, "Leave him alone, let him do his asceticism."

Hierodeacon Cristofor the Hermit

Grazing the sheep through the forests of Sihla, brothers Vasile and Constantin encountered several hermit monks near Saint Theodora's cave and Coroi's Gorge, three kilometers away from Sihla.

Once they found a hermit's hut under pine tree roots deep into the mountains. They knocked on the door, but no one answered. Entering in, they saw a table with a paper on it that read, "Here

---

[22] Building on a monastery's premises, inside which priests do the service for the holy water *(t.n.)*.

lives the beast of the earth, D. C.[23]" One of the brothers said, "How many hidden servants Christ has in this forest!"

Brother Constantin (Cleopa) as a Rasophore.

After a few days, they discovered the mystery of the hut. One evening the Father who had been living in asceticism in that cell arrived at Sihăstria's sheep stable. He was Hierodeacon Cristofor. He came with a knapsack on his back, in which he carried the skull of a saint he had miraculously found in the forest, and which gave off a sweet-smelling fragrance. Then this blessed hermit went together with the brothers from the stable to Sihăstria's Igumen, Protosynkelllos Ioanichie, and told him how he found the relics, saying,

"While I was returning to my hut under Coroi's Gorge, coming from Sihla Skete, where I had served the Divine Liturgy with its Igumen on the feast day of the Holy Prophet Elijah the

---

[23] i.e. Deacon Cristofor.

Tishbite, I fell asleep on the foot trail under a pine tree. Suddenly, an unseen hand woke me up. Not seeing anyone around, I went back to sleep. After a little while, someone awakened me again and I saw a saint in the air who said, 'Father Cristofor, walk 100 steps to the right and you will find my bones near a small cave. Please, take my skull only and carry it with you throughout your life as a blessing, but bury the other bones in the ground.'

"Then I made the sign of the Holy Cross and left to find those holy relics. After I found them, I began to pray. I kissed them, then fulfilled the command and left for my hut with the skull. I felt very pleased and full of spiritual joy. But I was thinking, whose skull is this? After much prayer, the pious saint appeared to me and said, 'Father Cristofor, thank you for burying my bones and for obeying, taking my skull with you. And if you wish to know my name, I am Hieroschemamonk Pavel.' He was Saint Teodora of Sihla's Spiritual Father!"

This pious hierodeacon spent three days at Sihăstria Skete, serving the Divine Liturgy together with Igumen Ioanichie, and everyone kissed the holy relics of Pious Pavel.

Then Father Cristofor went back to the forest, taking the hermit's skull with him. To no avail did the Fathers of Sihăstria search for the hut later, as no one was able to find it. Local tradition mentions a place between Sihla Skete and the nearby Coroi Gorge, hidden by God, that no one can discover. Many holy hermits lived in asceticism there throughout the ages. Perhaps that is where Father Cristofor fell asleep in the Lord with Pious Pavel's skull in his arms, unknown to all.

The Psalter's Power

Elder Cleopa used to tell us how the three brothers traveled to Cernăuți in the summer of 1930. Since Gheorghe did military service there, they decided to go together to pick up his military license.

After taking the blessing of Father Ioanichie, the Igumen of the skete, they set off on foot from Neamț towards Northern Moldavia. They agreed to walk ten to fifteen steps apart from each other along the path in order to ceaselessly repeat the Prayer of the heart and utter David's Psalter by heart.

They first stopped at the Monastery of Saint John the New in Suceava. Then, leaving for Cernăuți, they arrived at a village in Dorohoi County, but did not find a place to spend the night. Yet a faithful woman, seeing that they were strangers, asked them,

"What are you looking for, brothers?"

"We are searching for a house where we could stay overnight, and we can't find any."

"We have a house at the edge of the village where no one lives. But I don't know if you can sleep in it since it is haunted by devils because of some witches."

"If you accept us, we will sleep in it!"

"Ok, brothers. Come on, I'll take you there."

Having arrived at that house, the brothers ate some food and, as they were tired, they went to bed. After a little rest, the evil spirits woke them up, raising a ruckus. So, the brothers pulled out the Psalter, lit candles and the three of them prayed for several hours. In the beginning, loud sounds, cries, and screams could be heard. Then, as the brothers prayed fervently, the devils fled, ashamed by the Psalter's power.

Before dawn, they again drifted off a little, but the demons no longer dared to come close. In the morning, when the owner of the house arrived, she asked them how they slept, and finding out what had happened, she asked them to advise her how she could deliver the house from evil spirits. The brothers told her to read the Psalter in the evening, at midnight and in the morning, to bring a priest to do the service for the blessing of the water in the house, to fast and to confess, and that is how the demons would flee.

Having arrived at Cernăuți, they got the necessary military documents from the regiment, and they returned home again through the same village where they had stayed overnight. The owner of the house received them with joy and told them that since they had prayed in the house, it was no longer haunted by devils. That is how the woman understood how great the power of the Psalter is over unclean spirits and witches.

Brother Vasile's Asceticism

For three years, rassophore Vasile, Father Cleopa's eldest brother, did his obedience at the sheep stall. He was so meek and full of love that everybody loved him, even the birds of the air, the dogs, and sheep.

This was his ascetic work: he would eat only once a day, in the afternoon at three o'clock. He knew the Psalter, the seven Lauds and many Akathists by heart and would say them daily, while walking bareheaded behind the sheep. At night he would do hundreds of prostrations and read the Lives of the Saints, always thinking of God's judgments.

Another ascetical work this Christ-loving soul undertook was taking care of the hermits in the forest. At that time, over 40 hermits, monks, and nuns lived in asceticism around Sihăstria and Sihla Skete. Brother Vasile was the hermits' friend. When he met one of them in the mountains or forests, even if he did not know them, he would do a prostration and say, "Your blessings, Father, pray to God for me, a sinner! Do you need some food from the sheep stall?"

If the hermit nodded, the next day brother Vasile would bring cheese, potatoes, vegetables, salt, and flour. He had a number of hermits that he knew and would visit in their huts.

One time he asked a hermit, "Father, what should I do to be saved?"

"Brother Vasile," answered the Elder, "pray ceaselessly, do obedience with love, and have humility. If you keep these three, surely you will be saved!"

Holy Bishop John's Prophecy

In the fall of 1930, rassophore Vasile was herding sheep together with his brother Constantin, on a slope of the Sihla Mountains. Vasile was walking ahead of the sheep and was praying, Constantin following them. At that moment, a holy and amazing hermit passed by, Bishop John accompanied by a deacon. He had fled from Kiev, around 1918, because of the atheistic persecutions. After he blessed them both, Bishop John, having the gift of foresight, said to the younger brother through the deacon, who knew Romanian:

"Brother Constantin, tell your brother Vasile to prepare to go ahead, because he has a long journey to take!"

Bishop John speaking with Novice Constantin.

The deacon translated these words to novice Constantin. Then the blessed bishop left towards Sihla to see his own spiritual father, Hieromonk Vasian, who was a hermit near Saint Theodora's Cave. Constantin, however, did not understand what the bishop meant to say. However, meeting up with his brother who was ahead of the sheep, he told the latter the holy hermit's words.

Brother Vasile understood Bishop John's prophecy, which was that he needed to prepare for the hour of his death, which was drawing near.

Brother Vasile's Amazing End

I n the spring of 1931, this humble, obedient man, Father Cleopa's elder brother, got sick and was brought to the Skete. Once, while he was praying in front of the church after the Holy Liturgy, he had a terrifying vision. Out of fear, he began to weep and called out in a loud voice:

"Most Holy Theotokos, have mercy on me and don't let the devils beat me! Don't leave me!"

He said to the Fathers who had gathered around him, "Make the sign of the cross, brothers. Do it! Because, look, our Lady has come! The Mother of the Lord is before us, with the Savior in her arms! Here she is above us!"

"Brother Vasile, why were you yelling so loud?" the monastics asked.

"Fathers, while I was praying in front of the church, a host of very ferocious devils suddenly appeared, with staffs of fire in their hands, and they began to beat me terribly and to scream, 'In vain are you praying, as you won't be saved! You are ours because you are sinful!' Then I began to call out with hope to the Mother of God. In that instant a white cloud full of light descended from heaven until it was above the church. And in the cloud, I saw the Mother of God with the Infant in her arms telling me, 'Do not be afraid, for you have three more days to live and then you will come to us!' Then the Savior blessed all of us and the cloud rose up to heaven… Fathers, the Mother of God has great power and boldness before our Savior Jesus Christ, and He listens greatly to her prayers."

After this, Igumen Ioanichie told him, "Brother Vasile, don't let the enemy deceive you! Be careful with yourself and guard your mind, because many are his traps!"

Then he said to the other novices, "If, three days from now, brother Vasile leaves us and our world, then truly the Mother of God appeared to him. If not, then he was deceived by the devils."

After three days, at exactly the same time, rassophore Vasile Ilie departed in peace with prayer on his lips.

Who knows how many holy hermits were praying for the repose of his soul at that moment.

Monk Gherasim Ilie's Asceticism and End

Monk Gherasim Ilie was Father Cleopa's elder brother. He herded the Skete's cattle for four years and was a solitary and ascetic soul. After receiving the monastic schema, Father Gherasim intensified his ascetic strife. He would say the Psalter and the seven Lauds of the church daily, which he knew by heart, and at night he would do hundreds of prostrations while repeating the Jesus Prayer. His soul was very zealous and mysterious, and he had great reverence for the Theotokos. He would speak little and had the gift of tears.

Father Gherasim always carried with him an icon of the Theotokos. He would wrap it in a clean towel, put it in his peasant's shoulder bag next to the Lives of the Saints, and take the cattle to graze. In the woods, he would hang the icon from the trunk of a beech tree, read the Akathist Hymn of the Annunciation, and do prostrations.

Once, while he was praying, he began to weep intensely before the icon of the Theotokos. A forester who was passing by stopped and asked him,

"What happened to you, Father, that you're weeping so much?"

"I stubbed my toe."

"Never mind, brother, you'll get over it!"

"May God grant that I'll get over it!"

This young soldier for Christ had another secret ascetic practice. He always contemplated the thought of death and the hour of His dreadful judgment. When he heard that one of the Fathers was very ill, he would draw near him, comfort him and pray for him, read to him from the holy books, and then he would begin to shed tears.

"Why are you crying, Father Gherasim?" the sick person would ask him.

"I'm crying because the hour of my death is drawing near, and I have not prepared yet!"

Monk Gherasim would often go into the cemetery at night and there he would pray and weep alone by the Fathers' graves. And in his cell, he had made a coffin that he was using, instead of a bed, in which he would rest for a few hours.

Father Cleopa was also telling us about him, "My beloved brother Gherasim knew the whole Psalter by heart, including the Song of Moses and the Paraklesis of the Theotokos, from cover to cover, and all the names for commemoration. He pastured the cattle for three years. He knew the whole Psalter, all of it, from *Blessed is the Man...* until the end. Poor him, what a great battle he fought. I could hear him arguing with the devils. They would snatch his prayer ropes, pull his hair and tell him, 'What do you have against us? You're burning us with the Psalms!' And he would weep. When he was drowsy at night, he would slap himself, saying, 'Don't sleep, you horse! Here's your coffin!' His coffin was leaning against the mason stove. Father Gherasim did not sleep at all in the night before Matins. He would say three kathismas and make 33 prostrations, then another three kathismas, and again 33 prostrations, and so on until the midnight service.

"I, however, was sleeping. I did not like doing so many prayers. So, he would suddenly say, 'Wake up! Let's go to Matins!' But he didn't sleep before Matins. After Matins he would sleep in the coffin from his cell on a little bit of straw, placing a stump under his head. One day a Father told him, 'How many coffins like this are going to rot by the time your holiness dies!' And he answered, 'I believe in the good Lord that this one will be my eternal house!'

"He would sleep three or four hours at the most after Matins. I went to the Starets and told him, 'Father Starets, I can't stay with Gherasim anymore! He is slapping himself and is weeping all night long! Sometimes he begins to cry and sobs for two hours, so intensely that his shirt bounces up and down on his back.'[24] 'Well, son,' the Elder said, 'leave him alone. That's

---

[24] This is a Romanian expression, "de sare cămaşa de pe el", meaning extreme sobbing and heaving *(t. n.)*.

his work! You don't know what he's going through. He has great work with the Psalter. He fights with the devils!'"

That is why neither he nor brother Vasile lived long, nor did Costandie Uricaru. He too knew the Psalter by heart. Do you know why? Listen to what the prokeimenon says, "*He was caught up lest evil change his understanding or deceit deceive his soul.*"[25]

That is how Father Gherasim lived! He got sick once and the Igumen said to him, "Should we get a doctor so you can get well?"

But he answered in tears, "Forgive me, Fathers, I prayed to God to give me trouble and illness, so that I could be saved. So, if He had mercy on me, should I resist it now? Leave me in the hands and will of God, because the illness is for my salvation!"

As he was sick, Father Gherasim could no longer come to church. But he was never absent from the Holy Liturgy. The brothers would carry him on a blanket and lay him down in the narthex.

The others would ask him, "Father Gherasim, why don't you stay in your cell until you get better?"

"Forgive me a sinner, Fathers. I've come to attend one more Holy Liturgy! Maybe this is the last one of my life! No other service is more necessary for our salvation than the Divine Liturgy!"

One day an old monk died. Then Father Gherasim said to everybody in tears, "You should know, Fathers, that after Father Vasile, it's my turn to leave this life."

Indeed, on September 14, 1933, the feast of the Exultation of the Holy Cross, the great ascetic Gherasim gave his soul into the hands of Christ, lying in the coffin that he himself had made. Under his head they found this letter addressed to his younger brother.

"My beloved brother Constantin, you should know that God will keep you alive for a longer time in this life. So, I beg you not

---

[25] Wisdom of Solomon 4:11 *(t.n.)*.

to forget me, a sinner, in your holy prayers. For I, too, have prayed to God for you with many tears, and for all the brothers, that the Lord would bring you on the path of salvation."

Brother Constantin's Amazing Vision

After the death of his brother, Constantin began to read the entire Psalter daily and to fast for 40 days in a row, praying for the salvation of his brother.

The 40 days having come to completion after Father Gherasim's death, novice Constantin returned from his obedience and slept for a little while. In his dream, he saw that his brother's grave from the old cemetery near the church was opened and the coffin lid had moved aside; a fountain of crystal-clear water began to flow from the Holy Altar over the grave, and his brother's face was turning white as snow. Then Gherasim awoke as if from sleep and said, "Brother Constantin, the prayers of the Church have saved me...!"

Father Cleopa with a disciple near the graves of his brothers Gherasim and Vasile.

The same year, after his brothers departed for the Lord, Constantine was extremely saddened by their untimely end. But he prayed with tears for God to reveal to him where their souls were. And behold, one night he fell asleep in his cell, and did not wake up until morning.

After he awoke, his soul was very calm and peaceful. Then he went to the Igumen of the Skete and told him the dream that he had that night. He said that he had met his brothers, Vasile and Gherasim, together with his sisters who had departed to the Lord, in an amazing garden full of sweet-smelling flowers and trees loaded with fruit, where birds were singing praises to God in the sky. He spent that whole night with his siblings walking together and singing with great spiritual joy in the garden of heaven!

Finally, his siblings said farewell to him, promising him that they would continue to pray for him that they would all be together eventually. They urged him to be obedient and to pray ceaselessly, adding that after a while he would be a spiritual guide for the souls and then he would come to be with them. They departed leaping with joy and Constantin woke up from his deep sleep. It was already five o'clock in the morning.

Brother Constantin as a "Paraclisier" [26]

While he served as a *paraclisier* in 1932, Father Cleopa witnessed several miracles that took place during the Holy Liturgy in Sihăstria Skete. Here is what he told us:

---

[26] *Paraclisier* is an acolyte, who assists the priest in the altar and in the church *(t.n.)*.

"Now listen to what happened to me with a very good priest, Calistrat Bobu. As a spiritual father, he once went to visit a nun who was living in asceticism in the forest. At that time there were about 50 hermits in the woods. She told Father Calistrat, 'The Holy Spirit doesn't descend on you all because you have switched to the New Calendar!" From that moment on, Father Calistrat started to have doubts.

Once, when I was a paraclisier, I noticed that the antidoron from the Starets was white and sweet, while the one from Father Calistrat was greenish and sour. Then I asked Starets Ioanichie, 'Father Starets, why is it that when Father Calistrat celebrates the Liturgy, the antidoron is greenish and sour?"

"Well, my son, he is serving with doubt! He went to a hermit in the forest and she told him that the gift of the Holy Spirit doesn't come during the Liturgy because of the calendar. And I told him that he'll run into trouble, because he doubts that the Holy Spirit comes!"

Once Father Calistrat was celebrating the Holy Liturgy and when he invoked the grace of the Holy Spirit, he immediately saw that the Agnos had become flesh and was bleeding onto the Holy Paten and the Holy Antimension. And when he looked into the Holy Chalice, he saw blood. Then he called me,

"Brother Constantin, come over here! What do you see?"

"Woe, Father Calistrat! The Holy Communion has turned into flesh and blood!"

Then he sent me to call Father Starets. When he came, the Starets had the chanters read the Psalter in the Analogion, and he said,

"Well, Father Calistrat, now do you believe that the Holy Spirit comes and transforms the Gifts?"

"Forgive me, Father!" And he fell to his knees.

"Come, look! Did the Holy Spirit come? Did it become flesh? Did it become blood? Are you still going to have doubts, Father?"

"I do believe, Father Starets. Please, forgive me!"

"Well then, start gathering the Holy Mysteries!"

Then, with a chisel, he made a hole in the Holy Table's foot, because the Holy Table is the Lord's Tomb, and he buried the Holy Mysteries there, as the Holy Fathers teach us to do. Then he re-consecrated the holy chalice and washed it in the Altar's washing area[27] together with the Holy Antimension. And we waited a few hours until the entire Psalter was read. Then, the Holy Liturgy service started again, from the Proskomedia, "And one of the soldiers pierced his side with a spear…" And thus, the Holy Liturgy was celebrated and the miracle did not repeat.

"Do you believe now?"—the Starets asked him.

"I do believe, Father!"

Then, Starets Ioanichie gave him a 40-day canon and told him, "Why don't you believe me when I tell you, instead of going to old women to teach you about the calendar?" This happened in 1932.

It was also about that time that I witnessed another miraculous act during the Divine Liturgy.

Once, when Starets Ioanichie Moroi was serving, after the consecration of the Gifts, a drop of Holy Blood jumped out of the Holy Chalice onto the Antimension. That drop began to shine and then it gave off rays of light. Then Starets Ioanichie called me over,

"Brother Constantin, come over here!"

When I drew near, the Starets told me, "What do you see here on the Holy Antimension?"

---

[27] In the Orthodox tradition there are special rubrics and rules for washing holy things, especially the Holy Chalice and Disk, so that rinsing water does not flow into the gutter but goes into a blessed and sanctified area *(t.n.)*.

"I can see a drop of the Holy Blood. It is shining so bright that I can barely look at it."

"Do you see Whom we serve? That is why you should have great fear and reverence in the Holy Altar!"

Then Igumen Ioanichie used that drop of Holy Blood to partake from the Holy Communion. Later, when I still had the obedience of a *paraclisier*, in the monastery there was a priest who was celebrating and who had an ulcer. Due to his illness, he couldn't bear the smoke from the censer.

This priest told me many times to be more careful and use less incense, but out of inattention, I kept repeating my mistake. Seeing this, the priest stopped reminding me, but he was sad inside. So, one night after I came from Matins and went to sleep, I had a terrifying dream, and I saw the priest surrounded by rays of light.

Then I realized he had a holy life; I quickly ran to him and asked him to forgive me. Then I went to the Starets that night and I confessed, telling him my error.

Brother Constantin an Iconographer

Father Cleopa used to say, "When I was a novice, I had a gift for painting. A monk called Nil, from Secu Monastery, had taught me how to paint icons. After I learnt how to draw and paint in watercolors, I started using paints. Sometimes the Igumen would come to my cell to see how I painted, and he liked it. But I had begun to feel tempted by money, because I was buying the paints and everything I needed for painting holy icons myself.

Once Father Starets came to me to test me, 'How much does that icon cost?'

'It doesn't have a price, Your Reverence!' I answered.

'For this one, brother Costică, you should ask a good price because it is beautiful!' the Elder said, trying to tempt me.

"When I saw that I had to bargain with people to get money, I was afraid that pride and the love for money would conquer me. Then one day Father Chiriac, the skete's steward, came to me and said, 'Brother Costică, leave painting and come to do obedience!' So, I left everything and I was sent to pasture the sheep.

"That is how I was delivered then from two sins, pride and love of money!"

Monk Galaction Ilie, Novice Constantin's First Spiritual Father

This charismatic monk, originally from Săliştea Sibiului, through his ancestors, was born in commune Pripirig, Neamţ, of poor parents. In his youth he was a shepherd of the village's sheep.

Then, as he wished to follow Christ, in 1918 he entered the asceticism of monastic life in Sihăstria Skete, and was tonsured into monasticism in 1925. Here he had the same blessed obedience, pasturing the skete's sheep for 25 years. This blessed Father was a great ascetic. He greatly contributed to the spiritual formation of novice Constantin Ilie—the future Saint Cleopa—who was his disciple from 1930 to 1942.

Here are a few of the labors of this Elder blessed by God:

Elder Cleopa used to say that Father Galaction never ate anything until he finished his daily monastic canon. When the brothers were calling him to join them for meals, the Elder would reply, "Forgive me, brothers, I haven't done my duties to God today. So, how can I eat if I haven't done my duties?"

Then the Father would withdraw to the forest and finish his prayers and prostrations, and only then would he sit at the table.

Again, his disciple would say that the Elder did not eat on Wednesdays and Fridays until the evening, after the stars came out. Then the Father would cross himself, ask forgiveness from all, take prosphora and then eat in peace. His disciple, brother Constantin asked him once,

"Father Galaction, the day is long and Your Reverence, you are weak and old. Wouldn't it be good for you to allow yourself to eat earlier?"

"Brother Constantin, listen to what Father Atanasie from Neamț Monastery told me. Once a saint saw how a dead man was being taken to the grave, and two beautiful angels were going with the coffin, one in front and one behind it. The saint asked them, 'Who are you?' And the angels answered, 'I am named "Wednesday" and me, "Friday!" We came here by God's command to help this soul who fasted his whole life on Wednesday and Friday in honor of Christ's Passion.' Since the day Father Atanasie told me this story, I no longer ate anything on these days, so that Holy Wednesday and Friday would help me at the hour of my death."

This humble Father, if he saw someone passing by the sheep stall, would immediately say to his disciple:

"Go, brother Constantin, and call that man to eat with us because there is a spring here with the sheep, and if we don't give anything from it, the spring will dry up. But, if you give something, God will keep the sheep healthy and you won't notice the slightest loss because God's blessing will be over us."

His disciples used to say that they never saw Father Galaction eating by himself, or in hiding. If he received something to eat from the monastery, he did not taste it until he reached the stall. He would call everyone there and share with each one, with brotherly love.

"Why don't you ever eat by yourself, Father Galaction?"—the brothers asked him. And he would answer, "It is a great danger for a monastic to eat in secret!" Then with his heart full of peace, he would add, "Love and brotherhood far surpass wealth!"

Father Galaction was the poorest monk of the monastery. He had a single set of clothes, one winter coat, and a few undergarments. His disciple asked him once,

"Why don't you, Your Reverence, have some new good clothes made for you, like the other Fathers do?" And the Elder said to him, "Brother Constantin, I used to confess to a hermit that I met while traveling with the sheep on a mountain. He told me, 'Father Galaction, you should have as many belongings as you can carry on your back when you move from one place to another.' Then he added, 'Never leave your canon of prostrations unfinished, say the Jesus Prayer ceaselessly, and make peace with everyone before sunset! If you keep all these, God will provide you with His salvation!'"

Another time, the Elder met a holy hermit in the woods and asked him,

"Tell me, Father, when is the end of the world going to be?"

And the blessed hesychast answered him saying,

"Do you know when the end of the world is going to be? When there is no longer a trodden path between neighbors![28] That is, when love is going to be absent between people!"

---

[28] The idea is that the end of the world will occur when neighbors no longer love each other or visit each other enough to wear a path between their houses *(t.n.)*.

Father Galaction would have the brothers read in the evening, from the Paterikon and the Holy Scriptures, because he longed much to hear the word of God. Once he said to his disciple, "Brother Constantin, please read to me from the Holy Scriptures about Job's patience!"

The whole time brother Constantin read, Father Galaction shed tears. Then he added, "Look, this was a great man in the world, who didn't complain before God when He took away so many of his sheep, cattle and even his children. But me, the sinner, how weak I am in faith! Since if a sheep gets sick or dies, I can't even eat that day!"

"Why can't you eat then, Father Galaction?"—his disciple asked. "How could I dare eat when I see that God punishes my flock because of my sins?"

After 12 years of obedience looking after the monastery's sheep and doing other jobs, in the summer of 1942, monk Cleopa Ilie was appointed locum tenens Igumen of Sihăstria Monastery, and Elder Galaction remained with the sheep and his other disciples.

In the fall of 1946, after about 30 years of obedience, Father Galaction broke his leg. While he was lying in bed, awaiting his end, he heard that a monk named Nazarie had died, so he told his former disciple, Father Cleopa, who had now become the Starets, "Please, Father Starets, do not bury Father Nazarie without me! Don't spend money twice! Tomorrow evening at six o'clock, I will also leave this life!"

The next day, at the foretold hour, Father Galaction, the good soldier of Christ, gave up his spirit into the hands of the Lord. He was turning 64 years old on that day. And that is how this son of obedience came to an end, Archimandrite Cleopa Ilie's spiritual father who had lived with the sheep.

With the Sheep of Sihăstria

F ather Cleopa used to tell us, "During the years when I was a shepherd of the Skete's sheep together with my brothers, I had great spiritual joy. The shed, the sheep, living in quietness and loneliness in the mountains, in the middle of nature, these were a school of monasticism and theology for me.

"I read Saint John Damascene's *Dogmatics* then *The Theologikon* or *The Discovery of the True Orthodox Faith*.[29] Oh, brother, I loved it so much. When the weather was getting warmer, the older lambs and the rams would hide in the bushes. There was enough grass in Poiana Cireșului[30] and they stayed there. 'Stay there!'—I would tell them and continue reading *Dogmatics*.

Father Cleopa amongst the sheep, remembering the years of his youth.

"When I saw what was written there about the Holy Trinity, about angels, man and God, when I read about heaven and hell, about the other dogmatic teachings of Saint John Damascene, I would forget to eat that day.

---

[29] These titles are not exact, most likely *Elementary Introduction into Dogmas, The Fountain of Knowledge* and *An Exact Exposition of the Orthodox Faith (t.n.)*.
[30] Literally, Cherry-tree's Meadow *(t.n.)*.

"There was an old sod house where I used to take shelter and where someone from the monastery would bring me food. And in the evening, when I'd come home, I'd ask myself, 'Did I eat today?' Seeing the food there I'd say, 'I didn't eat!' I was occupied with Saint John Damascene's Dogmatics all day. There were different crocuses there since it was fall, and I would use a crocus as a bookmark.

"While I was tending the sheep, I read *The Paterikon*, *The Ladder* by Saint John Climacus, writings of Saint Macarios of Egypt, Saint Macarios of Alexandria, the books of Saint Theodore the Studite, Saint Isaac the Syrian, Saint Ephraim the Syrian, Saint John Chrysostom's *Fountain*, Saint Basil the Great's *Hexameron*, and the Lives of the Saints—I had purchased all of these volumes from Cozancea Monastery while I was at home, as a civilian. I had these books—and others—in my bag when I joined the monastery. I would read them, and it seemed like the day went by in an hour. The Lives of the Saints strengthen you greatly.

"So, my children, always have a book with you. Read the Akathist to the Savior, to the Mother of God and say the Jesus Prayer… And you should also carry something to protect you from the rain. In those years I prayed a lot, I read the Holy Scriptures and many works of the Holy Fathers. I would borrow these books from the library of Neamț and Secu Monasteries, and take them in a knapsack with me, while I was shepherding the sheep on the mountains.

"After I finished my prayer rule, I would pull out the books of the Holy Fathers and read them until evening near the sheep. It seemed like I could see Saints Anthony, Macarios the Great, John Chrysostom and the others speaking to me. I could see Saint Anthony the Great with a long, white beard, with a bright face, and he told me stories. And everything he was telling me would be imprinted on my mind like when you write with your finger on wax. I cannot forget anything I read back then.

"Later, I also began to write books, but because I wrote them without a blessing, I burned them. But when I went to Elder Ioanichie, our starets, to tell him what I had done, he gave me his blessing saying, 'Write it all!'"

Sometimes Father Cleopa would tell us about encounters he had with spiritual fathers that he met and the edifying words he received from them. Other times he would tell us about other events from his holy life—for example, how he learned to sound the talanton.[31]

"In those days, Father Vichentie Mălău was the spiritual father of Agapia Monastery. Once I found him teaching the nuns how to strike the talanton. The nuns weren't so good at it. Father Vichentie said, 'Look here, this little kid will learn how to strike it quicker than you.' And how did he do it? The Father had written, in different places on the talanton, certain words which he sang, so that the nuns could strike the talanton in those places according to the rhythm of the song. And he went like this, 'Hey come to me, hey come to me, hey come, hey come, hey come to me!'[32] And that's how I learned to sound the talanton."

Prayer and Obedience

While he was attending to the sheep, brother Constantin read in a book that every monk should read the seven Lauds. That is why he memorized them. But he wasn't able to say them because the sheep caused

---

[31] The talanton is a wooden plank struck by mallets to signal the start of services in the Orthodox Church. As tradition goes, Noah sounded the talanton to call the animals into his ark to save them from the Flood. Now, it is used to call God's rational animals into the ark of the Church *(t.n.)*.

[32] If any reader would like to try this rthythm, there is a blessed coincidence that the English translation has exactly the same number of syllables and patterns as the Romanian tune *(t.n.)*.

him trouble. Then he went to Father Starets and told him that he could not do the seven Lauds. And the Starets asked him, "With whose blessing did you learn them and who told you to do the Lauds? You should read the Morning Prayers and the Akathist Hymn to the Mother of God and constantly say, 'Lord Jesus…' The Church serves the Hours for everyone because they are read daily at the chant stand."

How Brother Constantin Was Healed

One spring Constantin had a hemorrhage due to a lung problem. Father Galaction, who was in charge of the sheep stall, sent him to pull up nettle roots, to boil them and to drink the tea. He was soon thereafter healed, and he never had any lung problems again.

After many years, having become Starets of Sihăstria, Novice Constantin went to Bucharest where he had to sort out some things and spoke with some believers in four different locations on the same day. Knowing that he had been sick, a faithful woman wondered how came he had gotten so much strength and brought him to see Doctor Atanasiu, who X-rayed his lungs and asked him, "What did you do, Father, to make your lung grow back like new?" And Father Cleopa told him how he had drunk nettle root tea and, with the help of God, he became healthy.

A Miracle with Saint John the New

Once, novice Constantin went over the mountains to his sister, Ecaterina, at Agapia Veche Monastery. In the forest, at a place named Poiana Trapezei[33], he noticed he was surrounded by a large herd of wild boars, which were a threat to his life. Seeing them approaching, he began to chant Saint John the New of Suceava's Kontakion, "The defender and support of the Christian faith…."

In that moment he no longer saw anything around him. After he climbed up and arrived at the hill's peak, he fell to the ground from fright and fatigue. After he recovered, he arrived at Agapia Veche Monastery with great difficulty.

The Encounter with the Rassophore Ilie Iacob (Saint John Jacob of Neamț)[34]

The blessed John Jacob of Neamț entered monastic life at Neamț Monastery in 1933, having been orphaned by both parents. At that time, the Starets of Neamț Monastery was Bishop Nicodim Munteanu, the future Patriarch of Romania.

---

[33] Trapeza Meadow, in translation *(t.n.)*.

[34] Saint John Jacob of Neamț, also known as Saint John Jacob the Chozebite, was Romanian by birth but he spent most of his ascetic life in monastic places that are under the jurisdiction of the Greek Orthodox Patriarchate of Jerusalem. Born in 1913 in Northern Romania (Botoșani county), he fell asleep in the Lord in 1960, near Chozeva monastery. He is known for his apocalyptic poetry. He was recognized as a saint by the Ecumenical Patriarch Bartholomew I in 1996. In 2016, he was also canonized by the Patriarchate of Jerusalim.

Bishop Nicodim, after blessing him and taking him to venerate the miraculous icon of the Theotokos from Stephen the Great's church, arranged for him to do obedience at the infirmary of the monastery together with monk Iov, who was leading a holy life.

Novice Ecaterina,
Father Cleopa's Sister.

Afterwards, Ilie Iacob was appointed assistant librarian for Neamț Monastery where he took care of ancient manuscripts and lent out books to the monks of the community's lavra, as well as to monks from the surrounding sketes.

Blessed John Jacob (left) on the
day of his Monastic Tonsure at
Neamț in the spring of 1936.

Novice Constantin Ilie from Sihăstria Skete would come to request spiritual books from the monastery's library from this blessed brother who would later live in the Holy Land. Once, in 1934, brother Constantin borrowed the Spiritual Alphabet, written by Saint Dimitry of Rostov, from rassophore Ilie Jacob. In the summer of that same year, rassophore Ilie Jacob came to Sihăstria together with the steward of the great lavra and asked novice Constantin, who was herding sheep in the valley,

"Brother Constantin, have you finished the book *The Spiritual Alphabet* yet?"

"I have a little to read, still. After I finish it, I'll bring it back to the library."

"All right, brother Constantin, may the Lord help you on the path of salvation! At Neamț Monastery there are many holy books. Read them now while you're young, because when you're older, you'll have other worries…!"

His Draft into the Army

In 1935, novice Constantin Ilie was drafted into the army. So, leaving his sheep on the mountains, he descended to the skete, confessed to the Igumen, received the Body and Blood of the Lord, and after praying for a long time, he asked for a blessing to leave for Botoşani to be incorporated into a communications unit.

Over there, he continued to pray and to lead a life of restraint and self-denial. He made a special request, as a monastery novice,[35] to be allowed not to eat meat, and the

---

[35] Even as a novice, Father Cleopa followed the rule of the monastery to abstain from eating meat *(t.n.)*.

unit's commandant agreed that he could take from the canteen whatever food was appropriate for him. He spent his days fasting and praying, and for that reason he never had a bodily impurity in his sleep as long as he was in the army.

For a long time, he wore the monastic garb during military service, since he was assigned to the infirmary. Here he helped the sick, observed his prayer rule, kept the infirmary clean and was honored by all, both officers and soldiers. The unit's commander rejoiced that he was there and protected him in everything, since he was saying the Evening and Morning Prayers in the unit's chapel with the soldiers, and during feast days he took everyone to the church. In this way, many rejoiced at his presence and his life dedicated to Christ.

For this reason, many times the military personnel had him speak to the other soldiers. Even officers gathered to listen and many found his words useful.

In special cases, when sick soldiers urgently needed a priest, novice Constantin would bring in the military chaplain to hear their confessions and give them Holy Communion. Some of them even asked him for spiritual advice, or how they, too, could join the monastic life.

Upon the completion of his military service, his higher-ups made a proposal to him to stay enlisted in the military, "Stay here. Your memory is so good that you'll become a general!" But he refused, saying that he was already, "a soldier in the army of Christ, the King of Kings!"

In 1936, young corporal Constantin Ilie, having been discharged from the army, went back to Sihăstria Skete, giving praise to God and the Theotokos for everything.

Schemamonk Paisie's Covenant with Novice Constantin

S aint Cleopa used to tell his disciples: "When I was a soldier and had a few more months until discharge, I stayed with Father Paisie during my leave and helped him with his work, because he was building a new cell with a chapel. He had my uncle, Father Ghenadie, as a disciple, a man of God who was a shepherd his entire life, never got married, and when he got old, he withdrew to Cozancea Skete.

"Father Paisie, seeing that my leave was ending and that I had to go back to my unit, took me aside and said, 'Tell me, brother Constantin, if you get discharged from the army, won't you come here to stay with me?'

"To which I answered, 'Reverend Father Paisie, I don't want to lie to you. I am spiritually bound to Sihăstria Skete where I went first and where my brothers fell asleep in the Lord. Here, in Cozancea, it is too close to my village, and I would like to live more like a stranger, and unknown by my relatives. After discharge, I'll return to Sihăstria!'

"Hearing this, he teared up and said, 'I had hoped that I would have a disciple from your family. But if you're not thinking about coming here after military service, then I, too, will go to Sihăstria, after a little while!'

'All right, Father Paisie! I'm going back to my unit now ...'

'If you're leaving, I'll come to see you out!'

"We went together until the place where the fields and hills of my village could be seen. Then Father said with tears in his eyes, 'Let's make a covenant! But first, let's make three prostrations!'

'Yes, Father Paisie! Let's do that!'

"After we both made three prostrations, he said this prayer, 'All-Holy Trinity, our God, through the prayers of the Most Pure Theotokos and of all Thy saints, arrange it that if brother Constantin should die before me, I would be at his side,[36] and if I should die before him, that he would be at my side! Amen.' "After that, we said farewell to each other. Our separation took place in the summer of 1936."

This covenant was fulfilled 54 years later, on the October 18, 1990, when the great spiritual father of Moldavia, Hierschemamonk Paisie Olaru, gave his soul into the hands of Christ, for eternity, in Sihăstria Monastery at four o'clock in the morning. Together with other Fathers, Archimandrite Cleopa Ilie stood by the Elder's bed and prayed for him in tears, reading the prayers for the departure of one's soul from the body, from the *Book of Needs*, since Father Cleopa had been his spiritual son since his youth.

Eight years after Hieromonk Paisie's transition to the heavenly dwellings, Archimandrite Cleopa Ilie gave his soul into the hands of the Lord on December 2, 1998, leaving hundreds of monastics and tens of thousands of believers as spiritual orphans, who had all been his spiritual children. We are convinced that these great spiritual fathers of Romanian monasticism are together now in the heaven of delights and pray with all the saints for the salvation of us all!

---

[36] Literally "head," since this is the Orthodox tradition, to stand at the head of the one departing and to read the Psalter.

Another Temptation by the Love of Money

Father Cleopa would tell us: "When I was a novice in Sihăstria, no one would lock their cell, since there was nothing to steal. Everything we needed was given to us by the community. But listen to how the enemy wanted to catch me once through the passion of the love of money. In 1937, when I was a cook, a faithful man came to us and told me, 'Father Cleopa, look at what new and beautiful coins have come out!' And he gave me one coin.

"I took the coin to my cell and I put it on the window sill under a piece of paper so that nobody could see it, and I locked the door. I would go all the time from the kitchen to my cell to lift up the paper on the sill to see if the coin had vanished, then I would come back. After a little while, I would go to the cell again!

"One day, seeing that the enemy had fixed my heart on money, to the point where I locked the door and was thinking only of it, I made the sign of the Cross, I unlocked the door to my cell once again and I gave the coin to a poor person.

"That's how I escaped the love of money!"

Saint Cleopa's Tonsure into Monasticism

Having been discharged from the army in the fall of 1936, novice Constantin Ilie was sent again to do the same obedience as before. Being the youngest shepherd, he helped the other Fathers, Galaction Ilie and Antonie Olaru. He led the sheep to the stall, milked them, cleaned the pen, added rennet to the milk in order to make cheese, and took the sheep to pasture.

All three shepherds were very meek, humble, quiet and loved holy prayer most of all. Everything took place smoothly and peacefully and they never had any trouble in their obedience.

In 1937, at the end of July, the Igumen established that rassophore Constantin Ilie was to become a monk. By then he had six years of discipleship in the monastery and had fulfilled his military duty. His tonsure into monasticism was approved by the Holy Metropolitanate of Moldavia and took place on August 2nd, 1937. His sponsor into monasticism was Schemamonk Proclu Popa, a great ascetic, full of love and humility, originally from Piatra Șoimului commune in Neamț County.

Novice Constantin asked the old schemamonk to take him under his mantle as his sponsor into monasticism. But the latter told him, "Brother Costică, I am very old, I'm 77 now, I have lost my strength. Please, search for someone else to be your sponsor!"

"Father Proclu, if you don't take me under your mantle, I won't take the monastic veil soon!" said novice Constantin.

When the old and meek Schemamonk Proclu heard these words, he rejoiced greatly and said, "Well, brother Costică, get ready, because I'll take you under my mantle tonight!"

The monastic tonsure service began, and his Godfather took him to venerate the icon of the Theotokos, according to tradition, while all the Fathers and brothers prayed to God for him to be strengthened on the path of salvation, and to be able to carry his cross to the end.

But when it was time to give him his monastic name, through the providence of God, a Father who was close to the Igumen, namely Schemamonk Nicolae, told him, "Father Starets, give him the name Cleopa, since we don't have any monk with this name here!"

"Well said, Father Nicolae!"

Then the Starets pronounced it:

"Our brother, monk Cleopa, is tonsured in the name of the Father, Amen, and of the Son, Amen, and of the Holy Spirit, Amen. Let us say, 'Lord have mercy' for him!"

After he was tonsured into monasticism, Monk Cleopa was blessed by his Starets and sat in the chant stand.[37]

That was how Father Cleopa was tonsured into monastic life, he who was to become one of the greatest Staretses and spiritual fathers of Romania!

Sihăstria Skete Burns Down

Through 1938-1941, Sihăstria Skete numbered over 35 fathers and brothers. All the cells were made of firtree wood and quite old, since Starets Ioanichie was an old man, over 80, and it was difficult for him to take care of all necessities of the Skete.

On May 30, 1941, the feast day of our Lord's Ascension drawing near, when thousands of pilgrims come to worship at the monasteries in Neamţ county, fathers and brothers in Sihăstria were trying to cope with the numerous believers who would stop for one night in every monastery.

It was a drought period, and a dry wind was blowing; one spark was enough to set fire to a wooden cell and within half an

---

[37] In traditional Orthodox Churches there are special seats surrounding the chant stand, called *strana*. This is where he was set, not precisely at the chant stand, but in the seats around it.

hour, all the Skete's grounds were caught up in flames. All the cells, the stone church's roof, and the wooden chapel dedicated to Saints Joachim and Ana burned down. Nothing could be saved from the chapel except for few liturgical objects.

In the tumult, some believers went through the flames and grabbed the Holy Gospel, the Holy Tabernacle that kept the Holy Mysteries, a few icons, and holy vessels. Not knowing where the holy relics were, they left them in the Holy Altar and ran outside. While the Starets was grieving over the loss of the holy relics, all of a sudden, a shining white silver box with a long, red ribbon could be seen up in the air, where the holy relics were kept. It had come out of the chapel by itself and after flying overhead, it fell in the middle of the courtyard.

Having witnessed this miracle, the fathers lifted up the box with the Holy Relics, kissed them and gave thanks to God with tears in their eyes. Behold, the God of miracles works miracles in all places and times if we have faith and pray to Him with tears and humility!

Then, the old Starets Ioanichie Moroi, having seen his entire toil of over 30 years destroyed in one hour, with tears in his eyes, made three prostrations in front of the stone church that now had no roof and uttered the words of Righteous Job, "The Lord gave, and the Lord hath taken away; Blessed be the name of the Lord! Amen."

These are the kinds of temptations, dangers, and troubles that the pious Starets was given to experience up until he went to celestial dwellings. However, Protosyngel Ioanichie did not lose heart, but strengthened everyone by saying, "Fathers, don't feel discouraged that the monastery burnt down. It burnt down because of our sins, and also to renew its founders![38] Your Reverends, bear

---

[38] The founders of monasteries and churches are especially honored in Orthodoxy and their names are always read during the Proskomedia service, just before the Divine Liturgy *(t.n.)*.

patiently all the temptations with strength and don't abandon this place sanctified by the prayers and tears of our forefathers. Just observe steadfastly the monastic order of this Skete. For whoever fails to observe the local rules, is driven away by this place! Keep the monastic traditions and don't allow the Divine Liturgy and the seven Lauds to be skipped, not even for just one day.

"If you do this, if you lead a pure life and have love between you, know that the Theotokos will raise this holy place up from its ashes and you will have peace and salvation in this place. But if you fail to diligently observe your prayer rule, fasting and monastic duties, you should know that this place will be deserted. Because God loves a deserted and pure place more than a place with many impure monks!"

While the then Patriarch of Romania, Nicodim, was paying a visit to Neamț Monastery, he discovered that Sihăstria Skete had burned down. So, he told the leading steward of Neamț Monastery, Archimandrite Teofil, to provide the Skete with wood construction material. But the steward said to Patriarch Nicodim, "Your Holiness, how can we help them, it is a distant skete in the forest…" However, the Patriarch said, "No, Teofil, we must help them, because Satan set fire to the monks' nest. And that place will be Romania's lavra."

How Monk Cleopa Was Chosen as the Locum Tenens Igumen

After the fire in the summer of 1941, it became increasingly difficult for Sihăstria Skete to survive. The old Starets Ioanichie Moroi, aged 82, became even sicker. He could no longer serve the Holy Liturgy, and it was difficult for him to hear confessions and to give advice. He was even beaten up by the Balta[39] thieves, who pulled out one of his eyes.

In the summer of 1942, only Hieroschemamonk Ioil Gheorghiu served at Sihăstria. He was a disciple of the old Starets, and was assisted by Hieromonk Calistrat Bobu. Then, because there were not enough cells after the fire, a large number of novices and monks went to Neamţ and Secu Monasteries. Food was cooked in a summer kitchen and it was served in a basement, which served as trapeza during the day, and as a dormitory for the fathers at night.

Despite the state of the Skete, Starets Ioanichie Moroi experienced some comfort, too. Once, when he was ill and was worried about the Skete's fate, a decently dressed woman entered the cell, drew near to him and said, "Don't be sad, Father Ioanichie. From now on we'll take care of this holy place!" It was the Most Holy Theotokos, the Skete's patron! Truly, from 1942 on, the Theotokos' protection and blessing could permanently be felt over Sihăstria.

During the same time, the spiritual fathers, together with the whole council, at Igumen Ioanichie Moroi's proposal, decided to appoint monk Cleopa Ilie as the locum tenens Igumen since he was young, determined and devout. The spiritual fathers and the elders prayed in the church in front of the icon of the Theotokos and they all climbed up to the skete's stall on Mount Tăciune[40] so as to invite Father Cleopa to come as locum tenens for the Starets until God would arrange an Igumen for it.

It was during the fasting before the Holy Apostle's feast day. When they all arrived at the stall, the novices, together with Father Cleopa, were sheering the sheep. Then Hierodeacon Ghemnazie Pristav, who was more daring, told him,

---

[39] Balt was the name of a band of thieves during this time *(t.n.)*.
[40] Literally, "Mount Blight" *(t.n.)*.

"Father Cleopa, the moment has come, as in David's time, for you to leave the breeding animals and now to pasture the speaking ones! Look, the Skete has burnt down, our Starets is blind and sick, and the monks are wasting their efforts! Come and help restore the Skete. All of us want you, and our Father, Starets Ioanichie, who has brought up all of us, spiritually, is calling you, too, because he can't manage any longer!"

Father Cleopa visiting the sheep pen where he spent the first years of his monastic life.

Hearing these words, Father Cleopa said,

"I am too young and can't be the skete's Igumen. Look for someone else because I'm not skilled at advising souls, and I'm a sinful man!"

"No, Father Cleopa, God is calling you now and you must be obedient, like you've always been! We will help you, too, and with the prayers of the Theotokos, we have hope that you can save our Skete's brotherhood from scattering more from day to day!"

"Please, Fathers," said monk Cleopa, "let me pray to God and think for a month, for I'm young and don't know what to do! If not, I will go to Secu Monastery."

"Fine, Father Cleopa, you can take a month to pray!"

Then, descending from the sheep pen, Father Calistrat, who was a confessor, said, "We approached Father Cleopa too abruptly! Let us pray to the Mother of God and let us give him the time to think it through!"

The next day, Father Cleopa wrote a postcard to Father Paisie from Cozancea Skete and asked for his advice what to do in this difficult trial. He fasted for three days and prayed to God for His will to be done.

After ten days he received a post card from hermit Paisie which read, "My beloved son, from me, a sinner, may you be as if you were neither giving nor receiving! Don't rejoice when they appoint you Starets and don't be upset when they remove you from this position! Obey to the old Starets and to the council of the Fathers, and leave yourself totally to the will of God."

Thus, Schemamonk Paisie blessed him to help with the renewal of Sihăstria Skete and after a month of prayer and waiting, Monk Cleopa took over the administrative lead of the community. The Fathers and brothers rejoiced at this change; everyone obeyed his words, and the Elder Starets was happy that his beloved disciple had been chosen by God to guide the Skete.

Locum Tenens Igumen

Father Cleopa's first concern was to renew the monastery grounds and the cells that had burnt down in 1941. With support from Neamț Monastery, which contributed hundreds of cubic meters of wood and timber for free, in the fall of 1942, they started building two wings of cells with more than 20 rooms, to replace those that had been destroyed by the fire. In the following years, 1943-1944, the faithful from the village Rădășeni, Suceava, who had been evacuated into the surrounding public forests because of the war, worked unwaveringly on these cells.

The new Igumen was revered by both the Skete's community and the believers who had taken refuge there, since he was pious, meek, committed to long fasting, and strengthened everyone—monastics and laymen alike. He also had a special gift for speaking, through which he guided and spiritually fed each listener.

After the army front went farther away and passed over to the West of the Carpathian Mountains, Father Cleopa continued to build cells and covered the stone church with a tin roof.

In this manner, by the grace of God and the blessing of the Theotokos, the protectress of this holy establishment, Father Cleopa proved from the beginning to be a very zealous monk, a courageous and spiritual Igumen, and a good steward.

The End of Starets Ioanichie Moroi's Life

After 33 years of harsh spiritual asceticism, Protosyngel Ioanichie Moroi grew very ill and could no longer lead Sihăstria Skete. Yet, he was joyful that his disciple, monk Cleopa, had been appointed to continue his spiritual activity.

The great Starets spent most of the last two years of his life in his cell, praying to God day and night, confessing and giving advice to his disciples. He was glad that the Skete was renewing itself both spiritually and materially.

In 1943, Starets Ioanichie's condition became more critical. He had two disciples that took care of him day and night. But in August 1944, his biological son, monk Nicanor, was shot by Russian soldiers near the front.

On September 3, 1944, sensing that his end was drawing near, the Elder called everyone near his bed and gave them his last advice: namely, to pray ceaselessly, to do obedience with love, to love the holy church and to live a pure life in Christ. Then, asking for forgiveness, he kissed them all and told them three times, "I am going to the Father on Tuesday!", thus prophesying the end of his life.

After a life of difficult trials and great suffering, on September 5, at 10 a.m., the great Starets Ioanichie Moroi gave up his soul into the hands of the Heavenly Father, leaving behind him a worthy disciple in the person of Father Cleopa Ilie. Mourned by the whole community, Father Ioanichie was buried in the new cemetery from the monastery's orchard.

The grave of Protosyngel Ioanichie Moroi (1859-1944).

How Monk Cleopa Was Chosen as Permanent Igumen

After the old Igumen Ioanichie Moroi moved to the celestial realms, the entire responsibility of providing for Sihăstria Skete weighed on the shoulders of monk Cleopa. He did not want to be ordained a deacon and a priest because he was afraid of this great responsibility before the Lord. Yet, look how God arranged it for him to be ordained and then appointed full Igumen of the Skete.

In October 1944, monk Cleopa, together with a few brothers, went to the skete's vineyard in Racova commune, Buhuși, in order to take the grapes. On the way, near Buhuși, a pious woman came out to meet them, holding a set of priestly vestments, a Divine Liturgy service book,[41] and a priestly staff, and she told him:

"Father, these vestments and holy objects were left in my house by a military chaplain that stayed with us during the war. Then, he went to the distant front, left them in our house, and I don't know what to do with them!"

"Sister, give them to a church or a monastery that needs them, because it's not good for you to keep these holy objects in your house!"

"Father, if I give them to Your Reverence, will you accept them?"

"Give them to us, Christian woman, so that we can take them to the monastery, because it's a sin to let them lie just anywhere!"

---

[41] *Liturghier,* in Romanian. This book contains the text of the Divine Liturgy, prayers and various hymns. It is customary to receive this book after ordination into the priesthood *(t.n.).*

"Here you are, Father: the vestments, the book, and the staff. Thanks God that I've met you and I am handing them over to you!"

Taking these objects, Father Cleopa placed them in the wagon and thought to himself, "Why did this woman bring these vestments, staff, and Holy Liturgy service book precisely to me? Could this be a sign from God that He wants me to be ordained a priest and to guide the Sihăstria Skete community with this staff?"

Having returned from the vineyard and going to confession, he told his spiritual father all of this. And his spiritual father, understanding that it was a sign from God, told him, "Obey, Father Cleopa, since this is what all of us vowed to do when we became monks; without this, we cannot be saved! And then, who will lead the Skete's community if we all run away from responsibility? The Holy Fathers say, 'Obedience is life and disobedience is death!'"

After two months, on December 27, 1944, when Saint Steven the Archdeacon is celebrated, monk Cleopa was ordained a deacon, and on January 23, 1945, when the Holy Martyr Clement is celebrated, he was ordained a hieromonk by Bishop Galaction Cordun, who was Starets of Neamț Monastery at that time.

After a little while, Hieromonk Cleopa Ilie was officially appointed as the Igumen of Sihăstria Skete

Sihăstria Skete Between the Years 1945-1946

As the war came to an end, the work of renovating the Skete, that had begun in 1942, continued for three more years. Thus, in 1945, the new trapeza was finished and blessed; over 100 people could eat there. Likewise, a good portion of the cells on the north side of the compound had been completed, containing ten large rooms and a kitchen for the whole community. Between 1945 and 1946, the southern wing of the compound's cells was rebuilt, comprising ten smaller rooms.

Here is what Saint Cleopa was telling us about the difficulties he encountered when renewing the skete: "When they appointed me Starets, it was very difficult. The skete lacked everything. Our feast day was approaching and we did not have anything prepared. The cells had burnt down, the bells had melted, and the church's large roof had been consumed by fire, too. So, I went to Neamţ Monastery to borrow some money. But they didn't give me any because they did not have funds.

"Then I went to Protosyngel Ioachim Spătaru, the man of God! A good Christian from Bucharest was with him, Constantine Vâlsan, the general director of the Telephone Company. Hearing that we had nothing for our feast day, he gave me 800,000 lei, which was a lot of money at that time. When I came back to Sihăstria, Father Ioil was waiting for me, our spiritual father, who had been praying to God that we would receive some help. When he learnt about the donation we received, he rejoiced and gave thanks to God."

In the spring of 1946, the faithful of Rădășeni commune, Suceava county, who had been evacuated during the war into the forests surrounding Sihăstria, decided to build, for free, a new winter chapel to replace the one that had burnt down in 1941, and which would have the same feast day, namely the Holy Ancestors of God, Joachim and Anna.

The founder of this new establishment was Hieromonk and Spiritual Father Gherasim Câmpanu, originally from the same village. By the end of 1946, the chapel was almost ready. It lacked only the iconostasis, which was still being worked on, and the interior frescoes. Through this work, the inhabitants of Rădăşeni and of other villages showed their gratitude to God and to the ascetics of the Skete, for being delivered from deadly dangers in Sihăstria, during the war in the summer of 1944.

During these two years, 1945 and 1946, God arranged for numerous people, young and old, to join the Skete's brotherhood, and so the number of its dwellers increased greatly. This happened for two reasons: firstly, because of the famine and poverty that were threatening the entire country, and secondly, because of the special renown that Protosyngel Cleopa had started to acquire. Sihăstria Skete thus began to have an extraordinary breadth, both spiritually and materially.

The soul behind this flourishment was, of course, Father Cleopa, the man of God, who had begun to be increasingly more famous in the area. For, while other monasteries and sketes were lacking personnel and especially spiritual fathers, Sihăstria was blossoming day by day thanks to the meek and merciful Igumen of the Skete. He was a priest, a father and spiritual guide for everyone: monastics, intellectuals, faithful laymen, poor people and the beggars.

He was sought after daily and he stood in the midst of the crowds helping, advising, reprimanding, feeding and reconciling each and every person. Thus, Father Cleopa became known throughout Romania, especially for his gift of the gab and for his homilies, then for his skills as a confessor and spiritual guide, and finally for his alms.

Due to his spiritual kindness and wisdom, God multiplied grace and gifts in him and poured out His blessings on the Skete's community through the prayers of the Most Holy Theotokos, the protectress of this holy establishment.

The Holy Bishop John from Sihla Mountains and Father Cleopa

T he blessed Bishop John met the brothers Constantin and Vasile for the first time in the fall of 1930, in the Sihla mountains at a place called "Râpa lui Coroi"[42], when he prophesied to Vasile, through his brother Constantin, that "he had to prepare for a long journey." Truly, after six months, his brother Vasile gave up his soul to the Lord.

We do not know about other encounters that Father Cleopa had with this amazing bishop, but we do believe that there must have been others. However, the turbulent times of the years 1940-1950 were such that this holy bishop was not spoken about publicly. He lived an ascetic life in this area until after 1951.

The three "meetings" between Agapia Monastery's Spiritual Father, Protosyngel Teodul Varzare and this holy bishop in Poiana Trapezei, on the footpath that descends from Agapia to Sihăstria, are conclusive enough.

The first encounter took place in the spring of 1946, when the bishop asked for paper and ink "because he had something to write."

Seeing the spiritual father, the bishop blessed him with both hands and told him in a prophetic voice, "Father Teodul, are you going to Sihăstria, to Father Cleopa? I go many times to Sihăstria, too, and stay for the service in the church, but by the gift of God, no one sees me!

---

[42] Coroi's Gorge *(t.n.)*.

"I know that Your Reverence wishes to withdraw from Agapia to Sihăstria, but don't go. Stay where you are and be obedient, because God did not send you to Agapia without a purpose. Your salvation is there!"

See what level of holiness this great bishop and vessel of the Holy Spirit had attained!

Blessed Bishop John participating invisibly at the Holy Liturgy served by Father Cleopa.

The bishop attended the holy services in Sihăstria, but no one could see him. However, he honored Father Cleopa in a special way.

The second encounter between Father Teodul and Bishop John took place in the summer of the same year, in the same place, when the former brought paper and ink, as the latter had asked for, but no one knows if the blessed Bishop wrote anything and if he did, what exactly he wrote.

The bishop blessed him again with both hands, kissed his forehead and said to him, "Father Teodul, are you going to Sihăstria? You'd better return to Agapia, because Father Cleopa is not in the Skete today, as he has been summoned to Neamţ Monastery to attend the council meeting!" See how amazing this bishop was, full of the grace of the Holy Spirit! He was praying for Father Cleopa and was helping him, through grace, to guide this holy place well.

This holy bishop, who lived ascetically in the Sihla mountains, had been a vicar bishop at the Metropolitanate of Kiev up until 1918, after which he took refuge in Romania. He was in close spiritual connection with Sihăstria Monastery and with Father Cleopa, with whom he probably met in secret at night or through the Holy Spirit, through holy prayer. Some spiritual fathers believe that the holy bishop met with Father Cleopa occasionally, when he had withdrawn in the Sihăstria Mountains in 1948, since both of them had hermit cells in that area.

We have been convinced that those who serve Christ with a pure heart know each other both here and beyond the grave, they search for each other, love each other, help each other, and pray for each other. For this is the joy of the pious, the praise of the righteous and the comfort of the saints, that both "in the body" and "out of the body" recognize each other through grace in Jesus Christ, the Savior of the world.

The third and last encounter between Bishop John and Father Teodul took place in the summer of 1947, when he wanted to return to his own country.

Sihăstria Skete Is Raised
to the Rank of Monastery

In 1947, since the name of Protosyngel Cleopa Ilie, Igumen of Sihăstria Skete, together with his spiritual and administrative activity, had become well known, the Romanian Patriarchate took into account the efforts towards the overall renewal of this monastic establishment.

The first who proposed that Sihăstria Skete should be elevated to the rank of an independent, self-ruling monastery was Archimandrite Teofil Pandele, the then general inspector and director in the Ministry of Cults, who was overseeing the activity of all monasteries in the country, both at the level of governmental administration and at the level of the Patriarchate.

Having investigated Sihăstria Skete's canonical and administrative situation, and noticing that this establishment met all legal conditions to be raised to the rank of monastery, Archimandrite Teofil Pandele drew an extensive memorandum that he handed to Patriarch Nicodim, to the Metropolitan of Moldavia, Irineu Mihălcescu, and to the Minister of Religions. Examining the monastery in person, he confirmed that Sihăstria Skete had a community of over 50 inhabitants, and that it was carrying out extraordinary missionary and spiritual activities in the area, being led by a self-taught Starets of great renown.

Taking all these aspects into consideration, at the proposal of the Metropolitan of Moldavia, the Patriarch of Romania approved the Sihăstria Skete to be raised to the rank of monastery, as well as Protosyngel Cleopa Ilie to be raised to the rank of Archimandrite. This decision was taken because within only five years, he had managed to turn a skete that had been totally consumed by fire into a renowned and well-organized monastery.

Archimandrite Cleopa Ilie in 1947.

Father Cleopa's as an Archimandrite was done by Bishop Valerie Moglan, the Vicar Bishop of the Metropolitanate of Moldavia, in Sihăstria Monastery on September 19, 1947. In his homily, Bishop Valerie addressed the following words to Archimandrite Cleopa, "Father Cleopa, receive this staff. Whoever obeys you, obeys God! Whoever doesn't obey, you could beat them with all the wood from the forest, and you still won't be able to make a man out of him."

We reproduce below the synodical document that raised Sihăstria Skete, Neamț County, to the rank of a monastery dedicated to the feast of The Nativity of the Theotokos".

The Patriarch of Romania
Nr. 298 Cabinet
1947, June 30

Decision nr. 299

Through the mercy of God, Nicodim, Archbishop of Bucharest, Metropolitan of Ungrovlachia[43] and Patriarch of Romania.

Considering report no. 83/947 of Holy Sihăstria Skete from Neamț County, which requests to be raised to the rank of Monastery;

Considering that the personnel of the Holy Skete is larger than 50 people;

Considering the love and abnegation with which the personnel of the Holy Sihăstria Skete from Neamț County fulfill their monastic duties,

We Hereby Decide:

Art. I. Sihăstria Skete from Neamț County, is to be raised to the rank of Monastery, to be named "Holy Sihăstria Monastery", Neamț County, in the future.

Art. II. The All-Pious Fr. Starets of the Holy Neamțu-Secu Monastery, Neamț County, is charged with bringing to fulfillment this present Decision.

Taken in our patriarchal meeting, today, June 30, 1947.

PATRIARCH,
NICODIM

---

[43] *Ungrovlachia* was the Greek term by which the Patriarchate of Constantinopolis referred to the Bishopric and then (from the 1350's on), the Metropolitante from Wallachia (Romanian principality north of the Danube) *(t.n.)*.

In parallel with this synodical decision, Sihla Skete, which was led at the time by Hieromonk Clement Popovici, was transferred under obedience to Sihăstria Monastery. Likewise, the meadow named Piciorul Crucii[44] and Tăciune mountain became property of Sihăstria Monastery.

These few facts have been written down lest they should be forgotten by those who will come after us.

The Tonsure into Monasticism of Father Cleopa's Mother

As she no longer had anyone at home, the elderly mother Ana Ilie often wept for her nine children who had departed early to the Lord. Her only solace was the village's church and the cemetery. She was never absent from the church during the feast days, and after services she would light candles in the cemetery.

Her last remaining support was now Father Cleopa, the Starets of Sihăstria, who had been chosen by God to serve Christ's Church.

Her children had all died at an early age, except for Father Cleopa, and her husband Alexandru had also moved to his eternal abode in 1943.

Regarding this moment, Father Cleopa would say, "When my father died, my mother sent me one telegram after another, calling me to the funeral."

Later, when we met, my mother asked me, "Why didn't you come to your father's funeral?"

---

[44] The Foot of the Cross, in translation *(t.n.)*.

*Father Cleopa and
Mother Agafia.*

*Nun Agafia in the last
years of her life.*

"I have joined the monastery and I no longer have a father or a mother!", I replied.

"How's that? Am I not your mother?" the old woman asked in tears.

"Come to the monastery and then you'll be my mother!"

In the late fall of November, in 1946, Father Cleopa brought his mother from his native village, Sulița, to Sihăstria Skete, so that she could join the sisterhood in Agapia Veche Monastery.

Here she prayed in the church day and night and rejoiced greatly for the young novices who had come to serve Christ, treating them like her own children.

In the fall of 1947, on September 21, Father Cleopa's mother was tonsured into monasticism for Agapia Veche Monastery, and her name was changed from Ana to Agafia. She joined the sisterhood of Agapia Veche monastery in the spring of 1948 and was entrusted to a spiritual mother named Olimpiada. Here she lived in monastic asceticism for over 20 years, praying to God day and night and sharing in the joys and sorrows of her three disciples, nuns Mihaela, Iustina and Iulia, who are still alive, in the community of Agapia Veche Monastery[45].

Every day Mother Agafia carried wood to the kitchen, though she was old. Her disciple would say, "Mother Agafia, why do you carry wood to the kitchen on your back?" And she would answer, "Well, should I eat for free?"

When a poor person came to Agapia Veche and Mother Agafia had no money, she would take some from her disciples and tell them, "I took a little from you because I don't have!" And they would answer, "It's good, Mother Agafia, that you took some." She, however, gave everything to the poor!

---

[45] This was true at the time when the book was written, at the end of the 20th century (t.n.).

Even as a civilian, Mother Agafia gave a lot of alms to the poor. Sometimes she mentioned that her husband would rebuke her saying, "Hey, woman, in vain do I bring stuff by the wagon, since you give everything away by the bag!"

From time to time, Mother Agafia went over the mountains and came to Sihăstria to speak to Father Cleopa and to pray by the graves of her sons, rassophore Vasile and monk Gherasim, in the cemetery. Then she would go back to Agapia Veche, comforted by the words of Fathers from Sihăstria.

One of the Miracles of the Theotokos

It was the summer of 1947. Archimandrite Cleopa left for Bucharest to bring ecclesial objects for the new chapel. Arriving in the capital, the Patriarchate's Fathers invited him to a spiritual meeting in the house of Alexandru Mironescu, a university professor, where many priests, professors and faithful had already gathered.

Among them were Archimandrites Benedict Ghiuş, Dosoftei Moraru, and Gherontie Ghenoiu, Rev. Professor Dumitru Stăniloae[46], and many other intellectuals. They were discussing spiritual questions. When Father Cleopa entered the room, the guests stood on their feet and, asking for a blessing, they were waiting for Father Cleopa to tell them words of spiritual benefit.

Since they asked him to speak, Father Cleopa began to share with them teachings of the Holy Fathers about honoring

---

[46] A confessor for Christ and the most influential 20th century theologian in Romania, perhaps in all of Europe, an authentic scholar and amazing spiritual force, who was canonized as a saint in the Romanian calendar by the same synodical decision as Father Cleopa *(t.n.)*.

the Holy Mother. While he was speaking to them, a miracle suddenly took place!

The large icon of the Theotokos on the wall, in which Prophet David was represented as well, began to shake powerfully and continued to do so for a few minutes, emitting a sound like a harp. The Fathers and the faithful gathered in the room were overwhelmed with emotions, not understanding what miracle that was. Some were weeping, others were making the sign of the cross, others were venerating the icon of the Theotokos, while others were praying with tears. Among them, Archimandrite Benedict Ghiuş was the most moved, repeating over and over, "Mother of God... Mother of God... A miracle! A miracle!"

After a few minutes, the icon stopped short, the pendulum swung normally, and everyone, moved, prayed to the Mother of God to take mercy on the country and the Romanian people. This miracle of the Mother of God with her Infant in her arms greatly strengthened the faith of those present, comforting their souls.

After Father Cleopa ended his speech, they all chanted the Axion of the Mother of God and each one withdrew thinking of the miracle that had taken place. Most of them believed this miracle to be a sign from the Mother of God to fortify and comfort the Orthodox believers at a time when Romania heavy trials disturbed the country.

The Consecration of the New Chapel

The new chapel in Sihăstria Skete, dedicated to the Holy Ancestors of God, Joachim and Ana, was built in 1946 by the Spiritual Father Calistrat from Secu Monastery. In 1941, since the old chapel had burned down, the faithful from Rădășeni commune built a new wooden chapel nearby, with the same feast day.

Then, the iconostasis was sculpted in oak wood, and the holy vessels, vestments and necessary liturgical objects were purchased. The other sculpted furnishings were made by the famous sculptor Gheorghe Gheorghiță from Târgu Neamț, between 1965 and 1980.

In the fall of 1947, the chapel was prepared for consecration. The date for the consecration was set for October 26, the feast day of the Holy and Glorious Great Martyr Demetrios the Myrrh-Gusher. The consecration service was celebrated by Bishop Valerie Moglan from Neamț Monastery, who also gave a beautiful homily.

In the same fall, after the completion of work in the chapel, Father Cleopa was looking for a painter to do the interior frescos. But he was not satisfied with those who were offering to do this job.

Then God arranged it for them to find a skilled painter named Ioan Protcenco, originally from Ukraine, who was painting icons for the churches near the capital. At Father Cleopa's insistence, the painter was brought to Sihăstria and in the spring of 1948, the chapel's mural painting began. The painter was a profound and contemplative Christian. He was praying a lot, speaking very little and practicing the Jesus Prayer. He only painted while fasting. After eating he would not paint anything else on that day, considering it to be a sin to paint after a meal. He would rest for a while on a bench in the orchard, always alone, then he would return to his room and prepare his paints for the following day. Though he could not see properly with one eye, this painter made exceptional icons thanks to the holy life that he led.

Before the end of his life, he received the monastic schema under the name of Irineu. His exemplary life urged his brothers in the monastery to toil more for their salvation.

Joys and Troubles

We cannot pass over in silence the troubles that Sihăstria Monastery, especially the Starets of this holy establishment, went through. In the fall of 1947, a year of famine, Archimandrite Cleopa strove to feed both the monastery's community and the faithful, bereft of everything, who were asking for food.

The Elder had asked for the oil in their pantry to be boiled so that it would not spoil over winter. While the pot of oil was boiling on the stove, through the negligence of the brother who was overseeing it, the oil got overheated and caught fire.

Hearing this, Father Cleopa went quickly, lifted the big pot off the stove with his bare hands, and took it out in the monastery's courtyard so that the kitchen would not catch fire. This was an act of great sacrifice, as Father Cleopa burned both hands to save the monastery from fire. He was in pain for a long time before he healed completely.

For a few years during this period, towards the end of 1947, an infamous band of thieves had been robbing households and monasteries in the Neamţ region, creating trouble, causing damage and scandals everywhere.

Since Sihăstria Monastery and Sihla Skete lay in the area where these brigands had made their shelter, and they were more isolated than other monasteries, they suffered significantly at the hands of these thieves.

Soon after the chapel was consecrated, the monastery's courtyard was surrounded by brigands. The faithful were held captive in the church under the threat of arms, and the thieves took all good provisions from the monastery's storehouse.

Father Cleopa told us about this event:

"One night when I was the starets and attended the vigil service in the church, Balta came with his gang, took me out from church and asked for wine, food, and money. Since we had nothing, they took me to the forest and tied me to a tree to shoot me. Then one of them said to their leader, 'Don't you remember how he was feeding us when he was at the sheep pen? And now you want to shoot him?' And they started to argue among themselves and walked into the woods. However, they untied me and I returned to the monastery."

The next day, Father Cleopa, saddened by all of this, went to Bishop Valerie from Neamț Monastery to ask for advice.

"Your Grace, what should we do to deliver the monastery from these brigands who have been robbing and troubling us for six years?"

"Father Cleopa, you know what you should do? Hold a Vigil service for the Holy Protection of the Theotokos every Tuesday evening and read the Psalter Day and night in the Church, for two hours, each person, from the Starets to the last novice. If you do this, the Mother of God will drive away these thieves and bless you with everything that you need, and the Monastery will be guarded from all danger!"

Hearing this, Starets Cleopa ruled that a Vigil service for the Holy Protection of the Theotokos be held every Tuesday evening, and that the Psalter be read ceaselessly in the church when there was no service. This rule is observed to this today. And those evil-doers were caught and punished according to the law. Since then,

Sihăstria Monastery has been spared from all dangers through the prayers of the Theotokos, the protectress of the holy place.

How Father Cleopa
Saved a Woman from Death

One night in 1947, Father Cleopa confessed many people up until after midnight and was feeling tired. When he wanted to rest a little, a troubled lady entered, crying, and said:

"Father, I've been standing here for six hours… I've come to confess because heavy sins are burdening my soul."

"Woman, I am tired. Please come in the morning."

"Father, if you don't hear my confession now, I'll go kill myself. Look, I've even got the rope on me. I have committed great sins and have aborted many children. Listen to me, 'cause I can't bear it anymore."

The Elder confessed the woman, encouraged her and strengthened her spiritually. He gave her a canon for repentance and absolved her of her greatest sins. The next day, after the Holy Liturgy, she took Great Aghiasmos[47], kissed the holy icons, and returned to her house in peace. Such difficult cases would arrive many times, yet Father Cleopa, with his meekness and wisdom, always succeeded in comforting and reconciling everyone.

---

[47] The holy water blessed on January 6, the feast of Theophany. Christians who committed great sins and are forbidden by their spiritual father to take Holy Communion can receive Great Agiasmos instead *(t.n.)*.

Father Paisie's Entrance into the Cenobium of Sihăstria

As Igumen and Starets, Archimandrite Cleopa wanted greatly to bring his first spiritual father, Hieromonk Paisie, into his monastic community. By the will of God, in the year 1948, on December 1st, the great Spiritual Father Paisie Olaru from Cozancea Skete joined the Cenobium of Sihăstria Monastery, to the comfort and joy of everyone.

From the start, Hieroschemamonk Pasie was appointed to guide and confess the faithful who were coming in ever increasing numbers. Thus, Sihăstria Monastery, through its Starets at that time and through its skilled spiritual fathers, created a movement of spiritual renewal in the monasteries from the Neamț area.

Every day, there were monks and faithful civilians who were coming to Sihăstria, waiting for their turn to speak with Spiritual Father Paisie and to open up their hearts before him. Priests, monks, Christian believers from villages and cities, intellectuals, young people of all ages would come out of his cell with a bright face and would give glory to God that He had arranged it that there should be such a meek and skillful spiritual father.

Friday was the day when monks would go for their weekly confession. Over half of the monastery confessed to Father Paisie and took comfort from his wisdom, silence, and humility. He did not speak much, but bolstered the people spiritually, especially through his kindness and steadfastness. He could confess, on average, between 50 and 100 persons per day, monastics and faithful from all over Romania.

Archimandrite Cleopa's First Refuge into the Mountains

Having gone on foot with the Monastery's sheep through the mountains for many years, Father Cleopa knew all the hermits' locations and cells in the Sihăstria and Sihla areas. Likewise, he knew numerous hesychastic monks that were very ascetic and labored deep into forests, completely unknown by anyone except God and their spiritual fathers.

In 1948, on May 21, when the monastery was celebrating the Holy Emperors Constantine and Helen, Elder Cleopa celebrated the Holy Liturgy with many priests and gave the sermon of the day, praising the zeal of the great emperors who granted freedom to Christians and built many churches.

Later, the Elder said to his disciples, "On the day of the Holy Emperors Constantine and Helen, I was giving a sermon and said, 'May God grant it that our current leaders be like the Holy Emperors, so that the Church could commemorate them unto the ages of ages!'

"One of the men who were present there recorded me and hardly had I taken off my liturgical vestments when a car drove up and I was told to go with the persons inside. They took me to Târgu Neamț and put me in a cellar with nothing in it except for a bed made of cement. They interrogated me for five days, without giving me any water or food. Then they released me."

After a couple of days, a Christian benefactor told Father Cleopa in secret to withdraw to the mountains or some other place for a time. Hearing this, the Starets took council with a few spiritual fathers and that night he withdrew into the Sihăstria

Mountains, in the place named Piciorul Cucului [48], deep in the forest, over six kilometers above the Monastery. He made a hut out of wood and earth and prayed unceasingly day and night, asking for help and mercy from God and the Theotokos.

Once a week, Hieromonk Macarie would come up during the night to confess him and bring him something to eat. Sometimes monk Antonie would also come, from the sheep pen, with whom he had done obedience when tending to the sheep.

Father Cleopa used to tell us that while he was making his hut, some birds would come and lie on the crown of his head. When he received Holy Communion for the first time in front of the hut, a flock of birds came to him such as he had never seen before. They had a mark in the form of a cross on their foreheads and sang beautifully the entire time he partook. Then they flew away.

Later, when he finished the Holy Gifts, he decided to celebrate the Divine Liturgy. After he prepared himself and read all the prayers, he placed the Holy Antimension on a nearby log and began the service. Upon giving the blessing, saying, *Blessed is the Kingdom of the Father and of the Son and of the Holy Spirit, Amen*, a flock of beautiful birds appeared again. The birds sat in a nearby bush and began to sing. Father Cleopa asked himself, "What could this be?" But a secret voice spoke inside him, "These are the chanters for the analogion."

Then he continued the Holy Liturgy and took communion. When he finished, the birds flew away. Father Cleopa used to say that since that moment, he never again saw birds as beautiful as those ones in the forest. Of course, the fact that he took communion and witnessed the miracle with the birds comforted him very much. So, he gave thanks to God from his heart for His great love for mankind.

---

[48] The Cuckoo's Leg, in translation *(t.n.)*.

For as long as he stayed in this place, he was also helped by Protosyngel Ioil Gheorghiu and by a Christian man from Metocul Bălan village. The signal for the meeting with Father Antonie was this: the disciple would strike a tree once and if the Elder heard the sound, he would strike another tree once, too. If one of them did not answer, the other would wait until he heard the previously established signal.

Father Ioil would bring him food supplies, salt, wheat, and bread rusks, and put them under a fallen tree, because no one knew where his hut stood.

Father Cleopa toiled a lot in his earthen hut, praying night and day. For this reason the devils would tempt and frighten him, either when he was awake or in his sleep, and through all kinds of delusions, as he would tell his disciples later.

"Once, around midnight, I was reading my prayer rule and had gotten to the Akathist Hymn to the Holy Protection of the Theotokos. All of a sudden, I heard a loud noise. 'Well,' I said. 'There's a big earthquake!' When I opened the door just a bit, I saw a wheel as tall as the fir trees with black figures around it, holding pitchforks of fire. One of them said, 'This is the Starets of Sihăstria! Put 'im on the wheel!' and immediately I realized I was on top of the wheel. The wheel was spinning and they stood ready with their pitchforks, so that I would fall off the wheel into their pitchforks.

"Clutching the Akathist book tightly to my chest, I cried out, 'Step aside for I have papers from the Theotokos!' Then I didn't see anything, neither the wheel nor anything… And I found myself in the hut."

Father Cleopa read the Akathist Hymn to the Holy Protection of the Theotokos daily. After the above-mentioned temptation, he noticed a fragrant smell of lilies and roses when he opened the book to read. Then, fearing it might be a deception from the enemy to push him towards pride, he prayed to God to take away the fragrance from him. For Father Cleopa used to say, "When you pray it is not good to receive any kind of fragrance or any sensory impressions, because then the devils come before you, wanting to push you to feel proud." He sensed this fragrance for over forty days upon opening his book to read the Akathist of the Holy Protection, after which the smell disappeared. That is how he escaped the devil's traps!

*

Forty years after these events, Father Cleopa went together with two of his disciples to search for the hut in which he had stayed in 1948. They went slowly through the forest for a few hours to the area where the Elder had lived ascetically, but they could not find it. Then they walked farther on. On the way back, feeling tired, they sat down on the edge of a ravine in order to eat something.

While eating, Father Cleopa noticed that they were sitting right where the hut had stood. It was now in ruins. They could only see pieces of wood, cardboard and iron. The Elder was very delighted that they had found the hut of his youth and said, "Look, a real miracle! When we thought we had wearied ourselves to no avail, God helped us rejoice by finding the hut!" Then, giving praise to the Lord, they returned to the Monastery.

Archimandrite Cleopa as Starets of Slatina Monastery

After about one year of peace, sadness covered the brotherhood of Sihăstria Monastery again. It was August 1949, and Archimandrite Cleopa had been called to the Holy Patriarchate by Patriarch Justinian, who respected him

*Protosyngel
Ioil Gheorghiu,
Starets of Sihăstria
Monastery between
1949 and 1956.*

very much. By the order of the Patriarch, Elder Cleopa was to go with a group of 30 monastics from Sihăstria Monastery to Slatina Monastery in Suceava, in order to renew its community and spiritual life.

When he returned to Sihăstria, Father Cleopa chose 30 fathers: spiritual fathers, priests, monks and novices, including Hierochemamonk Paisie Olaru. Then, leaving Protosyngel Ioil Gheorghiu, disciple of the great Starets Ioanichie Moroi, as Starets of Sihăstria Monastery, he established his departure for August 30, 1949.

Breaking the monastic community into two and separating one group from the other was painful for all. Everybody was weeping and praying, asking for help from the Theotokos. The entire community accompanied Father Cleopa and the other 30

Fathers, and brothers along the road; near Pârâul Alb[49], they said farewell to each other, embracing each other and shedding tears. In that exact moment, Archimandrite Maxim, the spiritual father of Agapia Monastery, a great protopsales and a skilled and determined priest, was coming to Sihăstria.

Witnessing this separation, he encouraged both groups saying, "Fathers, why are you so sad? The Holy Fathers gave their life for Christ and defended Orthodoxy, and Your Reverences are weeping here like by the river of Babylon? Listen to how the Church chants, 'Oh, holy martyrs who have contested well and have been crowned: Intercede with the Lord that He have mercy on our souls.' So, be obedient and God will help you through the prayers of the Theotokos." Then they chanted 'It is Truly Right' and 'O Champion General', and they separated.

The Community of the Slatina Monastery, pastored by Father Cleopa in 1950.

Slatina Monastery, founded by Alexandru Lăpușneanu in 1554, had only eight old monks and it was waiting for them. It was difficult in the beginning, but in a few months, the new community got adjusted and everything felt normal.

Father Cleopa began to renew the spiritual life at Slatina, setting the daily and nightly holy services and Divine Liturgy

---

[49] The White Stream, in translation *(t.n.)*.

in proper order. He likewise organized weekly confession, a monastic school for the brothers, and community life, according to the model of Saint Theodore the Studite.

In 1950, a few skilled theologians who especially esteemed Father Cleopa joined the Cenobium. Among these were Protosyngel Petroniu Tănase, Hierodeacon Antonie Plămădeală, the future Metropolitan of Ardeal, Archimandrite Dosoftei, Protosygel Gherontie Bălan, Hieroschemamonk Daniil Tudor, and Hieromonk Arsenie Papacioc.

They all helped Father Cleopa to successfully manage the voivodal[50] monastery, turning Slatina Monastery into a true spiritual academy, unique at that time in the whole country.

The news of the monastery's renewal spread out everywhere, to the point that numerous pilgrims, faithful, students, intellectuals, and people of all ages and social classes went there on pilgrimages to receive guidance from Elder Cleopa and the other spiritual fathers. Under the guidance of Protosyngel Petroniu, a beautiful church choir was organized, consisting of 30 young brothers whose singing moved souls.

And in this manner the renewal of Slatina Monastery began.

Spiritual Guide of Several Monasteries in Moldavia

Archimandrite Cleopa was then appointed by the Metropolitanate of Moldavia to supervise and guide the spiritual life of several surrounding monasteries—Putna, Moldovița, Râșca, Sihăstria, Sihla, and Rarău Sketes—according

---

[50] Voivode was the title of local princes in medieval times *(t.n.)*.

to the model of Slatina Monastery. He paid regular visits to each one of them to inquire about their life and give spiritual advice, after which he returned to Slatina. The Elder placed a particular emphasis on obedience done with love, on weekly confession, the Jesus Prayer, and participation in the holy services; as for the cells, he required that the established prayer and prostration rule be observed, and one's monastic canon be fulfilled.

*Archimandrite Cleopa Ilie
in 1950.*

This is the only way to form good, obedient, and humble monastics zealous for Christ. And when certain disturbances or temptations arose in these monasteries, the Elder sent one or two spiritual fathers from Slatina Monastery to restore peace. A monastic school operated regularly in all the monasteries mentioned above which maintained the same organization of spiritual life.

For three more years, these monasteries progressed greatly in their monastic life due to their respective Starets, but especially under the close supervision of Archimandrite Cleopa, who led their proper spiritual development for the glory of God and for the joy of the faithful.

How Father Cleopa Avoided Becoming Starets of Neamț Monastery

At the beginning of 1951, Partriach Justinian, wishing to spiritually renew Neamț Monastery, the largest lavra in the country, proposed to transfer Archimandrite Cleopa along with 70 monks from Slatina and Sihăstria to Neamț.

Hearing this, Father Cleopa was in great distress and prayed to the Theotokos to deliver him from this temptation. Then, remembering the advice of Spiritual Father Vichentie from Agapia Monastery, who would say, "Well, boy, when you run into great troubles, you should fast for three days and pray, and God will teach you what to do!", here is what he did.

One night he locked himself in his cell (only his disciple, Hieromonk Serapion, knew about this) and he prayed while fasting for seven days, from Monday to Sunday.

On the seventh night, while sitting on his stool, dozing off, he saw a heavenly light surrounding the icon of the Theotokos on the wall. Then the Mother of God spoke to him from the icon, saying "Don't be sad because of the troubles from Neamț Monastery, for I will quiet them. But do not be in doubt." For one thought was urging him to go to Neamț, while another was telling him to go off into the wilderness.

He then went to his spiritual father, Hieroschemamonk Paisie, he confessed and told him everything he saw and heard from the icon of the Theotokos in his cell. The Elder told him, "It is a divine sign. But don't tell anyone about this vision right now. Now, prepare to take communion tomorrow. If it is from

God for you to go to Neamţ Monastery, the Mother of God will help you. But if it is not His will, you will remain here."

The next day after the Divine Liturgy, Father Cleopa received word that the Patriarch had taken council with several persons and decided that things would remain as they had been before. Everything accordingly quieted down through the prayers of the Theotokos and with the blessing of Father Cleopa's spiritual father, Hieroschemamonk Paisie.

Starets Cleopa's Second Flight of Refuge into the Mountains (1952 to 1954)

Up until the spring of 1952, Slatina Monastery flourished greatly and it was among the best organized monasteries in Romania. It now had over 80 dwellers, 60 of whom were young. The faithful would come on feast days to participate in the holy services and listen to Father Cleopa's sermons, which were moving everyone's hearts. Thus, everything unfolded in peace and good order. Father Cleopa, however, would confide to his disciples, "I am here, in Slatina, only in my body since my soul is still there, at Sihăstria, where I took the veil and have lived for so many years."

The devil, however, who never sleeps, could not bear the good ascetic strife and harmony of the monks from Slatina Monastery. So, he urged the *Securitate*[51] to make a very detailed

---

[51] The Romanian Secret Police during communism, every bit as evil and to be feared as the more infamous KGB *(t.n.)*.

investigation of the monastery's community. At nightfall, the Secret Police came in great numbers; they interrogated and threatened the Starets as well as the most prominent members of the brotherhood. In the end, they held captive some of them, among whom were Father Cleopa, Hieromonk Arsenie Papacioc, and brother Constantin Dumitrescu.

They were taken to Fălticeni, where they were interrogated all night. They reproached Father Cleopa: "You are sabotaging our national economy because you say today it's George, and tomorrow it's Basil, it is a feast day and people put down their cant hooks[52] and stop working!"

Father Cleopa responded: "How can I not say that it is a feast day when it is written down in the calendar by our Holy Church?" In the end they asked Father Cleopa to quit spreading religious propaganda and they set him free.

Arriving at the monastery at night, Father Cleopa confessed to his spiritual father and, upon his advice, withdrew in secret together with Hieromonk Arsenie Papacioc in Stânișoarei Mountains and in other places unknown to us, until the troubles quieted down at Slatina. Up there they were not always together, but confessed to each other and they had the Holy Mysteries with them, from which they partook every two to three weeks.

They stayed hidden for a long time in the forests of the Negrileasa and Ostra villages, taking shelter in an abandoned sheep pen and receiving supplies once a month from a good Christian named Straton.

There were many wolves at that time in the Stânișoare Mountains, but the people who brought them food were not afraid of them because of the prayers of the two secret hesychasts.

---

[52] Most of the workers were loggers (t.n.).

Archimandrite Cleopa Ilie.

*Archimandrite Arsenie Papacioc,
a great spiritual father, guide and
co-ascetic with Father Cleopa in
the Mountains of Moldavia.*

After he returned to Sihăstria, Father Cleopa would occasionally retell episodes from his nomadic refuge in the mountains: "When I was in the forest, wondering about, my "friends" used to visit me: old Martin[53] and the sly fox. It didn't cost very much to escape from "old Martin". When I heard him growling, I would throw him a potato, and he'd leave. But with the fox it wasn't so easy. She would come at night to the door of his hut and if I happened to forget some food outside, it made her day! She would take care of it!

"Once I forgot the kettle that I was using for cooking. It still had some food in it. The fox came and began eating. I saw her through my little window and I went outside. When she saw me, she bolted away but the kettle's handle fell over her head. Now, I wasn't so upset about the food, but I felt sorry to lose the kettle, since I no longer had anything to cook in. I ran after her yelling, 'Leave the kettle!' But she was still sly. She got near a branch, hung the kettle on it, pulled it off her head and ran away. I was very happy that I still had my kettle!

"I had other friends that were even more terrific. They were the dormice and the forest rats. If you don't know how to organize yourself, these will leave you with no food in the dead of winter. I had a bag of rusks tied to a beam in my cell. No sooner would the evening fall than the 'parishioners' would show up, too. They had dug holes through the hut and would come for the rusks. I didn't mind the rusks so much, but I would be bothered because I couldn't do my prayer rule.

"Hardly would I start reading when they would start to crunch on the rusks. What could I do? I took a stick in my right hand and the Psalter in the left hand, and I would do my prayer rule like this: '*Lord, hear my prayer*,' and with the stick, 'whack'

---

[53] Name by which bears are referred to in folk literature for children *(t.n.)*.

at the dormice! After I hit, they pretended to be dead. Then I would continue, '*Listen to the voice of my supplication*' and other verses, and again, they would begin to crunch and again, I'd frighten them with the stick. And this is how I did my prayer rule until I plugged all the holes."

Once, late in the fall, while walking through the woods, a cold rain started to fall and he was soaked to the skin. Since he was very far from his hut, he had to endure most of his journey back in drenched clothes. Confronted with a severe chill wind on his way home, he became nearly paralyzed and fell down not too far from the hut, unable to move.

Father Cleopa was thinking to himself, "Now I'm going to die and I don't have Holy Communion on me." Then he prayed deeply and slowly, slowly, he crawled back to shelter. Once inside, he made a fire with great difficulty, sat next to it to dry off and so, little by little, he recovered.

But Father Cleopa had other kinds of temptations, too, as he used to say:

"Once, it was 1 o'clock at night and I was in the hut. I had done the Midnight service and I was finishing the Matins, when suddenly I heard, boom, boom, boom…! The ground was shaking. I went outside to see what that noise was about, and when I opened the hut's door, I saw a great light outside, and in the light, there was a huge brass car with many wheels.

A tall man with large, half-white, half-black eyes got out of it who said just this, seething, 'What are you looking for here?' I then remembered what the Holy Fathers say: if you have the Holy Mysteries, you have the living Christ! I had the Holy Mysteries in a hollow in a firtree, inside the hut. And when I saw how things stood, I hastened inside, I put my arms around the firtree with the Holy Mysteries and uttered only this, 'Lord Jesus, don't leave me!'

"You should see how strong prayer is when the devil is at your door! And when I looked outside again, I saw how he was stepping back, cast off by the power of Christ. Near the hut there was a deep ravine which that unclean spirit fell into. But how did it fall? When it reached the ravine, the car rolled over three times with the spirit in it and finally crushed down and made such a loud noise that my ears kept on ringing until 1 o'clock the next day."

Another time, while he was inside the hut, he heard some noise again. And when he went outside, it seemed as if a real war had started. He saw tanks coming towards him, armed soldiers running, and it seemed as if an entire army was trying to capture him. So, he began saying the Jesus Prayer and the whole deception vanished.

Father Arsenie also mentioned something that happened to him in the wilderness when he was with Father Cleopa. "A great rain caught us once in a forest that wasn't so high, as tall as a house. Father Cleopa was in one spot and I, in another. We were looking for thick bushes to take shelter in. Father Cleopa insisted that I should walk over there, where he was, hiding under branches. There were about 30 meters to his spot. I said that my place was better, and His Reverence said that his was better. Then I thought, 'No, wait, boy! Let me listen to Father Cleopa!' I ran away from there and a lightning bolt immediately struck the spot where I had just been. It marked me! See what obedience means!"

In 1953, when the winter was very heavy, Father Cleopa was received in the houses of the faithful, scattered here and there. Sometimes, in the evening, Father Cleopa would give a homily to those in the household. After some time, the host would say, "Father, I have a little nephew, could he come, too?" "Yes, let him come!" Then shortly after they would say, "Father, I have a niece. Can she come to listen to your talk?" "Let her come, too!" But when His Reverence saw that too many people were gathering, he would go to another room where he would leave a little written note on the table, that read "I have left. Forgive me!" And he would withdraw to the forest.

Once, when he was at a faithful's house, he had a different temptation. The evil one took the form of a squirrel and sat on top of an icon in the room where he was staying. Enraged by it, Father Clopa threw something at it. But immediately afterward he began to weep, because in fact he should have only used prayer to battle the devil.

Fathers Cleopa and Arsenie lived ascetically in Stânişoara Mountains until the summer of 1954, when Patriarch Justinian obtained approval for the two ascetics to either return to the monastery or to go to the Patriarchate.

When they came to get Father Cleopa from the wilderness and bring him to the Patriarchate, he was afraid that it might somehow be a trap. But he began to pray to God to show him if he should go or not. Then the word of Saint John Climacus came to his mind, "If obedience calls for death, a pastor who fears death should be ashamed!" So, Father Cleopa said to himself, "Who is calling me? The Patriarch of the Church is calling me! If he sends me to die, I'll go and die!"

Thus, after more than two years of ascetic labors as hermits in the wilderness, Fathers Cleopa and Arsenie left for Bucharest accompanied by Hieroschemamonk Daniil Tudor.

Patriarch Justinian received them there with great love, and he consulted with them spiritually every evening. They were then sent to many monasteries around the capital city in order to confess and give advice to monks and nuns. Fathers Cleopa and Arsenie returned then to Slatina Monastery, to the joy of the monastics and faithful from that area.

Fathers Cleopa and Arsenie embracing each other spiritually
at the Monastery of Sihăstria in 1996.

His Missionary Activity with Old-Calendar Believers

In the spring of 1955, activities were organized, especially in Moldavia, so as to clarify the issue of the Old Julian Calendar and to argue against those who still observed it. In this attempt at bringing the Old Calendar faithful back into the bosom of the Orthodox Church, ten theologians, Staretses and spiritual fathers were chosen to go through villages inhabited by Old Calendarists so as to try to bring them back to the mother Church.

Archimandrite Cleopa Ilie, the Starets of Slatina, made a special contribution to this movement. He was a renowned canonist, who knew very well the *Rudder* and the *Canon Law of the Orthodox Church*. The persons involved went to all villages that were affected by the Old Calendarist movement, organized advisory canonic meetings on the topic of the Old and New Calendars, gave ample explanations to the rebellious, and part of the Old Calendarists returned to the ancient Church's bosom, to everyone's joy.

Pilgrimage to the Holy Monasteries

I n 1956, Archimandrite Cleopa withdrew from his obedience as Starets of Slatina Monastery, leaving one of his disciples, Protosyngel Emilian Olaru, in his stead. Together with two disciples, he was called to carry out on a spiritual mission in Timişoara and Arad. Here he met the Metropolitan of Banat, Vasile Lăzărescu, who had just prepared the reliquary for Saint Iosif the New of Partoş's relics. From here, Father Cleopa visited the Vasiova Monastery, where the famous Spiritual Father Vichentie Mălău, one of the greatest spiritual fathers of Romania, served for many years. With reference to him, Father Cleopa stated that "he could be canonized anytime."

Then Father Cleopa, with his disciples, was sent to Gai Monastery near Arad, where he stayed for a time. Here he established the same spiritual rules as in Sihăstria Monastery. But when the bells rang for Matins, unaccustomed to midnight services, the believers called the fire brigade, thinking that the monastery had caughtfire[54]. Father Cleopa invited them in the

---

[54] It was customary to ring the bell in case of danger *(t.n.)*.

church and gave a moving sermon. Among the words he spoke were these, "Let the fire that has started burning here at Gai Monastery not be put out until the end of the world!"

From Gai, Father Cleopa was invited from time to time to visit the bishop of Arad, Andrei Magieru, with whom he spiritually conferred and who confessed to the Elder.

After he visited other monasteries in the area, he returned to Moldavia and lived in Putna Monastery for a few months. He was asked here to spiritually revive the monastery, where Archimandrite Dosoftei Morariu, a disciple from the Elder's youth, had been appointed as the new Starets.

At Putna Monastery he spoke daily with great love to pilgrims, from both Romania and abroad, about the bravery of the Orthodox Prince Stephen the Great of Moldavia, about his sacrifice in defending the country and the Orthodox faith, and about the numerous churches and monasteries that he founded and that still stand, to this day, throughout our holy territory.

Archimandrites Dosoftei Morariu, Cleopa Ilie, Victorin Oanele, and Hieromonk Paisie Olaru in 1984

At Putna he had the occasion to speak to both the youth and the elderly, Romanians and foreigners, about the beauty of Orthodoxy, the heroism of our forefathers, the beauty of the painted monasteries with wonderful exterior frescos, about the glory of God and the blessing of the Romanian people. During this short stay at Putna Monastery, Father Cleopa harmoniously combined in his sermons, the ancient Orthodox piety with the patriotism of our forefathers, and not to a lesser extent, with the sacrifice of so many generations of monastics who kept alive the vigil lamp of true faith in the soul of the Romanian people.

In 1956, Father Cleopa took his cojoc[55] and his spiritual books that he loved so much and returned to the place of his repentance, the Holy Monastery of Sihăstria, guided at that time by Protosyngel Ioil Gheorghiu, the disciple of Starets Ioanichie Moroi, with whom he also shared a cell.

The Monastery of Sihăstria from 1949 to 1959

The humble Starets, Protosingelos Ioil, Archimandrite Cleopa's successor, led Sihăstria Monastery's community with much wisdom for 10 years. His greatest virtue was his regular presence each day and night at every church service. He was the first to enter and the last one to leave. That is why when he saw a brother or Father had been late to the holy services, he would say to him, "Little Father, come to the church on time! Don't miss the holy services if you don't have another obedience, because that is why we have come to the monastery!"

His Reverence had a greater vocation for the church than all the monastery's brothers and Fathers, and he was a living icon for everyone . He was also the community's spiritual father along with Hieroschemamonk Paisie Olaru, who had returned from Slatina in 1953. These two Fathers, chosen by God,

---

[55] Iconic traditional shepherd's cloak made of sheepskin leather and the leather's natural wool *(t.n.)*.

adorned Sihăstria's spiritual life, maintaining the same measure of devotion as during the time when Father Cleopa was the Starets, gathering around them numerous Christ-loving youth.

In the fall of 1956, Father Cleopa returned to the monastery, with a clean conscience that he did his obedience where the Church sent him. After his return, the spiritual life at Sihăstria intensified even more. Father Cleopa would confess and advise the faithful from his cell on the hill; Father Paisie would confess and teach his spiritual children at the cells in the forest, as he was a great lover of silence and quietness, and Father Ioil was always present first in the church, and then in the Monastery's administrative building.

The three Fathers, advanced in prayer and grace, granted new spiritual dimensions to Sihăstria Monastery during those troubled years. The living model of each one of them inspired their spiritual children to pray more, to do God's will, and to prepare for the difficult days that were looking ahead.

Sihăstria Monastery's three great Spiritual Fathers: Paisie, Cleopa and Ioil in 1972.

Sihăstria Monastery's community counted more than 80 Fathers and brothers, who were all zealous, prayerful, and Christ-loving. The greatest joy for the community was the daily attendance of the Divine Liturgy and of the midnight services. The young members of the brotherhood would do obedience during the day and were present in the church at night, while the Elders were never absent from the church, day and night.

Everything was done in quietness, with peace, joy and counsel, and everyone obeyed the three great Spiritual Fathers of Sihăstria: Elders Paisie, Cleopa and Ioil. Elder Paisie would urge his disciples to lead a quiet and peaceful life of prayer. Father Cleopa would exhort everyone, monastics and laymen alike, to remember the hour of their death and to listen to their spiritual father or Starets and to always defend the true faith of the Orthodox Church. Starets Ioil, on the other hand, would urge them not to miss Church services.

Thus, Sihăstria Monastery became a spiritual fortress of Romanian Orthodoxy, a place of prayer for the children of Christ's Church, and a house of spiritual peace and joy, where you could meet with God more easily.

Between 1956 and 1959, Sihăstria, like the other Romanian monasteries, lived a few years of peace and quiet, and significant spiritual growth, but on the horizon, a great storm was looming against Christ's Church. Atheism and every nuance of sectarianism were preparing a new attack against Orthodoxy—so many times tested throughout history. For this has always been the destiny of the apostolic Church: to be permanently persecuted, permanently under surveillance, yet permanently alive, strong, victorious and salvific!

The Persecution of the Church from 1959 to 1964

The persecution from 1959 to 1964 was the most difficult period for Romanian monasticism in the 20th century. It began in April 1959. Firstly, all the Staretses and Spiritual Fathers who had a more intense spiritual activity and to whom many faithful were coming were excluded from monasticism for the rest of their lives[56]. In the same month all the young novices and rassophores were thrown out of monasteries throughout the country.

Towards the end of 1959, the atheistic government in Bucharest passed by vote a special decree which excluded all monks under 55 years of age, and nuns under 50 from monasteries. The decree was enforced severely, under the control of the Securitate forces and the surveillance of the political organs of every region. By the spring of 1960, 4,000 monks and nuns were expelled from their monasteries.

The monasteries in Moldavia took the hardest hit, since they were more numerous and they had a greater spiritual vocation. Some monasteries like Sihăstria and Slatina were transformed into monastic nursing homes: Sihăstria—for elderly monks, and Slatina—for elderly nuns. At Sihăstria, more than 40 old monks were brought from Moldavian monasteries, who, after many years, passed to the Lord. Their graves can be found in the Monastery's cemetery.

The small sketes and the monasteries that were left unmanned, as well as the mission monasteries, were either

---

[56] Decree no. 410/October 28, 1959 ordered the closing down of more than two thirds of Romanian monasteries, on grounds that their activity was counter-revolutionary (t.n.).

closed down or transformed into parishes where married priests served, and the entry of new young people in monasteries was interdicted and surveilled by the Securitate.

The Starets of Sihăstria Monastery Protosyngel Ioil Gheorghiu, together with Hieromonk Varsanufie Lipan, Archimandrite Cleopa's disciple, were excluded from monasticism on April 22, 1956, and they were under house arrest in their native villages: the former in Dumbrava Roșie commune, and the latter in Piripig commune, Neamț counry. Thus, Sihăstria Monastery lost its Starets and more than 40 dwellers under the age stipulated by the Decree, while Archimandrite Cleopa lost his closest disciple, with whom he was sharing his cell, and the majority of his spiritual sons.

The Third Flight of Refuge into the Mountains

Considering this difficult situation and knowing he was always under the surveillance of political organs, Elder Cleopa, urged by the Holy Spirit, withdrew for the third time to the mountains of Moldavia, to his much-loved peace and quiet.

He first went into the forests around Hangu commune. Then, leaving Hangu, he stayed for some time on Petru Vodă Mount, where he built a wooden hut not far from the mountain's peak, and he lived there more than two years, receiving help from a devout Christian in the area.

Finally, he moved to the forests around Pipirig. Here, every two to three weeks, he would meet with Father Varsanufie to confess to each other and partake of the Holy Mysteries. Occasionally, they would serve the Divine Liturgy there, in the forest. Father Varsanufie would also bring to Father Cleopa what he needed. Among those who especially assisted Father Cleopa during this withdrawal were Dumitru Niţă and Gheorghe Olteanu from Dolhesti, Pipirig commune, as well as Father Vasanufie's relatives from the same commune.

Archimandrite Cleopa and his disciple, Protosyngel Varsanufie.

By 1962, he was joined by his disciple, Father Varsanufie, and together, they lived ascetically in various places for more than three years.

With the passage of time, everybody was eagerly waiting from Father Cleopa's homecoming. Everyone wanted him to return, but maybe none as much as his elderly mother, Nun Agafia from Agapia Veche Monastery. She had not seen him for about six years and did not want to depart to the Lord without seeing him one last time.

Nevertheless, Father Cleopa would not come, thinking that if he returned to the monastery, he would be arrested. At the same time, he had become accustomed to peace and quiet, and ceaseless prayer, and the Holy Spirit's comfort rested his soul day and night. With the help of all his spiritual children's prayers, he remained healthy and occupied himself, along with prayer, with writing holy books "on the roots of fir trees," as he himself would later testify.

Here are some of the titles of the works he accomplished in over five years of hesychastic asceticism in the mountains: *Sermons for Monks*, also titled *Ascent towards Resurrection, Concerning Dreams and Visions, God's Miracles in His Creation, The Confession of Hierarchs, The Confession of Staretses, The Confession of Priests* and *The Confession of Monks.*

Archimandrite Cleopa also wrote other works of spiritual benefit, some of which were printed while others were eventually lost. But the ones that have been preserved to this day demonstrate that Elder Cleopa was a very zealous reader of the Holy Scriptures, of the writings of the Holy Fathers and the Holy Canons, and especially a fervent man of ceaseless prayer.

The Elder would pray in solitude for 10 to 15 hours a day. His disciple, Hieromonk Varsanufie, would later tell us that Father Cleopa used to read the following prayers in the morning: the Morning Prayers, several Akathist hymns, always including the Akathist hymn to the Savior and the Akathist hymn of the Annunciation, the Canon of Repentance to the Savior, the Canon to the Guardian Angel, the Canon to the Heavenly Powers and all the Saints, and a few kathismata from the Psalter.

In the afternoon he read Vespers, the Small Compline and a few canons for the Theotokos. Then, after a little break, he would eat his only daily meal towards evening and then continue with the Evening Prayers and the Paraklesis to the Theotokos. After midnight he read the Matins service. During any remaining time, he said the Jesus Prayer.

He slept very little, keeping vigil and cultivating spiritual thoughts day and night. He had become worthy of receiving the prayer of the heart, and often shed fiery tears and felt a great joy in his heart.

Sihăstria without Father Cleopa

During the period of persecution, it was extremely challenging for services to be held at Sihăstria Monastery because of the lack of celebrating priests. The number of spiritual fathers continued to decline and the faithful were fearful of going to monasteries, while the youth who wanted to remain in monasteries were received as workers in civilian clothes.

The absence of Archimandrite Cleopa and of Protosyngel Ioil Gheorghiu made spiritual life in Sihăstria Monastery even more difficult. Now the entire burden weighed down on the shoulders of the elderly Spiritual Father Paisie. More than anyone, this holy man confessed monastics and laymen day and

Father Paisie, the spiritual father of the Monastery, in the Sihăstria Cemetery.

night, comforting, strengthening, and giving hope to all who prayed to God with faith.

Everyone continued to ask about Father Cleopa, commemorating him in their holy prayers. Everyone would have liked at least to see him and rejoice in his words, but no one knew where he was toiling ascetically and praying to God. Yet, they all felt mystically the power of his prayers. And this conviction gave hope to all that, sooner or later, he would return to his spiritual children.

Sihăstria Monastery's new Starets, Protosyngel Caliopie Apetri, was providentially ordained to lead the community. He was, in fact, a disciple of Father Cleopa's with whom he had stayed together in Slatina Monastery, as well. At the same time, he was a very courageous, daring Father, zealous for holy things and full of kindness. All these qualities, together with God's grace, helped him to keep Sihăstria Monastery in order for 12 years.

Beautiful services were held, sermons were given, the faithful came in increasing numbers and the critical condition from 1952-1962 improved greatly after 1963.

Therefore, we could say together with Prophet David: *Who is so great a God as our God? Thou art the God who does wonders!*

Mother Agafia's Tears

It was the summer of 1964. The events in the lay world were unfolding towards the improvement of the situation of Christians. People were regaining hope for a better tomorrow. The monasteries, these fortresses of millennial Orthodoxy, were praying persistently for the victory of Christ's cross. More and more believers were filling up churches, pilgrimages to the monasteries had multiplied, and God had turned His face towards us sinners.

I was coming from Târgu Neamţ going to Sihăstria Monastery through Agapia Veche. I wanted to comfort Father Cleopa's mother and bring her something for her daily needs. When I reached the monastery's gate, old Mother Agafia was waiting there for pilgrims to speak with them. As soon as she saw someone enter the monastery courtyard, even if she did not know them, Mother Agafia would ask them, "Hey, listen, haven't you seen my Cleopa?" And the faithful would answer, "No, Mother, I don't know him!"

When other faithful came to worship, the old nun would draw near them and ask them, too, with tears in her eyes, "Haven't you, perhaps, seen my Cleopa?" But they would answer her, "We don't know, Mother! We haven't seen him!" Then the old nun, sighing, would wipe the tears from her eyes, looking into the distance. Understanding her great pain, I drew near Mother Agafia to give her what I had prepared for her and I told her gently:

"Mother Agafia, stop asking people where Father Cleopa is, because they don't know where he is to be found."

Then the old woman told me with tears of pain, "Well, Father Ioanichie, if you were a Mother!..."

Her words filled my eyes with tears and after I venerated in the church I told her, "Let it be, Mother Agafia, because Father Cleopa will come back to Sihăstria soon!" Then I departed, crossing the mountain to reach the Monastery.

The next day in the afternoon, Mother Agafia, overwhelmed with longing for her son, Cleopa, grabbed her staff and without saying a word to the other nuns, she set off over the mountain towards Sihăstria. But since she was alone and over 88 years old, she lost her way in the forest and in the evening a man found her and brought her to a forester's cabin. She no longer knew how to return or how to reach Sihăstria. The workers at the cabin gave her a room to sleep in overnight. During this time Agapia Veche's bells were constantly ringing and all the sisters were searching for her in the forest. They finally found her the next day around noon, and they asked her, "How did you get here, Mother Agafia?"

The grave of Mother Agafia, who fell asleep in the Lord in 1968 in Agapia Veche Monastery

"I wanted to go to Sihăstria, to see if my Cleopa has come! But I got lost. A man brought me to this cabin and I don't know which way to go."

"Come, we'll take you there, Mother Agafia!"

Upon arrival at Sihăstria, she knelt before the graves of her two sons, Vasile and Gherasim, and after she finished weeping, all alone, she stood up, kissed the crosses, venerated in the church and told the sisters, "I can die now. But won't you let me stay here?"

"No, Mother Agafia! Let's go back!"

"All right, let's go…"

Father Cleopa's Return to Sihăstria Monastery

In August 1964, the unspeakable joy caused by the release of all Romanians imprisoned by communism seized everyone. The prisons were now empty, those that had survived were released, the monasteries and the whole country were making thanksgiving prayers to God, and everyone was hoping for a better tomorrow.

At the end of the same month, accompanied by a benefactor, I arrived at Father Cleopa's hut, hidden from the view of the multitude. Kneeling, I kissed his hand, we embraced each other and wept together. It seemed to me that I was dreaming. Then, God strengthened us, we prayed for a long time, and I told Father Cleopa, "All Pious Father, I have come because the Fathers from Sihăstria have sent me to bring you home, after nearly six years of separation. The prisons have been opened and God has blessed our country with a little freedom. So, we are asking you to return to Sihăstria! All the Fathers are waiting for you with great joy. The faithful, too, are waiting for you, but Father Paisie, the spiritual father of us all, who raised you from your youth, and your mother, Mother Agafia, miss Your Reverence the most!"

Yet Father Cleopa was hesitating. He had become accustomed to hesychasm. He was waging a secret battle in his soul. To renounce hesychasm to be useful for others? Or to stay longer in the wilderness? Seeing him in this dilemma, I let him pray to God for two more weeks. On September 29, the feast day of Saint Chiriac the Hesychast, Father Cleopa, together with Varsanufie, his disciple, walking across mountains and dales, along trails known to them only, arrived back at Sihăstria Monastery.

With great joy, Fathers and novices kissed him with tears in their eyes and gave glory to God that he had returned to his cell again, in good health. Truly thankful, that evening they held a vigil service. And Father Cleopa spent the following day together with his spiritual father, Hieroschemamonk Paisie.

This is how Archimandrite Cleopa returned to the Sihăstria community.

Father Cleopa's Spiritual Activity

The news of his return to Sihăstria Monastery spread everywhere in just a few days. Little by little, groups of faithful from all over the country began to visit him, to ask him for council and receive his blessing.

Father Cleopa started once again to comfort the people, to give homilies daily, to confess people and draw many to Christ. Each day, tens and hundreds of faithful would come to his cell from all over Romania and even from abroad.

There they listened to the Elder's advice and encouraging words, asked spiritual and theological questions, ranging from the simplest to the most profound, and each one left his cell satisfied, rejoicing that at least they had been able to see him and receive his blessing. Thus, as he was known by many people, they all gave thanks to God that He had given him to us as a heavenly blessing.

The first duty that Father Cleopa requested the faithful of all ages and ranks to fulfil was to conscientiously preserve the right faith, i.e. the dogmas of the Orthodox Church. Without the right faith, no one can be saved, even if they have done good deeds.

Father Cleopa in Sihăstria Monastery's Garden

T hen the Elder emphasized the confession of sins, urging the faithful to confess at least four times a year. He said, "Brother, when you see that your mother or father or someone else in your family has become ill, don't call the doctor first but the priest. The doctor can't give them an extra moment of life. For if he could, he wouldn't give it to you, but keep it for himself. Everything happens according to God's will! Call the priest and tell him, 'Father, take your time and confess my father or my mother by the book.' And the priest should ask them if they have done such or such a sin, this or that…

"After confession, it is good for the one who confesses to say that he did it all the sins. Because if we do not err in actions, we err in our thoughts or with words. And at the end the priest can absolve all the sins through the gift that Christ has given him.

Father Cleopa admiring flowers in the monastery's courtyard.

"Then you can call the doctor. If the person dies having confessed purely, the Church can pull him out of hell in 40 days, or perhaps more, but it can pull him out. But if he has not confessed and has heavy sins, forgiveness is no longer possible and there is no service that can pull him out from hell. There is no salvation without confession."

The Elder recommended everyone to have a spiritual father in the parish that they belong to. And if someone wanted to confess in more detail, they could do it especially with an older spiritual father in a monastery. In this case, the faithful that confessed at the monastery had to get a blessing from their local priest and then to read the ordered canon.

We should mention here that the Elder heard the confessions of a large number of faithful, plus about 40 Fathers and novices from Sihăstria Monastery, and many more monks and nuns from other monasteries, married priests, and several Hierarchs.

Through confession, Father Cleopa won many souls for Christ, yet he asked each one if they were able to do the epitimion[57] that he had arranged. If someone said that they could not fulfill it, the Elder gave them an easier one, according to their age, strength and zeal.

Then he asked each faithful person to pray as much as possible as the Holy Apostle Paul commanded, saying, "pray ceaselessly." (I Thessalonians 5:17) The Elder recommended that, generally, each person should pray at least one hour in the morning and one hour in the evening. In the morning, one should say the Morning Prayers, the Akathist hymn to the Theotokos, and in the evening,

---

[57] "Canon" in Romanian. In the Orthodox tradition, after confession, the priest may give spiritual instruction for the healing of the soul. It is not (or should not be) viewed as punishment but as a spiritual medicine. This could include things like not receiving Holy Communion for a given amount of time, doing certain prayers, a prayer rule, prostrations, asking forgiveness from certain people or returning stolen property, etc. (t.n.).

the Evening Prayers, and the Paraklesis to the Theotokos with the vigil lamp lit. The Jesus Prayer should be said as frequently as possible throughout the day.

He prayed daily for himself, for the Church, for those that had fallen into grave sins, for the sick, for those who were suffering and for all the faithful. Thus, Elder Cleopa's prayers sometimes worked true miracles, and people's requests that were for their benefit would be fulfilled: they returned healthy from hospitals and journeys, or succeeded in examinations and in daily life.

He would ask them to go to church weekly or, in case of necessity, once every two or three weeks. If they could not go to church, at least one person from the family should go, a spouse or one of the children, whom he named the "family's apostle." At home, they should read holy books, pray and abstain from eating until the "family's apostle" returned with holy anafora[58] from church.

He also exhorted people to give alms. "Let no one leave your home without help, brother! If you don't have money, give them a potato, a crust of bread, a handkerchief, give them something, however little that is. If you give little and you are sad that you didn't give more, your alms arrive to God like lightning. Why? Because two great virtues have met: mercy and humility."

He advised each one to give alms in the name of Christ according to their means, since the one who gives alms has "given a loan to God" and it is the easiest way to be saved. Because God said in the Holy Gospel, "Blessed are the merciful, for they shall receive mercy (Matthew 5:7)."

Likewise, he recommended the faithful live in permanent Christian love and harmony according to the word that Christ

---

[58] Antidoron, the bread blessed during Divine Liturgy (t.n.).

Himself uttered, "By this all will know that you are My disciples, if you have love for one another (John 13:35)."

A principal obligation that he asked of Christian families in villages and cities was to have children. According to the Holy Canons, Father Cleopa interdicted abortions or murdering children in any way, for this is one of the greatest sins in the life of a Christian. Then he recommended young people live a life of virginity until marriage and obey their priests and parents, according to the commandment of Moses, "Honor your father and mother for it to go well with you and to live many years on the earth (Exodus 20:12). As for those who had lawsuits and fights over earthly things, the Elder asked them to make peace with each other and follow their priest's advice.

Finally, Elder Cleopa would give a homily according to their level of understanding, answering every question asked. Then he would bless them with the Holy Cross, anoint them with oil,[59] give them little icons and incense, and then send them in peace to their homes. After he rested briefly, yet another group of faithful would come and ask him for advice and a blessing.

There were days, especially in the summer, when the Elder received groups of faithful numbering in the hundreds.

Elder Cleopa dedicated himself to this great spiritual mission which he carried out, uninterruptedly, from 1964 until he gave up his spirit into Christ's arms on December 2, 1998.

---

[59] In Romania, many services end with the faithful being signed with oil on the forehead and the back of the palms, in the form of a cross. Typically, various fragrant and blessed oils are used, with the exception of Holy Unction. When the faithful go to visits Elders or venerate Saints' relics they can also be anointed *(t.n.)*.

Spiritual Advice for Monastics

Since Fathers and novices from both Sihăstria and other monasteries were coming to Father Cleopa for confession and spiritual advice, the Elder sought to give each one appropriate advice for their spiritual needs, as the Holy Spirit so guided him.

A group of monastics from Sihăstria Monastery in the summer of 1970.

The spiritual advice that one received depended on the answer they gave to the Elder. Because Father Cleopa knew well the Holy Scriptures, the Holy Fathers, the *Philokalia* and the Holy Canons, and because he was inspired by God, he always succeeded in giving the best answer, fitting the needs and spiritual struggles of each person. Thus, he who received the Elder's advice and fulfilled it had great peace and joy. If he promised to take his advice but failed to do so, his conscience bothered him and he needed to return to the Elder.

The advice that he most often gave to both monastics and the faithful was this, "If you want to go straight to God you need two walls. But not of bricks, or stone or clay, but two spiritual walls: You should have the fear of God to the right, since Prophet David says, 'The fear of God turns man away from evil ,' and to the left, the fear of death, since Jesus, the son of Sirah said, 'Son, remember your end and you will never sin.' These two good deeds, fear of God and mindfulness of death, save man from all sin."

Other advice for monastics included: doing obedience with love, while saying the Jesus Prayer in one's mind and heart and, depending on the obedience, participating each day in the Divine Liturgy and the Church's services.

Likewise, Father Cleopa urged monastics and novices to obey their spiritual fathers in everything. If they could not fulfill a canon, they were to ask their spiritual father for another canon according to their strength; they were to read a chapter or two of the Holy Scriptures daily, especially from the New Testament; to read the life of the saint commemorated on that respective day, and one fragment from the *Paterikon* and other holy books.

Again, he recommended that those who lived in the monasteries should be as stable as possible in their monastic life; not to go from one place to another, from one monastery to another; not to have personal possessions and to never do anything without the blessing of the Starets and of their spiritual father.

If some monks or novices came to him scandalized by certain things, the Elder would urge them to be mindful of themselves, "What do you think? When the helmsman of a ship on the sea goes through dangerous rocky coasts, do you think he looks to see where other boats are headed? He has his eyes on the helm. What someone else is doing is their business. Each one is saved according to how he navigates his soul. Let me tell you what happened once:

There were three brothers at Neamț Monastery. They were disciples of Gheorghe Lazăr, an old and holy man, who worked miracles in these parts. They went to him and said,

'Uncle Gheorghe, we are leaving this monastery because we've got scandalized!'

'Well, why, beloved?' said the old man.

'There is no longer salvation in this monastery!'

Then old man Gheorghe, who would never get angry, yelled three times, 'Don't you do that! Don't you do that! Don't you do that!"[60] and he left them there to think."[61]

If anyone of the monastic yoke observed a more serious offense in their spiritual father, without judging him, Father Cleopa recommended them to choose a different spiritual father.

This is just a fraction of the advice that Archimandrite Cleopa used to give his spiritual children that came and asked for counsel.

Spiritual Advice for the Faithful

Father Cleopa was a skillful spiritual father for both monastics and the faithful. Primarily, he strove to awaken zeal and longing for God in people's souls. Through this process, the soul grew and became spiritually renewed.

He generally recommended his spiritual children to observe the following advice:

---

[60] Nicolae Steinhardt, a famous literary figure, came to Father Cleopa once complaining of some mistreatment he had suffered at the monastery he was living at. Father Cleopa said, "You must become the monastery." It is in this sense that Elder Gheorghe was telling the monks, "No, you make it!" (t.n.).

[61] These monks were clarified and remained in the monastery (t.n.).

Children should be raised from infancy in the fear of God. They should learn prayers by heart, confess, and receive Holy Communion monthly; they should be brought regularly to the Holy Church and listen to their parents; do their prayers and prostrations for their father and mother, siblings, and relatives; learn religion in school, observe the holy fasts, and not steal.

The young people should have their own spiritual father. They should confess once a month and receive Holy Communion with great devotion, when they are worthy of the Lord's Body and Blood, following their spiritual father's guidance. Then, they should obey their parents in all things, avoid all scandals and the ugly sins of our times, read holy books, and those who have a special calling, should make themselves available in the service of the Lord, either by studying in theological seminaries or Faculties of Theology, or by embracing monastic life. Those who steered away severely from Christian morality should confess to experienced spiritual fathers and follow the canon they are given.

Those who want to get married should be canonically examined by their priests to make sure they are not distantly related or getting married against their parents' will. Afterwards, they are to respect the commandments of God for those married, that is, not to murder their children, to listen to their parents, to be good Christians, to give alms and to fulfil the advice of their spiritual fathers with a pure heart.

Married couples should make their house a true church. They should give birth to and raise children in the fear of God, pray a lot, give alms to the poor and to widows, confess at least four times a year, and if permitted, receive Holy Communion. They should not welcome sectarians or people of other religions in their houses,[62] live in peace with each other, take scrupulous care of their parents and the elderly of their family, and obey their spiritual pastors in all things.

Father Cleopa's Spiritual Fathers

Up until 12 years of age, Father Cleopa—a pupil, then, in the primary school, confessed to the parish priest, Gheorghe Chiriac, who baptized all the children in Alexandru Ilie's family. Thereafter, young Constantin started confessing to the spiritual fathers from the nearby Cozancea Skete, particularly to Father Conon Gavrilescu who was a renowned exorcist and spiritual father in the area.

Since the fall of 1929, when Constantin entered monastic life at Sihăstria Skete, he had the Skete's Igumen, Protosyngel Ioanichie Moroi, as his spiritual father. The latter was also the spiritual father of all those who dwelled in the monastery, as he was the only serving priest of Sihăstria.

Around 1937-1938, monk Cleopa occasionally took the sheep close to Agapia Veche and confessed his sins to the famous Spiritual Father Vichentie Mălău. After 1938, when Protosyngel Vichentie went as a missionary priest to Banat, Father Cleopa

---

[62] After the fall of the Soviet Union, many well-intentioned Protestants came to evangelize the Orthodox country of Romania which had just suffered the greatest persecution of the Church since the persecutions of Rome. Many naïve Romanians invited the leaders of these sects into their houses to preach and start house churches, helping them carry out their missionary activity. This is what Father Cleopa referred to: he did not interdict having Protestant friends (or people of other religions) over for dinner or being friends with them. Rather, he emphasized that the Orthodox should not help promote those of other faiths in their missionary activity (t.n.).

confessed to both old Starets Ioanichie and to Hieroschemamonk Ioil.

As of 1942, after he was appointed Igumen locum tenens, Father Cleopa usually confessed to Hieroschemamonk Ioil Gheorghiu, the spiritual father of the skete, since the old Igumen was bedridden. Even after his ordination into priesthood, in 1945, and even after he was appointed as Sihăstria's Igumen, he still confessed to Hieroschemamonk Ioil, and sometimes to Hieromonk Calistrat Bobu.

Towards the end of 1948, Hieroschemamonk Paisie Olaru was transferred from Cozancea to Sihăstria Monastery's community, becoming the spiritual father of Father Cleopa and of many fathers. This great Elder was the most skilled spiritual father in Moldavia in the second half of the 20th century. Even when he had withdrawn to the mountains, Father Cleopa would still sometimes confess to Spiritual Father Paisie, who would meet him in the middle of the night in a place known only to them.

On October 18, 1990, when Hieroschemamonk Paisie moved to the Lord, Father Cleopa chose his disciple, Protosyngel Varsanufie, as his spiritual father, to whom he had already confessed when he had withdrawn to the mountains.

In the spring of 1997, Protosyngel Varsanufie moved to the Lord, and Archimandrite Cleopa chose the one who would be his last spiritual father, Hieromonk Iacob Savin, to whom he confessed until his death.

These were Archimandrite Cleopa Ilie's spiritual fathers, from his childhood until the end of his life, whom he always commemorated with piety in his prayers at church and in his cell.

Two Old Monks with the Gift of Prayer

A round 1968–1970, several older monks lived ascetically in Sihăstria Monastery, all of whom were Father Cleopa's disciples.

They attended Matins every night. After the midnight service finished, they would each withdraw to their cell. Only two old fathers would remain in the Church and waited for the others to leave.

Then, when no one else was in sight, they would lie flat down in the form of a cross and start praying in tears to the Savior Christ, asking for mercy and the forgiveness of sins.

They would do this every night after Matins, without being seen by anyone. But one night, there was a priest who led a holy life, who was praying in a corner of the church, whom no one had observed. He was Father Dimitrie Bejan,[63] a parish priest in Ghindăoani village, Bălţăteşti commune, Neamţ County, who used to come to Sihăstria from time to time.

The two Fathers who were lying on the floor, faced-down, did not observe that there was someone else in the church. Having begun to pray from their heart, flames of transparent

---

[63] Father Dimitrie Bejan was indeed a holy confessor, having been taken prisoner for 6 years in the Russian Gulags (1942-1948). After 1948 he was an inmate several times in the Communist prisons or he was in home arrest. He was tortured for his faith and for upholding the historical truth that Bessarabia and Bukovina, which had been incorporated into the Soviet Union, were Romanian territories. He saw the Holy Mother and to him the testimony was entrusted of an old Russian who had witnessed and miraculously escaped the martyrdom of 20,000 Orthodox monks and priests with a holy bishop as their leader. The 20,000 monks were given three days to choose either to renounce their faith and join the communist party or receive the death penalty. The holy bishop left to consult with the monks. He returned in five minutes and announced, "We have all chosen death!" And so, they were slaughtered *(t.n.)*.

The community of Sihăstria Monastery in 1970.

light kept growing and rose above their heads. They were flames of the grace of the Holy Spirit that was growing according to the measure of the two Elders' prayers. The priest, who had never seen such a thing, was amazed at this miracle and, falling to his knees, he was praying, too.

After a short while, that flame of grace shrank little by little until it went out. Then the two Elders got up on their feet, did three prostrations, kissed the holy icons and each one went to his cell.

So, here we see that even in our days there are still monks with a holy life, who have the gift of fiery prayer! Their names are unknown to us even to this day. But some spiritually gifted Elders tell us that they were Fathers Ianuarie and Casian, disciples of Father Cleopa. However, this remains one of God's mysteries.

Concerning a Christian Woman Who Had the Gift of Divine Prayer

Father Cleopa told us about another mystical miracle that also happened in the Church of Sihăstria Monastery: "In the winter of 1971, it was my turn to serve in the Holy Altar. I came to the church at four o'clock in the morning and I read my Holy Communion prayers in front of the Holy Altar Table. Not long afterwards a woman came in to pray, who had come to the monastery the previous evening. She prayed quietly before all the icons and did prostrations continually. She did not know there was someone else in the church, since it was dark, being winter. Noticing that she was praying so earnestly, I looked out through the Holy Doors to see who was praying with such faith. The woman was on her knees in the middle of the church, with her hands up, and was saying with all her heart, 'Lord, do not leave me! Lord, do not leave me!'

"Then I saw a yellowish light around her head and I got frightened. The woman fell, face-down, and prayed without saying a word. The ray of light over her became increasingly large and lifted up over her head. After a little while the light slowly went out and the woman got up and left the church. She was a woman from the countryside.

"So, see who has the gift of prayer! Look, laymen surpass us monastics! I was doing the Proskomedia and overcome with emotion, I began to weep with the spear in my hand. Only God knows how many chosen ones He has in this world!"

Pilgrimage to the Holy Sepulcher and Mount Sinai

In the fall of 1974, ten years after his return from the wilderness, many pilgrims from our country, together with Father Cleopa and Protosyngel Ioil Gheorghiu, left so we could worship at the Holy Sepulcher and other holy places. This was one of the greatest joys of Father Cleopa's life.

The first and most holy path we walked together in the Holy City of Jerusalem was to go and worship at the Holy Sepulcher. Then we went up to Golgotha and we kissed the Holy Cross on which Christ was crucified for our salvation and the salvation of the entire world. Then we participated in the Holy Liturgy and giving thanks to our Savior Jesus Christ, we walked on a pilgrimage to the other holy places in Jerusalem with our souls full of joy and emotion.

In the following days we worshiped on Mount Zion, where the Mother of God fell asleep, as well as at Prophet David's tomb. Then we descended to the Garden of Gethsemane and we worshiped at the Mother of God's tomb and all the holy places there. Holding the New Testament in hand, we ascended the Mount of Olives and stopped there at the two large Orthodox convents, Saint Mary Magdelene and Eleon, where ten Romanian nuns were living in asceticism.

Continuing our journey, we ascended Mount Tabor where the Savior was Transfigured before His disciples.

We went through the Holy Land up to Galilee, the city of Nazareth, where the Mother of God received the Annunciation of Christ's incarnation.

*Father Cleopa with a group of Fathers from
Sihăstria Monastery on Mount Tabor.*

We were all joyous, but Father Cleopa rejoiced the most of us all, he who had gone through so many troubles in this life!

We made another stop in Cana of Galilee and at the Samaritan woman's well. From there we traveled to the Jordan River in which Jesus Christ, the Savior of the world, was baptized, and we returned to Jerusalem.

Then we left for Bethlehem, the city where Christ Our Lord was born. We stayed there one day, praying for the Savior to be born spiritually in our hearts and souls, as well.

After a few more days we all left together on a trip of over 300 kilometers, to Mount Sinai where Moses received the Tablets of the Law. Moses led the chosen people through that place on their way to the Holy Land. Lord, what a wasteland that place is and how blessed our Romanian country is, overshadowed and protected by Thy goodness!

On the horizon the Orthodox Monastery of Saint Katherine, inside which lie the great martyr's relics, looked like an unconquered fortress. We were received with much kindness by Metropolitan Damianos, the monastery's Starets.

The next day we climbed up to the peak of the mountain where the Holy Prophet Moses received the Tablets of the Law. Then we returned to the Holy City of Jerusalem, magnifying God for it all!

After we worshiped at the Holy Sepulcher again, we visited the Ein Karem village, the birthplace of Saint John the Baptist, then Jericho and the monasteries on the Jordan Valley where our Savior Jesus Christ was baptized. On October 30 we returned to Romania, giving glory to God for everything. Father Cleopa confessed to his disciples that he had not felt fulfilled until he worshiped at the Holy Sepulcher and the other shrines in the Holy Land.

Pilgrimage to Mount Athos and Other Holy Places

Three years after the first pilgrimage, in September 1977, a group of four Fathers from Sihăstria Monastery, with Archimandrite Cleopa Ilie as their leader, left for Mount Athos by train.

Athos, also dubbed the "Garden of the Theotokos," is the second holiest place for the Christian world, after the Holy Sepulcher. Athos is the paradise of Orthodox countries, unique in the Christian world. It is a monastic country, overshadowed by the grace of God, where over 1,000 monastics from all over the world live in ascetical struggles. The Holy Mother is the ruler here and no other woman can enter this place.

We arrived in Thessaloniki, the capital of ancient Macedonia, where we were welcomed by a few Romanian monks. For a whole day we visited the monasteries and ancient churches of Northern Greece, and then we left for Mount Athos.

In Ouranoupoli we boarded a boat for Mount Athos. Some contours could be made out on the horizon: a few Athonite monasteries, the Port of Daphne, and the over 2,000-meter mountain peak. Everything seemed to us to be a divine miracle. Mount Athos is a narrow strip of earth, with an area of 339 square kilometers, over 80 kilometers long which shelters about 20 large monasteries on both sides, over 15 sketes and about 200 large and small cells in which over 1,500 Greek, Serbian, Russian, Romanian, and Bulgarian monastics live ascetically.

After a two-hour journey on the boat, we docked at the port of Daphne, then ascended to Karelia, Mount Athos' capital. After we received visas to enter Mount Athos, we set out for the Romanian Skete Podromu where we stayed for two days. On Saturday night, during the Matins service, a novice Ioan was tonsured into monasticism; he had been one of Father Cleopa's disciples, whom he also received under his mantle. The tonsuring service was officiated by Archimandrite Victorin, the Starets of the Sihăstria Monastery, who gave him the name Ioanichie.

Then the Divine Liturgy was celebrated and Father Cleopa gave a beautiful sermon. After the meal we visited all the caves and desert cells around Prodromu Skete, and the next day we departed to worship in the great Athonite monasteries renowned throughout the world.

We made our first stop at the Great Lavra Monastery. Here we worshiped at the tomb of Saint Athanasius the Athonite in the church's narthex.

The tonsuring into monasticism of the monk Ioanichie Mutrescu
(Mount Athos, 1977).

After that, we visited the Romanian *Kelis* at Lacu Skete and then Iviron, Koutloumousiou, and Stavronikita Monasteries. All of them had been renewed by the Moldavian and Wallachia voivodes[64] who provided assistance and donations year after year. What moved us the most was the Icon of the Theotokos named Portaitissa at Iviron Monastery, where we all venerated, with Father Cleopa leading us. On the road to Karyes we made a short stop to the *Keli* of the famous hesychast Paisios the Athonite[65], a great devout man, honored and sought-after throughout Greece, who amazed us with his holiness and humility.

Then we worshiped the miraculous icons at Protaton Monastery in Karyes, at Pantokrator, Esphigmenou and Vatopedi Monasteries, where many relics and several miraculous icons

---

[64] Romanian nobility along the lines of princes or even kings.
[65] He was canonized in 2015 by the Holy Synod of the Ecumenical Patriarchate, celebrated on July 12 *(t.n.)*.

are found. Stephen the Great[66] built a watchtower at Vatopedi's port, still in good condition to this day.

We continued the pilgrimage to Hilandar Monastery. From here we crossed the mountain and stayed in Zographou Monastery, built from the ground up by Saint Stephen the Great between 1475 and 1502, and which is dedicated to Holy Great Martyr George.

We then worshiped at the monasteries on the Western slope of Mount Athos, which were Docheiariou Monastery, built in its entirety by Alexandru Lăpușneanu[67] in the 16th century, and the Xenophontos and Panteleimon Monasteries. Continuing our pilgrimage, we visited the following Monasteries: Xeropotamou, Simonos Petra, built by Michael the Brave;[68] Philotheou, Grigoriou, built by Saint Stephen the Great, Dionysiou, built by Neagoe Basarab;[69] and the Monastery of Saint Paul.

The Athonite Igumens heard about Archimandrite Cleopa's arrival in Mount Athos and as such, quite a few of them solicited him to speak to their monastic communities, for their spiritual benefit. He gave five spiritual sermons with special patristic and philokalic content, which comforted many young souls and echoed throughout Greece, a large part of them getting published.

Leaving Holy Mount Athos, we visited Athens and its surrounding monasteries, then we went to the great Spiritual

---

[66] Saint Stephen the Great ruled Moldavia from 1457 to 1504. He defended the Orthodox faith and the Moldavian territory from attacks by the Ottoman Empire, and his spiritual father was Saint Daniel the Hermit. He was glorified by the Romanian Orthodox Church in 1992, with a feast day on July 2.

[67] Another Prince of Moldavia, who lived from 1499 to 1568.

[68] Voivode of Wallachia, he managed to unite the three Romanian Principalities, Wallachia, Transylvania, and Moldavia, in 1600, for a very short period of time. He lived from 1558 to 1601.

[69] Romanian Prince who lived from 1459 to 1521.

Father Porphyrios, who had the gift of clairvoyance—a true saint of our times. He lived his ascetic life in a small skete in Attica.

Next, we stopped on the island of Aegina, which was under the guidance of Metropolitan Hierotheos. From there we went to the island of Kerkira (Corfu), to the relics of Saint Spyridon, to whom Father Cleopa had great devotion.

The next day, being Sunday, we served the Divine Liturgy together, and Father Cleopa was invited to give a homily to the Platytera Monastery in the city. Late that evening we departed on a ship to Italy to the relics of the Holy Hierarch Nicholas, the Great Wonderworker, at the earnest desire of Father Cleopa, who wanted to kiss them at least one time while he was alive, and to ask for his help.

At ten o'clock the next morning we arrived in Bari, where the cathedral stands, with Saint Nicholas' relics. We all worshiped here in tears at the casket with his relics, which is kept under the altar of the large church, and we prayed for his help and intercession for us and for our country. Then Father Cleopa read the first part of Saint Nicholas' Akathist hymn in tears, and we all continued it and sang all together, "Rejoice, Saint Nicholas, Great Wonderworker!" It was a moment of great emotion, which we cannot forget.

From here we left for Rome where we visited the catacombs of Saints Callixtus and Sebastian. We then made a stop at Celie Monastery in Yugoslavia to the great Serbian Theologian Justin Popović.[70] We all wanted to speak with this world-renowned theologian and expert in Dogmatics, who was on house arrest in this monastery.

---

[70] Saint Justin lived from 1894 to 1979. He was glorified by the Serbian Orthodox Church in 2010 and his feast day is celebrated on June 14 *(t.n.)*.

*Metropolitan Hierotheos together with Archimandrite Cleopa
on the island of Aegina.*

*Archimandrites Cleopa Ilie and Justin Popović
at Celie Monastery (Serbia).*

For two days Archimandrites Justin and Cleopa held spiritual conversations through a translator. Then Father Cleopa asked for some personal advice. He would have liked to remain on Mount Athos until the end of his life, but he was in doubt. In response, Archimandrite Justin told him: "Father Cleopa, if you go to the Holy Mountain, you will add a flower to Theotokos' Garden. But who will you leave the faithful with? Over there (in Athos) you'll only gain spiritual benefits for yourself, but in your country, you can also help others, bringing many guideless souls to God. I, too, lived ascetically for a time on Mount Athos, but in the end, I returned to do mission work in my own country.

"I'd say that you should remain in your country, to save yourself and help others to be saved. This is the greatest good deed for monks these days. Especially now, while we battle against faithlessness, sects and religious indifference!"

Following his advice, Father Cleopa returned home in peace!

Hieroschemamonk Paisie and Archimandrite Cleopa

Of all the spiritual fathers of our monasteries in the second half of the 20th century, two have been recognized throughout the entire country as being the most skilled. They were Hieroschemamonk Paisie Olaru (1897-1990) and his disciple, Archimandrite Cleopa Ilie (1912-1998).

TThey were both visited by countless faithful and monastics; they both had the gift of the counsel and of tears. They both cultivated thousands of disciples of all ages, from children and peasants to intellectuals, priests and Hierarchs. They were both charismatic and clairvoyant. They were both men of prayer who sacrificed themselves for the salvation of the many.

These two skilled spiritual fathers typically used the same spiritual means, but each one had his own particularities.

Father Paisie had a meek, calm, and very sensitive nature. He could not turn down anyone who had come for confession, nor would he set any particular conditions. He spoke very quietly and slowly, forgave easily, and shed tears for each person, especially for mothers, children, and sick people. He confessed day and night, since he had a lot of people waiting at his door, and strove to reconcile and please everyone. For this reason, he did not usually sleep on a bed, but napped briefly on a chair in order to continue.

Father Cleopa and Father Paisie, the two pillars of Sihăstria Monastery.

Often one called him or knocked on his door and he would respond, "Who's there?" If no one was confessing to him at that time, he would say, "Come on in!"

There were two things in particular, among others, that I could never really find out about Father Paisie: I never knew how much and when he ate and, similarly, when and how much he slept. A disciple would bring him something to eat every day and place the container on a chair. Yet, Father never ate anything until he finished confessing all the faithful that were waiting for him.

When he was free, the Elder would take his shovel and go out into the garden, since he had a small plot of land around his cell. A spiritual father asked him once, "Father Paisie, why do you weary yourself so much with that garden?" And the Elder answered, "I go out in the open air and work a bit in the garden to forget about the worst sins I've heard in confession! Because the devil has the habit of always bringing to mind what spiritual fathers hear during confession, especially sins of the flesh, in order to tempt them. I mostly work alone, so I can say the prayer of the mind and spiritually strengthen myself. Otherwise, we can't cope with so many people, and our words and prayers have no power to change the faithful's souls".

Father Paisie did not give very harsh canons to his spiritual children and took into account their age, zeal and love for Christ. Generally, he told them to repeat Psalm 50 seven times a day, 'Our Father' fifteen times, or to do prostrations while saying the Jesus Prayer, and to say Evening and Morning Prayers, the Canon to the Savior, the Paraklesis and the prayer to the Theotokos, "Under Your Mercy." Precisely for this reason he was sought by many and succeeded to save not just a few souls but many for the Kingdom of God!

The Elder would tell the faithful who came to confess, "Have patience! Don't even think of cutting a piece from your cross!" In other words, do not grumble and despair during the troubles of life. He wept with those that wept for their sins and rejoiced with those that had been saved from passions. Even more, Heiroschemamonk Paisie had the gift of clairvoyance. Sometimes he would tell people not to leave that night so that they would not suffer some event. Other times, he would tell them not to leave without receiving Holy Communion at the monastery; if they obeyed him, everything went smoothly with his blessing. As such, none of the Elder's disciples strayed from his word.

From 1973 to 1985, Hieroschemamonk Paisie was a hermit at the Sihla Skete near Saint Theodora of Sihla's Cave, which depended, from the point of view of church administration, on Sihăstria Monastery. Here, he continued the same ascetical work of hesychasm and spiritual guidance. Because more faithful came to him here than at Sihăstria Monastery, he had no rest day or night. He was nonetheless at peace as people returned to their homes calm and joyful.

One of Father Paisie's disciples told us that when he would descend from the cells to go to the church, the Elder often murmured the words, "Let's go to heaven, to heaven of course, riding a wagon pulled by two horses!" When his disciples asked him about these words, the Elder told them that humility and love are the two horses on which Christians ride in the easiest way to heaven.

In 1986, he fractured his leg and was taken to Sihăstria where he remained bedridden until the end of his life. The Holy Spirit strengthened him to satisfy everyone, as he continued confessing monastics, faithful, priests and even Hierarchs.

Archimandrite Cleopa, having been raised and guided by Hieroschemamonk Paisie at Cozancea Skete, had many common features with his spiritual father.

The same zeal for Christ, the same love for holy prayer, the same mercy for each person, the same almsgiving to the poor. But he also had some spiritual traits that differentiated him from Father Paisie.

Father Paisie in front of his cell at Sihla.

Father Cleopa was a very decisive and categorical person, hard on himself and a great ascetic. He was providentially endowed by God with a fantastic memory and with a great love for the teachings of the Holy Fathers, to the extent that he knew more patristic and practical theology than many of those that had a theology degree. He knew the Holy Scriptures, the Lives of the Saints, Dogmatics, Canon Law, the *Philokalia*, and even more patristic literature very well. He was thus sought out by many theologians and intellectuals and held authentic patristic and canonical lectures, at any level.

As a spiritual father, Elder Cleopa was often more severe, especially with monks and priests who were not proficient in the teachings of the Holy Fathers and the Holy Scriptures or with those who did not pastor Christ's flock with the fear of God.

In such cases, the Elder was always harsh and categorical. He required priests and monks to lead an exemplary Christian life to be a source of light and guidance for the people.

However, towards children, mothers, the elderly and the poor, Father Cleopa was very meek and merciful and no one left his cell without a small gift, an icon, a book, a little cross, a few pieces of incense, money for those in want and his usual blessing upon departure. In severe cases, according to the canons of the Church, he asked those with great sins to go to the local bishop, for the appropriate absolution and canon of repentance.

For about 54 years, as long as he was Starets and a spiritual father, Elder Cleopa raised and formed thousands of souls for Christ—priests, monks, laymen—who always respected his advice and, according to their strength, fulfilled the commandments of our Savior Jesus Christ.

This is why Elder Cleopa was so much loved and sought after by all. Because he openly told each person, in a few words, everything that was necessary for their salvation.

Similarly, a disciple asked him, "Father Cleopa, if someone sent by God were to come and you were allowed to ask him one question, what would that question be?"

Elder Cleopa took some time to think it over, then answered, "Even though I know what to do, I would still ask, 'What must I do to be saved?'"

So, we can state that these two great spiritual fathers, Hieroschemamonk Paisie and Archimandrite Cleopa, revivified Sihăstria Monastery in the second half of the 20th century, granting it an unprecedented missionary dimension.

We have hope in God that this spiritual aspect will endure for many years ahead.

The Books Written by Archimandrite Cleopa

Since Father Cleopa was well-educated in the Holy Scriptures, the writings of the Holy Fathers, and the Canons of the Orthodox Church, he began, at the insistence of some Hierarchs and theologians, to write sermons and books with patristic, theological, and moral content. He was encouraged especially by Father Dumitru Stăniloae, whom he was very close to, and by Metropolitan Antonie[71] of Ardeal, who was his disciple.

He scribbled down something in his youth, as he himself told us, while doing obedience with the monastery's sheep. But knowing that he had written without a blessing, he repented and burnt his notes. After he became Igumen at Sihăstria, he started again making a record of some of his sermons and words of advice for the brothers, to spiritually strengthen them.

After he left to be Starets at Slatina Monastery, being surrounded by many theologian fathers among whom were Protosyngel Petroniu Tănase, Hierodeacon Antonie Plămădeală, or Hieromonk Arsenie Papacioc, Father Cleopa was urged to write down his homilies and other useful counsel for the monastics and faithful. However, it was difficult for him to write, as he was very busy as the Monastery's Igumen. Eventually, he found the time and wrote down a few books in words that sprang from the wisdom and grace that God gave him.

---

[71] Metropolitan Antonie Plămădeală was arrested for "activity against the communist government" when he was a priestmonk in 1949. The original sentence was seven years, but he served only four. In 1970 he wrote "Three Days in Hell," a novel that criticized the communist party. The book was banned then republished after the revolution of 1989 *(t.n.)*.

Father Cleopa writing in his cell.

"...all who have received from God the gift of counsel have the duty to use it in three ways for the salvation of human souls: firstly, they are obligated to preach through live speech and to sow the seed of God's word in the hearts of man. Secondly, they must preach with the hand, that is to write books with spiritual teachings for the use of the faithful. And thirdly, the greatest sermon is preached through the example of their life and all their good works ."

A fragment from Father Cleopa's writings.

A page from the manuscript of Father Cleopa's book:
"Guide to the Orthodox Faith."

In what follows we will briefly present Father Cleopa Ilie's works:

1. The first book on which Father Cleopa collaborated directly, together with other theologian fathers in Slatina Monastery, is entitled *Letters to the Holy Monastery Vladimireşti.*[72] It was put together on October 14, 1954, with the scope of combating certain grave canonic and dogmatic deviations from the Orthodox faith established by the Holy Fathers.

2. Clarifications on the Old Calendarists Straying is the second work by Father Cleopa. It was written in 1955, being commissioned by the Holy Synod of the Romanian Orthodox Church, so that the schismatic Old Calendarist Christians in Romania would be clarified and return to the bosom of their mother Church.

3. Sermons for Monastics (Philokalic Sermons) is Father Cleopa's most famous work. It was written in hesychasm, on the "roots of fir trees" during his third refuge in the mountains, between 1961 and 1962; it was printed by the Publishing House of the Metropolitanate of Moldavia and Bukovina under the title *The Ascent Towards Resurrection* in two editions: 1992 and 1998. The book contains 50 sermons of a profound philokalic character, meant especially for monastics and Christians who had reached a high spiritual level. This volume of sermons was translated and printed in Greek in Thessaloniki, in 1988.

4. The Confession of Hierarchs. After he returned from the mountains, Father Cleopa told us privately: "One Saturday I was in my sod hut, when this thought came to my mind, to write a guide for confessing Hierarchs, but I was in doubt if it was good or not to write it. The afternoon sun was glaring in my face. I did three prostrations and prayed to God for the wisdom to accomplish this work. While I was making the sign of the cross

---

[72] Vladimireşti Monastery was a convent in South-Eastern Romania that stirred some controversies because of a few atypical practices *(t.n.).*

and preparing to begin, against the sun rays, I saw a Hierarch clothed in vestments that radiated light, who blessed me with both hands. Then I understood that God blessed me to do this work and signing myself with the Cross, I began to write."

In the same years of hesychasm, 1961-1963, Father Cleopa, encouraged by his spiritual father, compiled additional confession guides for monastics and the clergy:

5. *The Confession of a Starets*

6. *The Confession of a Hieromonk Spiritual Father*

7. *The General Confession of Monastics*

8. *The Confession of Married Priests*

9. *On the Orthodox Faith* is another essential book compiled by Father Cleopa, which details, in simple language, the dogmatic teachings of the Orthodox Church, with a preface by the great Romanian theologian Fr. Dumitru Stăniloae. It was written between 1975 and 1976 and appeared in four editions. Two editions were issued by the Biblical Institute of Bucharest, in 1981 and 1985, the third edition was printed by Dunărea de Jos Episcopacy in 1991, under the title, Guide to the Orthodox Faith, and the fourth edition, in its final form, was published in 2000, bearing the same title.

10. In 1984, when the first volume of *Spiritual Conversations*, signed by Archimandrite Ioanichie Bălan was published by the printing house of the Roman and Huși Episcopacy, Elder Cleopa was one of the sixty fathers that collaborated to that work. Elder Cleopa contributed ten significant conversations that had a great impact among the faithful throughout the entire country, since they addressed many spiritual and canonical problems in the life of the Church.

In 1993, the same publishing house issued the volume's second edition. The first volume of Spiritual Conversations was translated in its entirety into the Greek language in 1985, and partially, only Father Cleopa's conversations, in Italian, in 1991, and in English, in 1994.

11. In 1988, the second volume of *Spiritual Conversations* was printed, to which Father Cleopa contributed four extensive conversations on various dogmatic, canonical, and moral themes.

12. In 1994, Father Cleopa's conversations, numbering fourteen, from the two volumes of Spiritual Conversations mentioned above, were reedited in a special edition entitled *Light and Works of Faith* by the Metropolitanate of Moldavia and Bukovina, Iaşi. The volume was reprinted in 1999.

13. Another much expected work, useful for all priests, was the volume *Sermons for the Great Feasts and Saints Throughout the Year*, published in two editions, in 1986 and 1996, by the Roman Episcopacy Publishing House.

14. After *Sermons of the Great Feasts and Saints Throughout the Year*, a volume of *Sermons for Sundays Throughout the Year* was published in two editions, in 1990 and 1996, by the same Roman Episcopacy Publishing House.

Father Cleopa's other books are:

15. The Value of the Soul, Galaţi, 1991, Bacău, 1994.

16. On Dreams and Visions, Bucharest, 1993, Bacău, 1994

17. The Miracles of God in Creation, Roman Episcopacy Publishing House, 1996

18. Book of Akathist Hymns, Archimandrite Cleopa Ilie and Hieroschemamonk Paisie Olaru, Pelerinul Publishers, Iaşi, 1996 and 1998.

19. Verses to the Mother of God, Metropolitanate of Moldavia and Bukovina Publishing House, 1999.

20-31. Conversations with Elder Cleopa, in 12 volumes, Roman Episcopacy Publishing House, 1995-2002.

Archimandrite Cleopa's "Universities"

The first school of spiritual formation where Father Cleopa studied was in his family, in his tender youth. His mother's piety and tears, his father's manliness, faith and stability, the moral authority of Father Gheorghe Chiriac of his native village, they all laid an authentic foundation for the spiritual formation of Father Cleopa and of his siblings.

When the children grew up, they began to draw closer to God through prayer and good deeds.

Departing from their childhood home, the children became spiritually close to Cozancea Skete and Schemamonk Paisie Olaru. The three brothers, Vasile, Gheorghe and Constantin, remained under the guidance of Father Paisie for five years. In this period, the Elder taught them to be obedient, quiet, humble and ascetic, and to practice the Jesus Prayer.

The seed sowed by Father Paisie fell on the good soil of their hearts and began to bear fruit. In 1929 the three brothers became members of the Coenobium of Sihăstria, completely serving Christ, far from their childhood home. Thus, they ascended to a much higher spiritual level, each of them having their own obedience and spiritual ascetic life.

In 1931 and 1933, Father Cleopa's spiritually-advanced elder brothers, Vasile and Gherasim, departed for the Lord. Constantin was tonsured into monasticism in 1937 receiving the name Cleopa, and he improved spiritually through good works with every passing day. In 1945, he became Starets, and in addition to other good works, he gave alms to the poor and saved many from death during the famine.

After Father Cleopa withdrew for the third time in the mountains, from 1959 to 1964, by the gift of Christ, he attained a high level of spirituality, that few in our days can reach. He prayed ceaselessly with the prayer of the heart, spoke with no one, constantly contemplated death, had no possessions, no money, no other comfort but the mercy of God and the prayers of the Theotokos. Here he obtained the gift of tears and peace of heart and he would have liked not to return to the monastery because he had acquired the sweetness of stillness and prayer. This constituted the loftiest spiritual university from which Father Cleopa graduated!

But the good Lord did not leave the faithful lovers of Christ completely without comfort. So, urged by the Holy Spirit, Father Cleopa eventually returned to Sihăstria Monastery, remaining obedient to men and God, and he continued his spiritual missionary activity for yet another 34 years, burning slowly for Christ like a candle of pure wax, awaiting the hour of resurrection night and day.

When people from high society came to the Elder—professors, theologians, dignitaries—and asked him what education he had and where he graduated from, Father Cleopa answered them with a smile on his lips, "You see that staff above the door over there? I walked the sheep with that. You see that knapsack hanging on that nail? I carried the books I took from Neamț Monastery and I read them while tending the sheep. Look at the opinci! Do you see them? That is my science! And my schools are at Tăciune, Piciorul Crucii, Răscoalele, at Chita Mică, Chita Mare, Dubau's Mound, Fagii Rari, Pârâul Solomâzdrelor, Piciorul Cucului, Piciorul Rotunzii, Pârâul Ruginii, Râpa lui Coroi, Piatra Dediului, Poiana lui Iosif, Poiana lui Serghie, Poiana Arșiței[73] and wherever I journeyed with the Monastery's sheep for over 10 years."

---

[73] Place names in Romanian (t.n.).

Spiritual Asceticism

Prayer

Father Cleopa, when he was little, prayed abundantly saying prayers from books; he knew many of them by heart and said them continuously. In his youth he especially loved the Psalter, from which he read daily. He knew by heart the Akathist Hymn to the Savior, the Akathist Hymn to the Annunciation, the Canon of Repentance to the Savior, the Paraklesis to the Mother of God, and other prayers which he recited daily.

In addition to his prayers, he did hundreds of prostrations and semi-prostrations every day. Recalling his childhood years, Father Cleopa said to his disciples, "Sometimes my brothers and I would even have competitions to see who could do the most prostrations in an hour. It seemed like I had springs on my legs. I could do 500 prostrations in an hour."

Likewise, he forced himself to master the prayer of the heart which he practiced day and night when he had more peace and quiet. His brothers, Vasile and Gherasim, had already learned this hidden prayer, since they were more advanced in its work.

As Igumen and then Starets of Sihăstria Monastery, Archimandrite Cleopa Ilie, being very busy during the day, prayed extensively at night. After he slept for two hours before Matins and two more hours after it, he would do his entire daily prayer rule for three hours until morning. He further increased his holy prayer during his 10 years of asceticism in the mountains, praying to God day and night.

Many times, Father Cleopa would speak to his disciples about the pure prayer of the heart, speaking as if on behalf of someone else who had lived in the desert, "I met someone who had been tormented by hunger, thirst, cold, or lack of clothes in the forest, and he told me that he once stayed at a faithful person's house overnight. Since it was Sunday eve, he was doing his rule of prayer. The neighbor's house was hosting a wedding party with loud music.

"The hermit at prayer had before him an icon of the Theotokos. Standing in front of it and thinking, he remembered the words of Saint John Climacus who said, 'Some worldly songs can uplift the spiritually advanced persons to the highest contemplation.'

"So, hearing this wedding music, he said to himself, 'If these people can sing so beautifully, how about the angels who praise the Theotokos, how do they chant in heaven?' From this feeling, his mind descended in his heart, and he remained in this spiritual state for over two hours, sensing great sweetness and warmth. Tears were rolling down his face continually, his heart was warm and he could feel how Christ was speaking to his soul. So much fragrance of the Holy Spirit came then to him and he felt such spiritual warmth that he said, 'Lord I wish I could die this very moment!'

"After two hours his mind left his heart and a sweet sorrow, joy, comfort, and special spiritual warmth lingered for a month in his heart—undisturbed by anything from this world. Tears that flow during this type of prayer, being from the Holy Spirit, wash away every stain, every sinful imagining, and the soul remains pure."

Father Cleopa also said this about prayer:

"When the mind descends into the heart, the heart opens and then closes. That is, the heart swallows Jesus and Jesus swallows our heart. In that moment, Christ the Bridegroom meets with the bride, our soul."

If someone asked Father Cleopa for advice on how to achieve the prayer of the heart, he spoke as if he were referring to someone else, so that no one would be aware of his work. For that reason, his disciples at Sihăstria Monastery did not know how he was praying and what level he had attained. Actually, the gift of tears did not abandon him until he departed into the heavenly realms.

Father Cleopa prayed for everyone who asked him for help. If someone was tormented at the moment of their death and he was called to read the prayers for the departing soul, the moribund always gave up their soul in peace to the Lord exactly when Father Cleopa was reading the prayers.

Through much prayer and extended fasting, Father Cleopa obtained the gifts of patience, obedience, wisdom, and eloquent speech from his enlightened memory, which amazed many.

Father Cleopa in his private cell at the monastery's apiary.

During the last years of his life, Father Cleopa prayed exceedingly and had deeply intimate moments when he no longer wished to speak to anyone, not even to his cell attendant. He also had secret places of prayer. While he still had strength, he would pray in the forests or in the mountains. During old age, he prayed more in his cell, alone. Another preferred place was the monastery's apiary, where he had a small cell in which he kept his books and manuscripts.

His most powerful prayers, however, were those at night, standing alone in his cell or at the edge of the forest, since he loved nature, the sheep and all of God's creation, deeply.

Otherwise, each phrase and word of his was a prayer and a blessing for the one who entreated him for help. Nevertheless, his prayer life will always remain, for us all, an unknowable mystery of his soul.

Fasting

B eing used to fasting, praying, and doing obedience from his childhood, Father Cleopa was spiritually prepared from his early years for a select monastic asceticism.

In his childhood home, they practiced prayer and fasting especially. None of the children ever broke the fast by eating what was not permitted on fasting days. Likewise, when they were older and herded the sheep near Cozancea Skete, none of the three brothers ever ate non-fasting foods on Mondays, Wednesdays or Fridays, being convinced that if any of them dared to do something like that, God would punish them. Usually, at the beginning of Lent, they kept three days of complete fasting, according to tradition.

At Sihăstria, all the novices and fathers fasted the first three days of Lent, completely, according to the typicon. It was only on Friday evening that they had their second meal. During the rest of Lent, they only ate once a day, food without oil, with the exception of Saturdays and Sundays. In the last week of Lent, they received one meal per day in the evening, and from Holy Thursday to Holy Pascha, they kept a complete fast.

The greatest faster in Sihăstria Skete was Igumen Ioanichie Moroi, who fasted from Monday to Saturday, being satisfied with just Holy Communion and the prosphora meant for the serving priest.

In imitation of his Starets, Archimandrite Cleopa would eat nothing during the first week of Lent, from Monday until Saturday. For the rest of Lent, he ate with the community.

He respected this arrangement of meals for his entire life. As for those who were old, sick or too young, he allowed them to eat twice a day on Tuesdays, Thursdays, Saturdays and Sundays, and to have just one meal at three o'clock in the afternoon for the rest of the days. Those who could not observe this rule were permitted, through a blessing, to eat twice a day.

Sometimes Father Cleopa would withdraw to his hut in the forest, in quietness and prayer, for a day or two. Also, during fasting periods, he spoke very little and prayed in isolation to the Lord, usually in tears. Yet, he never spoke to us about this ascetic work.

While in the wilderness, oftentimes he only ate one potato per day, and some wild edible plants that he could find. He told his disciples that on the eve of the Nativity Fast, he had two potatoes and a beetroot, and it seemed to him like it was food for a feast day.

Obedience

Father Cleopa was a man of obedience, from his childhood to the hour of his death. Whatever command his Starets would give him, he fulfilled it religiously and without complaint. Whatever word of advice he got from someone, he sought to fulfill it with joy and humility. Whichever brother asked for his help, he came immediately. No other dweller of Sihăstria was more obedient, more determined, or more stable than him. For this reason, he was more loved than all the other young novices and everyone could benefit from his spiritual stability. It is enough for us to recall how he was chosen as Igumen.

Then, even though Sihăstria Skete had burnt down, was poor and lacked all necessities, through his obedience and sacrifice, being overshadowed by the grace of the Holy Spirit, he succeeded to renew the entire skete in just a few years and to raise it to the rank of monastery, while gathering around him tens of young novices to establish a special monastic community. He fulfilled all this with the help of the Theotokos, first of all thanks to his accomplished obedience: to God, to the Hierarch of the area, and to his spiritual father.

If we add to obedience his zeal for all things holy, his hidden asceticism, and his gentleness, we will better understand Archimandrite Ilie Cleopa's personality.

Tears

From his youth Father Cleopa had the gift of tears while praying, though he often hid so that no one around him would notice it. In the church he would shed tears while he served the Divine Liturgy, especially during the Holy Epiclesis. But God visited him the most during the years of his refuge in the mountains, especially when he was saying the prayer of the heart. Sometimes his disciples saw Father Cleopa weeping while praying in his cell, for tears gave him much joy and comfort.

The thought of Death

Following his older brothers, Father Cleopa often contemplated the hour of his death, especially at night. When he was younger, he stood in vigil for one to two hours in the monastery's cemetery, near the tombs of his brothers, where he lit candles and prayed for their souls' rest. Reading *The Lives of the Saints*, he would be amazed at the tortures of the martyrs and the pious, who accepted death with manliness for the love of Christ, and he was further strengthened spiritually.

Patience

Father Cleopa was a man of patience and endurance. It was only through patience, stability, and prayer that he succeeded to cultivate so many souls for Christ and to guide the monastery entrusted to him for so many years.

Even when surveilled by the secret service, he never hated anyone since he had Christ in his soul and knew that without suffering, temptations, and patience we cannot be saved . That is why when a troubled Father came to him for advice, he would remind him of the words of the great Spiritual Father Vichentie Mălău who often told his disciples, "Listen brothers, patience, patience, patience.... And when it seems that you've run out of it, start from the beginning: patience, patience, patience... Patience to the door of your tomb."

Stillness

After finishing confession, Father Cleopa withdrew to stillness, especially at night, to the edge of the forest or to the cemetery where he prayed by himself. There he would say the Jesus Prayer, which he had been practicing since his youth. Stillness rested his soul, urged him to pray, and filled him with spiritual peace.[74] But when God visited him with the gift of tears, he withdrew to a hidden place and prayed fervently until God refreshed his soul.

Father Cleopa in stillness under a hornbeam tree near his cell.

After tasting the joy of stillness in the years of his refuge, Father Cleopa wanted to remain forever in this life of solitude, stillness being the mother of prayer, tears and spiritual joy. But the command of obedience urged him to return to his community.

---

[74] Father Cleopa sometimes told us how he himself received this advice:
"Father Vichentie was leaving on a mission in Banat and I went too to ask him for a last piece of advice. Father Vichentie told me, 'Hey, listen to my last advice, 'Patience, patience, patience, and when it seems to you that you've run out of it, again: patience, patience, patience… and when it seems to you that you've run out of it again, you start all over, from the beginning: patience, patience, patience….' And I asked him, 'But until when, Father?'
"'Not until spring time, but until death time!' That was Father Vichentie's last advice."

Humility

Another great gift of Father Cleopa was humility, one of the principal traits of holiness. The Elder said, "I am nicknamed amonk; I happen to be called a monk. But I have never become a monk in my life, since being a monk is a great thing. How can I call myself a monk before men, if before God I am not? A monastic should be an angel in the flesh, not lead a worldly life, like I lead, in sins and weaknesses!"

Holiness' main characteristic is humble thinking and repentance. Elder Cleopa humbled himself, often recalling the words from the Holy Scriptures: *I humbled myself and I was saved.*

I humbled myself and I was saved.

"I am a barren man," the Elder once said. "A tree with leaves only. You die of hunger near it. Saint Isaac the Syrian said, 'A word that does not work is like the one who paints water on the wall yet can die of thirst near it.' That's how it is with me. With me you die of hunger. I'm telling you what to do but I don't do anything. Why do you come to a barren milk cow? You come here for me to talk to you to no avail? But you don't tell me, 'Father, you sleep all night, you eat all the time, you don't guard your heart, you are not prayerful, you don't have tears, you don't have a broken heart' You don't ask me about watchfulness of attention, you don't ask me about my inner work…'"

Father Cleopa:
A Great Missionary Starets

Sermon

After Father Cleopa was appointed Igumen of Sihăstria Skete in the beginning of 1945, the first thing he did was to adorn the Church with services and some of the best chanters. Then he began to give sermons, inspired from the Holy Fathers, feeding monks, novices and the faithful spiritually. Truly, there was no other spiritual father from Neamț Monasteries who spoke more beautifully, more warmly and more convincingly than him. Father Cleopa had a fantastic memory and knowledge of patristics and scripture which he had accumulated since tender youth, and which was made even more prominent with the grace of the Holy Spirit that radiated and worked through the Elder.

A spiritual rest with Father Cleopa.

His living word, which fed all, brought increasingly more faithful to Sihăstria from nearby villages and cities, who came to participate in the holy services and hear Father Cleopa's sermons. Due to both his philokalic and hagiographic teachings, numerous youths embraced monastic life, who later became good monastics and skilled priests.

Defending the True Faith

The second virtue that adorned Father Cleopa's soul was that of steadfastly defending the true faith. The Elder combated all kinds of sects with wisdom and determination, as well as those who had been deceived by them.

Many times, it happened that whole large groups of Christians returned to Orthodoxy, especially in Bukovina, who had been tricked by various sects. This was a major reason why Archimandrite Cleopa was recognized throughout the entire country as a great missionary and defender of Orthodoxy in the second half of the 20th century. His writings confirm this; they strengthened many doubtful Christians in the right faith, a large part of them being compiled under the orders of the Holy Synod, or at the insistence of Hierarchs and significant theologians.

For the same purpose, the Elder was called to missionary services, to church consecrations, or to meetings with the faithful throughout villages and cities, and he always succeeded in attracting multitudes of people to the right faith, combating sectarian teachings. Likewise, whenever groups of Christians of different faiths would come to speak with him, they would leave ashamed.

Alms

Another fundamental virtue which characterized Archimandrite Cleopa throughout his life was giving alms. The Elder had no personal possessions at all but gave many alms from what the faithful would bring. Widows, beggars, poor people, mothers with many children, orphans and the sick came daily and received from Father Cleopa money, clothes, provisions, or words of comfort, and they all returned home thankful and giving praise to God.

Wherever he served as a Starets, Father Cleopa arranged for the faithful who came to the monastery, irrespective of their number, to eat a common meal.

One of his disciples from Slatina said that once, when there was a feast day, many people had come, and there was only a little food. If they were to offer food to every faithful, they would have no food left. The cook told the Starets:

"Father Cleopa, if we serve everyone a meal now, we won't have anything left to eat. What should we do?"

Then Father Cleopa, who never placed his hope in perishable things, said:

"Brother, serve all you have! Serve everything!"

And according to God's providence, after three hours some faithful people came and brought a wagon of provisions that sustained the community for a long period of time.

Yet, the Elder's greatest alms were still spiritual: prayer for all, confession, homilies, advice, and his writings.

Spirituality

Father Cleopa was one of the most skilled spiritual fathers in the country during the second half of the 20th century. He knew how to win over souls for the Kingdom of God. The Elder not only confessed people, but also gave great hope to his spiritual children, proving to be a true guide on the path of salvation. None left from under his epitrachelion troubled, unsatisfied or in doubt.

Through the example of his life, the Elder attracted many souls to the monastic life, who later became his disciples for their whole lives and became grace-filled monastics and enlightened priests. He urged spiritual fathers to take great care of their spiritual children, to visit them in their cells, to give them canons according to their strength, confessing them weekly and giving them communion with the Holy Mysteries.

Father Cleopa – the Father of spiritual comfort.

Thus, even from his youth, he had become a great spiritual father, to whom many priests, Staretses, and even Hierarchs confessed.

For over 50 years the Elder was the spiritual father with the largest number of spiritual children in Romania. He was ordained by God to be a Father of comfort, joy, hope and good advice, and like from a true spiritual mother, they all left his cell spiritually strengthened.

From 1945, when he was ordained as a priest and blessed as a spiritual father, up until the end of his life, on December 2, 1998, Father Cleopa received people of all ages and social classes daily, encouraging them all along the path of salvation and joy through the grace that God had given him. He urged them to abandon the sins they had committed, to repent, and make a new beginning through repentance, he himself being a man of repentance.

Because of this, he became known throughout the entire country, and even abroad, and enjoyed special respect. For the majority of the faithful who knew him he will remain for a long time to come, not just a theologian, not only an unsurpassed preacher, not only a man of prayer before God, but an unparalleled spiritual father!

The Gift of Discernment

Another great gift of the Elder was the gift of discernment. He did not give identical advice for two people that had the same problem. To one he would say one thing, and to the other something else. He knew the hearts of the faithful and what each one needed, through Christ's gift.

He knew if someone was coming out of inquisitiveness or faith. He knew how much we could bear, so as not to give us something too difficult that would then make us grumble. Because of this, many came to Father Cleopa to ask him what path to take in life, and the Elder gave each one an answer as the Holy Spirit inspired him; and those who listened were always spiritually thankful and blessed in Christ.

FFather Cleopa – a Father full of grace from our times.

Father Dimitrie Bejan's Letter to Father Cleopa

Father Cleopa and Father Ioanichie,

I kiss the hand of you both.[75] Your right hands. I have always felt love for you and felt close because you know what you want from God. May Father Cleopa forgive me, but that is what my conscience has told me since I first saw him up until now, as I make this declaration, that he is the most pure monk at this time in Romanian Orthodoxy. Maybe people superior to our monks can be found on Mount Athos. But Father Ioanichie still searches for God. He is very occupied with books. He

writes! He has the gift for writing and for spreading the word of God! Especially in the practical aspects of our Christianity. May God help him to have disciples!

If Father Cleopa and Father Ioanichie do not leave disciples in their wake, Sihăstria will be like a desert. So much Spirit: Paisie, Cleopa, Ioanichie, and there was their Starets, Father Ioanichie Moroi…

Missionary Priest Dimitrie Bejan
(1909-1995).

---

[75] In Orthodox culture one kisses the priest's right hand (since through it the Holy Liturgy is performed) or a Hierarch's hand for their blessing. In Romanian culture it is still not uncommon to kiss a woman's hand when meeting. There is even a common form of thank you, said after a favor or meal, which translates to, "I kiss your hand." Here it is used as a respectful greeting *(t.n.)*.

There was a good spirit from the very foundation of this skete which has become a monastery now. I would have liked to die there, but I think that God has decided that I should die here. I'm not upset. We remain in the body, Father Cleopa and Father Ioanichie…. Because the body is given to the God-created nature. Until when? Maybe in a thousand years, maybe less. We are transformed. Flowers spring up from us; trees, nettle, thorns spring up!

If our soul is good before God, a plum tree or an apple tree springs up near our head; if not, nettle and thorns. In a thousand years, no one will know about Cleopa and Ioanichie. You will be in heaven! You should look out from there, without binoculars, at the monks of Sihăstria; the future monks. You should come and with God's help, you should guide them. It is our only monastic community that has found the direct path to salvation! Maybe, maybe this holds true for the monks from Frăsinei, too! Maybe there, they might be more advanced spiritually, since women do not enter the monastery.

Father Cleopa in his cell, together with his biographer,
Father Ioanichie.

Father Cleopa and Father Ioanichie, tonsure monks, but later, after they are 30 years old. Let them pass through fire first. Can you take them from school desks and make them priests at 18? There are even priests here that are very young, they do not know and have not even heard about canons. They need to be raised for years under the shadow of a spiritual father, and a good one at that, who is as spiritual as possible and has full knowledge.

Some are children. Some young. They do not know that they have stepped with one foot in heaven! They don't know! They do not know what heaven is! No! They have no way of knowing. They should be told!... It is not obligatory to have a lot of people in a monastery. But monasteries should remain as always, as the place where we, the others, go to commune.

I kiss your hands, Father Cleopa and Father Ioanichie, and when I die, I will go to God and I will tell Him that you are doing good work, and I will wait for you in heaven! If our suffering on earth will count as 51% on God's scales and our sins will only be 49%, then we'll go to heaven! So, our Good God presses on the balance of our good and evil deeds, he presses down with one finger and says: "Let it be! Enter into My goodness!"

I say this for you, Father Cleopa and Father Ioanichie, who are dear to me and superior in formation and spirit. We cannot enter God's kingdom except through love! That is what the Holy Book says. With kindness, I would say. Only with that. We must be good not just with those who give you food and clothing. Be good with the downtrodden...

I kiss your hand and I thank you and I say, may you keep living on earth because you are needed. Amen.

Father Dimitrie Bejan, January 1ˢᵗ, 1995

Bodily Suffering

For many years Father Cleopa enjoyed bodily and especially spiritual health, having been blessed by God with a very resistant organism. But from the age of 70, the Elder felt increasingly fatigued and ill. The years spent in the mountains, as well as the trials through which he passed during the atheistic period, marked him greatly.

His first difficult suffering was a double hernia, for which he was hospitalized in the Saint Spyridon Hospital in Iași, and operated on two times in 1985. After a few years he was operated on for kidney stones, again in Iași and, likewise, he endured a facial operation because of a dental infection. He also suffered a fracture in his right hand.

In June 1996, he had an operation for a bladder tumor at the Urology Hospital in Iași. The doctors discovered that his left kidney was inactive. During the checkup in September, they found no tumor lesions but proposed a supplemental surgical intervention, which the Elder refused.

In May 1998, after enduring great pain, he accepted with difficulty to go for a consultation in Iași. He stayed a week, but he did not want to be hospitalized saying, "My friends are waiting, and I am preparing to go to them!" He said the same words in November 1998, when they again suggested a consultation.

This suffering kept Father Cleopa focused, always awaiting his final hour, with his mind on Christ and with unceasing prayer of the heart.

The Last Year of His Life

As early as 1996-1997, Father Cleopa was feeling more and more fatigued. Nevertheless, he was persistently approached by faithful pilgrims from Romania and abroad. His memory and voice were still healthy, and he always succeeded in comforting the faithful, the sick, the elderly and his spiritual children in the monastery.

He walked with great difficulty, only accompanied by his disciples, both in his cell and outside, in the open air. As for the adjacent hall, where for decades he held edifying talks and homilies for the faithful, he could only get rarely, in the summer.

The Elder was very frugal with food. He tasted only a little, then said, "It's enough! I'm full! Glory to God for everything!"

He did his prayers regularly, sitting on his bed or chair since he could no longer stand. His preferred time for prayer was in the morning from four to eight, after which he rested a bit. Then he spoke with the Fathers that came for confession and with the faithful. Around four o'clock in the afternoon he would finish his rule for the evening: the Canon of Repentance, two or three canons to the Theotokos from the book, the Paraklesis to the Theotokos, the Small Compline and others.

In the evening, his disciples brought him out into the fresh air on the verandah where he prayed the Jesus Prayer and admired the nature that God had adorned so beautifully. After an hour or two he withdrew to his cell for rest and would wake again towards the middle of the night.

The Last Days

The months of September and October foretold the approaching end of Father Cleopa. He spoke less and less, with a muffled voice, and always repeated the words, "Now I am going to my brothers!" "Let me go to my brothers!" Then again, he would say, "I'm going to Christ! Pray for me the sinner!"

Towards the end of September, one day at sunset, the Elder asked to go to the cemetery for the last time to see the graves of his brothers, of the great Starets Ioanichie Moroi, of his Spiritual Father, Hieroschemamonk Paisie Olaru, and of the other fathers and spiritual fathers older than himself. He was brought by car to the cemetery gate and from here his disciples took him from one grave to another to visit all his dear ones and acquaintances, those who had been his disciples, brothers, spiritual children or spiritual fathers.

At all graves he made the sign of the cross, and supported by his disciples, kissed the holy crosses and said a holy prayer, saying, "Pray for Cleopa the sinner, for tomorrow or the day after we'll meet before Christ!" Then he ended by saying, "Mother of God, have mercy on us and on all the Fathers in this cemetery, and pray before the throne of the Most-Holy Trinity that we obtain forgiveness from the Righteous Judge."

The Departure to Christ

On Friday and Saturday, the 27th and 28th of November, Father Cleopa still gave advice and blessings to those that came to him, monks and faithful. He was tired, but his face was calm. He spoke gently and beautifully to those who asked him questions and refused no one who wanted to see him. He comforted and strengthened them as always, in peace and joy.

Sunday, November 29th, on the eve of the feast day of Saint Andrew the Apostle, he was again surrounded by people. He spoke to them warmly, in short sentences, and with great gentleness. Some came, others left, and his disciples took care of everything.

At 11:30 p.m. a brother came to our pious Elder to get a blessing to be tonsured into monasticism saying,

"Bless me, Righteous Elder Cleopa, because tonight I will become a monk!"

After he blessed him and put his hand on his head, the brother asked for some counsel for his monastic life. Then Father Cleopa said:

"From now on, you no longer have a father, you no longer have a mother, you no longer have brothers, relatives, friends, land, house, you no longer have anything but Christ!"

"Father," said the disciple. "If you obtain boldness before God , remember me in your holiness' prayers!"

"May the mercy of the Theotokos be with us all!

At four in the afternoon another brother came to ask him for a blessing to become a monk, but Father Cleopa did not say anything and just put his hand on his head.

From Sunday afternoon, Father Cleopa no longer answered his disciples' questions and stayed unmoved with his eyes half-open on his confession chair, as if in ecstasy, for more than 11 hours.

On Monday morning at 3:30 a.m., the Elder awoke as if from a deep sleep, and was well disposed and spiritually thankful. Then he asked for something to eat, saying, "Have you ever seen a monk eat at such an hour as this?"

On Monday, November 30, and on Tuesday, December 1st, the Elder stayed with the faithful and gave spiritual advice as usual. On Monday evening, however, unexpectedly, Father Cleopa began to read the Morning Prayers, even though his disciples told him, "Father, it is evening now. Read the Morning Prayers tomorrow!" But the Elder did not listen to them.

On Tuesday evening, he went to bed late, signaling great fatigue. At 2:20 a.m. on Wednesday morning, a disciple heard the Elder breathing increasingly slower. When he drew near to him, the Elder breathed deeply one last time and gave his soul into the hands of Christ. Seeing that the Elder had fallen asleep in the Lord, his disciple ran to tell Father Starets and the Ecclesiarch.

The Fathers gathered immediately, together with the Starets, and they prepared him for burial. Then they brought down Father Cleopa's soulless body from his cell and placed it in the monastery's old church to the sound of bells. There they had a vigil with priests, monks, and numerous faithful.

The news of Father Cleopa's departure to the eternal dwellings spread quickly in the country and abroad. In the days before the Elder's burial, the faithful from every corner of the country came to say their final farewells to him, and the monks read the Psalter continuously in the church where he had been laid.

That is how the great Starets and Spiritual Father of the Romanian monasteries, Archimandrite Cleopa Ilie lived,

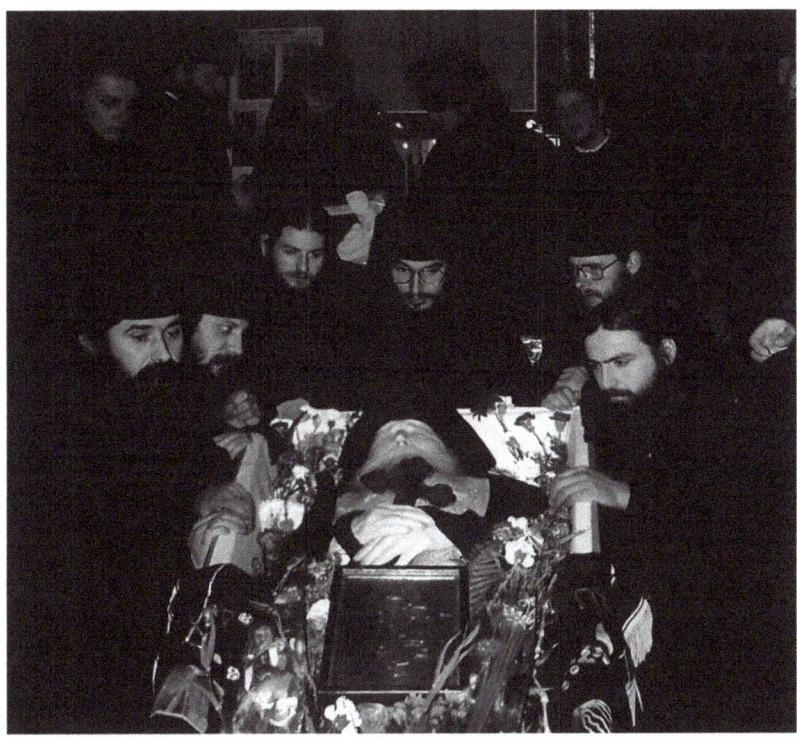

Father Cleopa waked by his disciples.

strived, and came to an end; he was mourned by all the Fathers and faithful who had him as a counselor, priest, spiritual father, and guide.

May his memory be eternal!

The Funeral

For three days and nights the entire monastery and the faithful that were close to him prayed for the rest of Father Cleopa's soul. The funeral was set for Saturday, December 5. By a miracle of God, the day of the funeral was beautiful, sunny, and warm, after many days of dark and frigid weather.

The Divine Liturgy was served by an assembly of Hierarchs made up of His Eminence Daniel, the Metropolitan of Moldavia and Bukovina,[76] His Eminence Bartolomeu, archbishop of Vad, Feleac and Cluj; His Grace Ioan, bishop of Huși; His Grace Calinic, the vicar bishop of the Archdiocese of Iași; His Grace Visarion, the vicar bishop of Ardeal, and His Grace Gherasim, the vicar bishop of the Archdiocese of Suceava and Rădăuți.

After the Divine Liturgy was served, the Lamentations service was officiated in the monastery's courtyard by the same assembly of Hierarchs. Numerous Staretses, hieromonks, priests and over ten thousand faithfuls from all over the country participated in the service. The monastery's courtyard, balconies, the road to the cemetery and the surrounding areas were packed.

The Assembly of Hierarchs and Priests at Father Cleopa's Requiem

Then they circled the church with the coffin held by twelve priests and walked in procession to the monastery's cemetery. With bells ringing, tender hymns, the sound of long flutes from Bukovina, Father Cleopa was laid down by

---

[76] The current Patriarch of Romania *(t.n.)*.

the priests in the place prepared for his burial in the middle of the cemetery, next to his beloved spiritual father, Hieroschemamonk Paisie Olaru.

With tears in their eyes, the attendants gathered around Father Cleopa, desperate to touch his hand one last time—the hand that had imparted such blessings in his over 50 years of priesthood. Through the cemetery's fir trees, the sun shone on the freshly dug tomb. The chant "Christ is Risen" was repeated many times as a victory hymn, erupting from everyone's bosoms.

Everyone attending the funeral experienced the pain of the temporary separation from a great father, spiritual father, and guide for the souls.

That is how the funeral service took place for the greatest Romanian spiritual father of the second half of the 20th century, who departed from us into God's heaven to receive the reward for his many struggles.

The soulless body of Father Cleopa mourned over by Thousands of faithful mourning over Elder Cleopa's soulless body.

With Father Cleopa's departure to the Lord, a rich chapter of Romanian hesychasm and monasticism at the end of the second millennium came to a close, a golden page of the history of Sihăstria Monastery and of our local indigenous Church.

We hope that in the years to come, both Elder Cleopa and Hieroschemamonk Paisie of Sihăstria will be placed beside other great righteous people of our country: Saint Paisie of Neamț, Saint Vasile of Poiana Mărului, Starets Gheorghe of Cernica, Saint John Jacob the Hosevite, and many others whose names are written by angels in the Book of Life for the praise of the All-Holy Trinity.[77]

The 40 Day Memorial Service

O n January 9, 1999, on the fortieth day since Archimandrite Cleopa's departure to the Lord, the Divine Liturgy was celebrated together with the memorial service according to tradition, in the winter church of Sihăstria Monastery. The service was led by His Eminence Daniel, Metropolitan of Moldavia and Bukovina, together with an assembly of

Father Cleopa's grave.

---

[77] Fathers Cleopa and Paisie of Sihăstria were glorified by the Holy Synod of the Romanian Orthodox Church on July 12th, 2024.

priests from the area. His Eminence Metropolitan Daniel gave a speech commemorating Father Cleopa.

Then the monastery's community, led by the Metropolitan and Archimandrite Victorin, went to the cemetery where they chanted the trisagion by the grave of our good and unforgettable Spiritual Father, Archimandrite Cleopa.

Afterwards, Sihăstria Monastery offered a common meal at the refectory for all those present—monastics, faithful, the poor—for the repose of the soul of Father Cleopa, who was and will forever remain in our hearts.

The Last Homily Father Cleopa Gave to the Community of Sihăstria Monastery, Delivered in the Refectory

– March 1, 1998 –

In the name of the Father and of the Son and of the Holy Spirit.

Mosteverend Father Starets, reverend Fathers and brothers, as I now see you here, my dear children, may I see you like this in heaven, in heaven's endless joy, since you are all in the service of the Lord and of the Theotokos, and each one, poor you, does obedience in his own direction, where he is asked to.

I love seeing you! But I don't know many of you. I rarely come here. I have so many people coming to me over there and I am sick. But I know some of them, who come to confess and who are older disciples... I would like that everyone, everyone would go to the eternal joy and not one, God forbid, to torment.

Dear Fathers and brothers, you should know that the Church as your spiritual mother. She gave birth to us upon baptism through water and Spirit. You have heard what the Holy Apostle Paul said: you received the grace of adoption at the second birth and renewal through the Holy Spirit. From that moment we are all sons of God by grace since we have been baptized in the name of the All-Holy Trinity.

That is why I'm asking you, with my whole heart, to love the Church, beloved! May the Church be dear to you, and as much as you can, day and night, go to the holy services. Those of you who are older, poor you, and who don't have strength, you can stay for less time. Those of you who are young can stay longer, because the services of the Church enrich one's memory and the gift of the Most-Holy Spirit comes over those who listen piously to the Church's holy services.

Dear ones, I, a sinner and unworthy man, am old, 86 years; I have had six operations, my right hand is broken, I was in a cast for 32 days—tomorrow or the day after you will be chanting Memory Eternal for me! What awaits me? Psalm 90 says it clearly, "The days of our years are threescore years and ten; and if by reason of strength they be fourscore years." And the verse continues, "yet is their strength labor and sorrow." I have entered the years of pain. I have grown old; I will be 86 years old now on April 10.

My dear Fathers, I ask you with my whole heart, whoever has love and strength, do not forget me in your prayer. Remember my name!

I feel love when I see you all serving the Savior and the Theotokos. May I see you so in heaven, dear children, all of you! You are all serving the Savior and the Mother of God.

Our monastery has a canonical order: we don't eat meat, confession is regular, the services are arranged according to Saint Savva's typikon...

When I came here, I found 14 Fathers, shod in opinci, with beards down to their belts, with wooden-bead prayer ropes in hand… My brother Vasile brought me here. When I came here, I was 15 and a half years old, I didn't know…

And when I saw the Elder, the Starets, at the head of the table, together with all the monks, he was reading words of instruction from Saint Theodore the Studite, and I asked a brother, "Is there a feast day today?" Because I had stayed at Cozancea, and it was idiorhythmic[78] there; each one had their own meal, their own house. "Hey, brother, it's not a feast day! Here we have community life. That's how monks sit at the table together, all the time!" The Elder was reading words of counsel …. He served the Liturgy and all he ate was Holy Communion for nearly 20 years. Only on Saturdays and Sundays did he take a bite from food in bowls. I know because I was a cook. May the Lord rest his soul, poor man! He had such great fear of God and he had such strong faith! I was tonsured in 1937 during the Dormition fast. I remember…

There was a Father, Nicolae Gradinaru, with a long beard; maybe some of you met him. He said when he led me before the altar: "Reverend Father, let's give him the name Cleopa, since we have no one named Cleopa here!" And the Elder put his hand on the scissors, and I was called Cleopa. That's what was meant for me!

---

[78] Monastic life in Orthodoxy has no different orders per se, but there is an idiorhythmic life, where each monastic is more or less independent, and the coenobitic life, centered on community. Today the consensus is that the coenobitic monastic life is more appropriate for the vast majority of monastics *(t.n.)*.

May the Lord grant him rest! I have a prayer list at home with the names of those that died here; I have many names of bishops and patriarchs on it. As long as I have a spark of life in me, I commemorate them every day!

But I ask you, my dear children, all of you, don't forget me in your holy prayers! As I see you here, may I see you like this in heaven, in the eternal, boundless joy!

May the mercy of the Most-Holy Trinity and the protection of the prayers of the Most Holy Theotokos be with you all, my dear ones, and may they take you all to heaven. Amen.

In Golia Monastery, in Iași.

Part Three

Wise Words from the Holy Fathers that Father Cleopa Used

Archimandrite Cleopa and Hieroshemamonk Paisie in a private spiritual conversation in the cemetery.

Wisdom has two ends. The first is fear of God and the second is love of God.

The **Holy Fathers** say: "Whoever would like to be saved should journey ahead by asking questions."

The good advice will guard you and the right thinking will defend you. One brother helping another brother, and advising each other, they are like a well-founded citadel and like an unconquered empire.

The **Holy Fathers** tell us likewise, that prayer is the mother and queen over all good deeds.

Saint Maximus the Confessor tells us similarly, "All good deeds help man to earn the love of God, but none of them as much as prayer."

Saint Hesychius of Sinai says: "During prayer there are three minds that squirm in battle against each other: the mind of the Holy Powers, the diabolical mind, and the mind of man."

Saint Ephraim the Syrian says: "When you sit and pray and receive unclean thoughts, you are like a bride committing adultery in front of her groom."

Coldness in prayer almost always comes from forgetfulness, the **Holy Fathers** say. And forgetfulness is the primary sin from the rational part of the soul.

Saint Nil the Ascetic says in the *Philokalia*: "Blessed is that mind that has attained prayer in Christ without imagination and without form!"

Saint John Chrysostom says: "You, when you pray, don't theologize, because you are mocked by demons!" When you pray, you must have a broken and contrite heart, the pain of the heart for sins and humility. This mystery is God's, the Source of rational minds in heaven and on earth.

Saint Makarios of Egypt says in his homilies: "Oh, man, I know that you don't know how to pray, yet I'll give you some advice: pray as you can, but pray often. Because from frequent prayer man begins to learn true prayer."

Saint Theophan the Recluse also says: "Prayer itself becomes the greatest teacher for the one who prays often."

Saint Isaac the Syrian says: "The sign of God's mercy at prayer is tears."

The same **Holy Father** says: "He who has discovered the sweetness of prayer will run from crowds like a wild donkey!"

The **divine John Climacus** says: "He one who has found the sweetness of prayer always wants to be alone."

Saint John Climacus also says: "The one who remains with his mind beyond this world and prays constantly to God, he is a monk!"

Saint John Chrysostom says: "The strength of one who lives in a monastic community is obedience; the strength of the emperor lies in a large army; and the strength of the hermit lies in much prayer. The fall of the one who lives in community is disobedience and the fall of the one who lives in stillness is decrease of prayer."

Saint Nikodimos the Athonite says: "The extent to which you pray for the one who does evil to you is the extent to which you leave him in the hands of God."

The **Holy Fathers** teach us, saying: "As water extinguishes fire, so forgetfulness extinguishes prayer!"

Hear what **Saint Maximus the Confessor** tells us, "The more you pray from your soul for those who defame you, the more God shows the truth to those who are scandalized by what they say."

And **Saint Isaac the Syrian** says, "The unrighteous mouth is gagged through prayer."

Saint Maximus the Confessor says, "No small battle is required to save someone from vainglory. And they are saved from it through the secret practice of virtues and through frequent prayer. The sign of delivery from it is to no longer remember the evil done to you by the one that defamed or defames you."

Saint John Climacus says: "Do not abandon quantity since quantity leads to quality." He says later: "Abandon, man, quantity, when the gift of God comes to you!"[79]

"To the extent that man prays, **Saint Nikodimos the Athonite** says, "He is like a church within a church. The mind is the priest, the heart is the altar, the sacrifice that is brought to this altar is choice and good will—since I willingly choose to pray to God —, and the sweet-smelling fragrance, the incense which arises from the altar of our heart, is prayer. *Let my prayer be set forth before thee as incense, from the altar of the heart.*"

See what **Saint Ephraim the Syrian** says: "Churches were on their tongues and altars in their hearts."

Righteous Isaiah says, "As many times as you have sighed, you have been saved."

Saint Theophan the Recluse says: "Woe to those that have become frozen in the church's order of the typikon and don't have their own prayer!"

Saint Gregory of Sinai says: "Whoever has the prayer of the mind has the Liturgy and has the entire order of the Church at all times."

The cemetery is the faculty of faculties and the school of schools, for listen to what **Saint John Chrysostom** says, "Go to the cemetery, oh brother, because the soul's loftiest school is there, which speaks to us about God!"

Jesus, the son of Sirach, says, "Son, remember your end and you will never err."

---

[79] The point here is that when the grace of God comes to us, we should feel free to abandon for that moment the typical structure of our prayer *(t.n.)*.

Saint John of Damascus says, "Oh, Death, it would be better if we called you life, for he who always meditates on you, always lives."

Saint Basil the Great says: "And Solomon, the lover of wisdom, if he had not forgotten death, women would not have conquered him, to become their mockery, and you wouldn't have built temples for them, denied God and worshipped idols."

The **Divine Fathers** teach us: "Man, if you want to have a counselor and a teacher in life to guide you surely along the path of salvation, don't take anyone other than death!" The greatest counselor that can guide us to the Kingdom of Heaven is death.

Hear what **Saint John Damascene** chants with great wisdom:
All things are more helpless than shadows
All are more deceptive than dreams.
In an instant all these are seized by death…
But come my beloved brothers,
For the one who has reposed let us ask for rest from Christ
And great mercy for our souls.

Sihăstria Monastery's cemetery in winter.

Saint Ephraim the Syrian says, "The man whose conscience is pricked by his very terrible sins is afraid of death, but the righteous man awaits death as a great celebration!"

The **Divine Father John Chrysostom** says, "None who remembers Gehenna will arrive in Gehenna!"

Again, he says, "Go, Oh, man, to the grave; stay there and meditate on the one who died, because you should know tomorrow that you will become like him."

And so, says **Saint Ephraim the Syrian**, "Why do we leave aside thinking of God, reading the Scriptures, going to the church, meditating on Gehenna and death, which comes unexpectedly? Because we cast ourselves into the tumultuous sea of this age, we cast ourselves into limitlessness in order to inherit the ages and death comes and finds us unprepared!"

When **Basil the Great** was asked by the philosopher Euboulos of Alexandria, "O, Basil, what is the greatest wisdom in the Christian world?" Did you hear what he said? "To always see death before us."

The **divine Hierarch Basil** said about fasting: "Conquer yourself, humble yourself, Oh, man, with the ancient wisdom of fasting because it is as old as the world!"

Again, **Saint Basil the Great** says, "If a man is sick and has been withered by an illness so badly that someone else must turn him over on his bed and he cannot turn over by himself, for him it is permitted to eat dairy, but not meat, only milk and cheese."

Saint Basil the Great also said this: "Oh man, do you want to live long? Fast a lot! Fasting is the mother of health and length of life."

Again, **Saint Basil the Great** says in the fourth chapter of the *Hexaemeron*, "much food and fatty food cannot be consumed by the stomach and have brought many illnesses into the world. Health always follows fasting and refrain."

Saint Isidore of Pelusium, too, says, "Whoever unites the spiritual fast with the bodily one becomes an icon of all philosophy."

Saint Basil the Great says: "The measure of self-denial is according to the strength of each."

Saint Ephraim the Syrian in "A Word about the Pharisee and the Tax Collector" says among other things, "Make yourself two carts, Oh man. Yoke one to justice and pride and the other one to humility and sin and you will see that humility and sin enter the Kingdom of Heaven before good deeds and pride."

Some **divine Fathers** say that the loftiest meditation is to know your helplessness. Because Christ says, *"When you have done all I have commanded you, say, 'We are your worthless servants, because I have only done my duty.'"* But does anyone do everything that Christ ordered us? It is only through humility that they can do it.

According to **Saint Isaac the Syrian**, there are two kinds of humility: humility from sin, which is barely knowledge of self, and humility from righteousness.

If someone asks what humility is born from, we will say what **Saint John Climacus** said, from obedience and renouncing one's own will.

If again someone says, "What is humility?". I will answer not in my words but in the words of **Saint Isaac the Syrian**, "Humility is Divinity's garment, because it is with this that God clothed Himself, when He agreed to come into the world and He clothed Himself with our humble nature."

And what it is, precisely, we hear it also from **Saint Isaac the Syrian**, "Humility is a hidden power which the perfect saints receive after perfecting their entire lifework. This power is only given to those perfect in virtue, through the power of grace as much as the limits of nature can contain."

Again, **Saint Isaac the Syrian** says, "Blessed is the man who knows his helplessness, because this knowledge becomes his foundation, root and beginning for all good deeds."

Saint Isaac the Syrian also says, "The mind's sadness is greater than all the soul's toil, which is prayer, if man feels sorry."

Saint Ephraim the Syrian says: "In a deep heart God will ascend."

Saint Hesychius says: "Do not trust your body until death."

The **Holy Fathers** say: "Nothing is poorer than a mind that philosophizes about good deeds without carrying them out."

Saint Basil the Great says: "Despondency is the drowsiness of soul and mind." Despondency is also named the "octopus of the soul" by the Holy Fathers.

Saint Maximus the Confessor says: "The abomination of desolation in a holy place is sin formed in the imagination."

Saint Pimen the Great says in the *Paterikon*, "We need nothing else to be saved but a watchful mind."

Saint Mark the Ascetic says: "There are three giants that murder the soul: forgetfulness, ignorance, and idleness."

Saint Basil the Great says: "reading in stillness illumines the mind."

Saint Maximus the Confessor says: "The mind's life is the light of consciousness, and lack of knowledge is the soul's blindness."

Saint Maximus also says, "Give your body food, rest, and drink, according to strength, but all your care should be for your mind, that your mind be with God. Always in prayer, meditation, spiritual contemplation and keep your body healthy and light."

Saint Clement says, "Place a guard at the gate of your heart, to receive neither that which comes from the outside, nor that which comes up from the inside!"

Saint Ephraim the Syrian says that sin is an evil demon that sneaks around and gradually takes control of our soul. But in order to escape this demon and to stop sin from entering our mind and heart, we must have great attention and watchfulness, that is born from the fear of God.

Saint Gregory the Theologian says in iambic pentameter,
"The mind is deceived and the truth is thieved
By love in excess or too much hatred."

Saint Isaac the Syrian says, "The man with many concerns will not become meek and peaceful." And again, he says, "Without estrangement from many concerns, don't search for light in your soul." And again, "a clouded mind will not escape oblivion and wisdom will not open its door to it." So, we should flee from the false cares of this age to obtain peace of heart and holy prayer which is the mother of all good deeds.

Saint Thalasie the Lebanese says, "Being wrapped up in the cares of this world, you cannot also have the fear of God with you!"

Saint Ephraim the Syrian says, "Don't cast me into carelessness, my brothers, as if sins of the mind are light! If sinning in the mind were not weighty, Christ Himself, the Wisdom of God, would not have reckoned lust as adultery and hatred of a brother as murder."

Saint Hesychios of Sinai says in the *Philokalia*, "No one, without guarding the mind, will escape the powers of the Tartars at the time of death when he passes through the toll booths, no matter how great a philosopher or how wise he is in the world."

Again, **Saint Hesychios of Sinai** says, "Guarding the mind is the path and gate to all virtue and good deeds before God."

Guarding the mind, according to the teaching of the **Holy Fathers**, consists of keeping our mind watchful, resisting sin in the mind and in calling "Lord Jesus…" through prayer of the mind.

Saint Maximus the Confessor says, "Watchfulness with attention gives birth to the fear of God, and the fear of God gives birth to faith. He who believes, fears, and he who fears awakens."

Also, **Saint Maximus the Confessor** says, "Govern your thoughts, Oh, monk! Because if you don't govern your thoughts, soon you will not be able to govern your actions!" All sins come from thoughts.

The **Holy Fathers** call imagination the bridge for demons. No sin passes from the mind to the senses if man does not first imagine it in his mind.

Saint Maximus the Confessor says in the *Philokalia*, "The one who has attained perfection in love has attained the height of dispassion. Whoever has been touched by the perfect love of God has attained the height of dispassion, has become the most blessed man in the world."

Saint Isaac the Syrian says, "It is a thousand times more useful to you, Oh man, to see your own sins than to see angels! It is of greater benefit to you to weep for your sins for one hour than to see angels and to raise the dead with prayer or to work miracles!"

Saint John Climacus says in the third chapter of *The Ladder*, "The demons of vainglory make the weak-minded into prophets, but he who does not believe any dreams or visions is a spiritual philosopher."

A **Holy Father** says, "If you receive heavenly appearances in this present world, you will become insane and lose your mind."

Saint Isaac the Syrian says, "The one who sees his own sins enters the Kingdom of God before the one who sees angels."

Saint Isaac the Syrian also says, "Don't compare the ones that work signs and miracles and powers in the world to those that work stillness in wisdom. Love the inactivity of stillness more than feeding the hungry in the world and more than bringing many people back to faith in God."

Saint Gregory the Theologian says, "It is good to theologize for God, but it is better still to cleanse yourself of passions for God."

Saint Isaac the Syrian says, "It is more useful for you to care about resurrecting your fallen soul from passions through moving your thoughts towards divine things than to raise the dead."

Father Cleopa in the last years of his life.

Saint John Climacus says, "Do not believe in visions and dreams because all of them are from the devil. Only the ones that announce death and judgment to you are from God. But if they lead you to despair, they too are from devils."

Saint Ephraim the Syrian says, "When the mind has abandoned the purpose of righteousness, of piety, then all good deeds are useless."

Saint Ephraim the Syrian again said, "Do not speak with a heretical man, don't receive him into your house, do not eat with him, don't even tell him 'good afternoon.' They are the forerunners of Antichrist!"

Let us listen to **Saint John Chrysostom**, who says: "If you want to find pure faith, you will find it in the lower class of people…" **Saint John Chrysostom** says again, "God is not glorified by the many, but by the few; not in the strong, but in the weak, who are sincere and faithful."

Saint Ephraim the Syrian says, "When the unfaithful wants to come to faith, speak with him with great meekness because the way to bring back and gain souls for Christ is meekness alone."

Saint Athanasius says, "*The Church will not be conquered by the gates of hell,* that is by the mouths of sectarians and heretics that blaspheme the truth."

Again, **Saint Athanasius** says, "The first time flee, the second time flee, but the third time make yourself a sword towards the one who wants to separate you from the right faith."

Saint Pimen the Great teaches us saying, "It is fitting for us to endure everything, even if someone were to pluck out our eyes or cut off our right hand. But if someone wants to distance us or separate us from God, then we should be angered" (*Paterikon*, Saying 118).

"If they want to attack our holy faith or the Holy Tradition of the Orthodox Church, then we must defend it with all our strength until death," says Saint Nikodimos the Athonite in *Unseen Warfare*.

Saint Gregory the Theologian likened inquisitiveness into the Holy Scriptures to an abyss, saying, "Gazing at lofty things without restraint can cast us into the abyss."

Saint Gregory of Nyssa speaks along the same line, "Do not break the bones of the Scriptures using your milk-teeth understanding so as not to be lost." That is, do not pry into the words of the Holy Scriptures beyond our power.

And **Saint Ephraim the Syrian** says, "If we read into the Holy Scriptures and we get to a place that we do not understand, do not follow our own mind saying that this is a hostile or unrighteous passage. But tell the devil of inquisitiveness, which leads to heresy and sectarianism, 'Listen here, devil! What are you telling me, that there is something incorrect in the Holy Scriptures here? I have heard the Holy Spirit Who says, *The Lord is righteous in all His words and devout in all His works.*'"

The **divine Maximus the Confessor** says, "Just as a garden is made to plant fruit trees and fruit trees are planted for the garden, so God made the Theotokos and He fashioned the plan ahead of time that from her Christ would be born at the fullness of time."

The Theotokos is the second heaven or the second world, as **Saint John Damascene** says. Through her the human race was renewed. She is the Empress of all the angels and of all the saints and our Mother, of all of the Orthodox faithful and of all downcast and saddened souls that call out to her for help.

Saint Maximus the Confessor says, "When you see that someone hates you or mistreats you, whether justifiably or unjustifiably, begin to remember him in prayer."

Our soul has two dominating parts, as **Saint John Damascene** reveals in *On the Orthodox Faith*: the mind and the heart.

True tears that spring from the love of God, have such power, says **Saint Gregory of Nazianzus**, that the fountain of tears after Baptism is greater than Baptism itself.

For the first Baptism washes away our sins but does not give us the power to sin no more. But tears after Baptism also wash away the sins we do. Tears of humility are better than Baptism because they wash away all the sins that we have done after Baptism up until then and they leave you pure.

Saint Dionysius the Areopagite says that the evil brought by the devil consists of this: mindless lust, anger without discernment, imagination or hasty delusion.

The Lord will preserve this world, as **Saint Symeon the New Theologian** shows, until the ranks of the fallen angels are filled by the souls of the righteous.

Saint Basil the Great reveals that priests hold the place of the 70 Apostles, and bishops hold the place of the 12 Apostles, until the end of the world—that is how Christ established the hierarchy from the beginning.

Saint Cyprian says, "Without hierarchs, the Church is not a Church and without a priest, a Christian cannot be called Christian."

One of the **Holy Fathers** says, "He who is outside of Christ is outside the Church! And he who is outside the Church is outside of Christ!"

Saint John Chrysostom says, "A woman is a man's shore."

Saint Ephraim the Syrian says, "What lioness or bear would ever kill its own cub? And you, rational and speaking being, do worse than wild animals and have come to killing your own children!"

A Christian woman, if she dies during childbirth, dies on the altar of sacrifice. She is like a martyr and all her sins are forgiven as Saint Paul says, "*Women are saved through childbirth.*"

Saint John Chrysostom says, "Just as a candle, set to serve all, sacrifices itself and spreads light, that is how a Christian woman does two works: silently shedding light, and sacrificing silently."

Saint Maximus the Confessor says, "The word of God is food, bread, water, dew and a river and life and everything."

Saint Basil the Great says, "If someone dying of hunger steals bread, it is not a sin."

Saint Maximus the Confessor says that "through the weightiness of the grindstone in the Holy Gospel, the Savior shows how heavy the sin of scandal is."

Here is what **Saint Mark the Ascetic** says, "Just as much as brass differs from iron or iron from kindling (brushwood), so is the difference between one body and another."

Saint Ephraim the Syrian says: "Whoever wants to save himself should ask skilled men when he lacks knowledge about something, so as not to misunderstand one thing for another and become lost."

Saint Isaac the Syrian says, "Your fruit is for your brother's benefit."

There is not a place where God is not present. **Saint Makarios the Great** goes so far as to say "God is in the devils and in Satan, too!" For all diabolical powers are fenced in by the power of the Godhead.

Saint Isaac the Syrian says, "The monk that does not give alms (be they physical or spiritual) is like a cursed and barren fruit tree."

Saint Dionysius the Areopagite says, "The science of pure thought is the joy of joys, and the science of impure thought is the torture of tortures."

Saint Isaac the Syrian says, "The most powerful causes of sin in the world, that lead many Christians to perdition are: wine, women, riches, lack of faith in God and perfect bodily health. If we remove these causes from us, with the help of God, we will be saved from sin, and so from death."

Saint Ephraim the Syrian says, "God does not look at the multitude of the gifts that you bring Him, but at the will with which you bring them to Him."

Saint John Chrysostom, in his book *The Well*, says, "If you ever hear someone blaspheming Christ or His Church, go to him and slap him because you will have sanctified your hands! And even if you suffer prison or beatings or punishment for it, rejoice, because this will be considered martyric for you if you suffer because you struck the one that blasphemes Christ!"

Again, **Saint John Chrysostom** says, "When you can, avoid danger! But in the end, if you fall into danger, do not lose courage! Confess Christ until the end!"

Here what **Saint John Chrysostom** says, "Let your anger not be towards your brother, but towards the serpent by which he fell."

Saint Basil the Great says, "Envy is worse than the devil."

Saint Anthony the Great says, "Satan loves nothing more than the one who conceals his thoughts."

Saint Maximus says, "Virginity, prayer, alms, obedience, and self-denial are an abomination before the Lord when they are not done according to His will."

Saint Andrew of Caesarea, in his *Explanation of the Revelation*, says about the great persecution that will be towards the end of the world in the whole Church, "In that time the desert of the mind and of the senses will help the Church of Christ."

The **divine John Chrysostom** says, "Contrary things are healed by contrary and similar ones are caused by similar, because through God's incarnation, everything that was fitting to human nature was overturned since Christ overturned the logic of this fallen world."

Saint Theodore the Studite says, "Woman, don't try to make your husband a saint all at once, because you can't! Little by little does one enrich himself both in matters of the body and of the spirit."

Saint Maximus the Confessor says, "Just as night follows day and day follows night, so in this present age, joy follows disgust and disgust comes again after joy."

See what the **divine Andrew** says about judgment day: "The quickness of God's wrath will come with no mercy or sparing upon the devils and upon all the people that did their will."

Saint Isaac the Syrian says, "If you thank God for little, you move Him to do something even better for you."

Saint Ephraim the Syrian says, "God asks two things from a sick man: to thank God for his illness and to pray ceaselessly."

And **Saint John Chrysostom** in the same spirit speaks of the sick: "The tongue of the ill is so pleasant when it thanks God in sickness, during times of suffering, that it is in no way lower than the voice of the martyrs who confessed Him in torments when they were crucified and cast in cauldrons and boiled. They suffered, too, and so do these sick people, to an extent." So, whoever gives thanks to God in illness is a voluntary martyr. The prayer of an ill man is the strongest, because he prays in humility with his whole heart.

Saint John Climacus says, "If God sees a monk or brother who is enflamed with love towards Him and has a lofty life from the start, He doesn't let him live long—for God knows the life of man ahead of time—, lest he should change."

In a monastery with community life, as **Saint Pachomius the Great** shows, a monk is a traveler with no burden.

Hear what **Saint Isaac the Syrian** says, "Everything is adorned in life by good measure."

The **divine Fathers** say, "The extremes are the devil's and the middle is Christ's, which is the Royal path."

Saint John Climacus says about obedience, "Obedience is a tomb for the will." Each one should bury his own will. And again, "Obedience is the total abandonment of your own reasoning."

Saint Theodore the Studite says, "The one who is obedient is like iron in the hand of the forger and clay in the potter's hand."

Saint Theodore the Studite says, "The one who obeys with love serves a liturgy."

Saint Basil the Great in his *Greater Monastic Rules* (rule 55) says, "In communal life the monk is both the sacrifice and the one who sacrifices."

"Whosoever obeys with love and has Christ in his mind becomes a son of God by grace," says **Saint Isaac the Syrian**.

Saint John Climacus shows that virginity through vows has the same value as that by nature.

Saint Theodore the Studite says, "Obedience and renouncing one's own will is the greatest fast in the world."

Saint John Chrysostom says, "Woe to the one who fears the ears and eyes of man!"

Saint Ephraim the Syrian, "As many sins man has in his heart and mind is as many demons, he has in himself."

Saint Mark the Ascetic says, "The devils strain themselves greatly to teach us to believe we have no devils in us," and says further on, "We have as many devils as we have passions!"

When we do not feel sinfulness, we are in the greatest sin, because then our blindness and lack of feeling is the death of our mind and the killing of the soul before the death of the body.

Saint Isidore of Pelusium says, "When a man who speaks about truth and good deeds acts upon what he says according to his strength, then that man becomes an icon of all philosophy."

Saint John Chrysostom says, "Yelling words upsets, but life in silence is useful."

And **Saint Isaac the Syrian** says, "A beautiful word is one thing, but a word born from one's work is something else. A beautiful word is a pawn of shame, but a word born of work is the chamber of hope."

Saint Basil the Great says, "Confession is of no use, nor does he really confess, if one only says during confession that he erred but remains in sin and does not hate it."

Saint Theodosius says, "If someone works little by little, he becomes wealthy both in physical and spiritual things."

According to **Saint Basil the Great**, the devil always goes to the death of the righteous and of the sinners, searching to find man in sin in order to take his soul.

The **divine Maximus** says in the *Philokalia*, "Christ is hidden in His commandments. Whoever fulfills a command receives Christ. And not only Christ, but the entire Holy Trinity."

Saint Cyril of Jerusalem says, "Oh, Christian, do not do anything until you've made the sign of the cross. When you go on a journey, when you begin to work, when you go to study books, when you are alone and when you are with many, sign your forehead, your body, your chest, your heart, your lips, your eyes, ears with the Holy Cross, all of you should be sealed with the sign of Christ's victory over death. And then you will no longer fear charms, enchantments, and sorcery. For those things melt through the power of the Cross, like wax before fire and dust before wind."

Saint Ephraim the Syrian says, "By your external composure, at the judgment, man's deeds will be known."

Saint Thalasie the Lebanese says, "You be quiet, so your deeds may speak". Or admonish and scold those close to you through your works not through much talk!

Similarly, **Saint Isaac the Syrian** says, "You be quiet, so your deeds may speak. Because good deeds ask rewards from God either in this age or in the age to come."

Saint John Damascene says, "Good is not good when it is not done in a good way."

Saint Ephraim the Syrian says, "Oh, the malice of Satan! When he sees man accustomed to sin, he attacks with the double-edged sword of despair!"

Saint Hesychius of Sinai says, "Just as water extinguishes fire, so forgetfulness extinguishes the good work of the mind."

Saint Isaac the Syrian says, "Just as fire cleanses rust from iron, so illness cleanses sin from man."

Saint John Climacus says, "It is fitting for the one who does not do what he teaches, being ashamed of his words, to also begin to do his work one day."

Saint Ephraim the Syrian says, "Even if you were as pure as the angels and as holy as John the Baptist, you would still not be worthy to be a priest!"

Saint John Chrysostom says, "The priest needs just to open his mouth and grace works."

Again, **Saint John Chrysostom** says, "Great abyss and danger rule where the priest does not know the canons. The priest, on the confession seat, is father, doctor, and judge!"

Saint John Chrysostom says in his 53rd Saying, "…And you priests, who distribute the Most-Holy Mysteries, no small torment is upon you if you know someone to be unworthy and you give him these awesome, Most-Holy and divine Mysteries.

And if you are afraid, oh, priest, that the one who comes to you is a general or a prefect or a prince, or one with a crown on his head, that is the Emperor, and you are afraid that he will be upset with you if you do not give him Holy Communion, if you are afraid, bring him to me! I would rather give my body to the flames before giving the Most-Holy and Most-Pure Body to someone unworthy! I would spill all my blood before giving the Blood, so terrifying and All-Holy, to one who is unworthy!"

Saint John Chrysostom says in his *homilies*, "When pastors are absent, wolves will gather."

Saint Nikodimos the Athonite says, "If you absolve a man without him promising to do his canon, all of his sins pass on to the priest."

Saint Athanasius the Great says, "Do not partake from the hand of a priest who does not keep the four fasts and Wednesdays and Fridays."

Conscience is a righteous judge. The **divine Saint John Chrysostom** says, "God did not place an exterior judge for you, whom you could bribe with coins, whom you could give a certain amount so that he would make you just. This judge has been placed inside you; you cannot bribe him with anything!"

Saint Gregory of Nyssa says in the *Life of Moses*, "Like a trumpet from the high heavens, creation cries out and speaks to us that there is a Creator."

Saint Ephraim says, "Just as a trumpet at the time of war rallies the soldier's heart to march forward, so does the Holy Scripture, which awakens the Christian's mind."

The **divine John Chrysostom** in one of his *Homilies* said this, "I speak from this cathedral—that is of the Holy Apostles in Constantinople—, and I see a multitude of people here. If 100 were to return to Christ, I would have a hundredfold reward. If 60 or 30 were to return, there would be no small reward; and even if only one returned, for this one Christ would also give me a great reward, because a single soul is more precious than the entire world, according to the word that says, 'What can man give in exchange for his soul, even if he were to gain the world?' But if not even one returns, I will not stop teaching and preaching because even the fountains and springs flow whether someone drinks of the water or not; they do their duty."

Father Cleopa thinking of eternal things in the twilight.

With Father Dosoftei, Father abbot Victorin and Saint Paisie.

In front of Holy Three Hierarchs Monastery, in Iaşi.

Deeds and Words
of Teaching

1. Father Cleopa had great devotion to the Theotokos, "The Queen of the Cherubim and of the Seraphim and our Lady…" He would not let a day pass without reading the Akathist hymn of the Annunciation and other Canons to the Holy Mother of God.

2. Father Cleopa would say, "Do you know who the Lord's Mother is? She is the Queen of the Cherubim, the Queen of all of creation, the chamber of the Word God's incarnation, the door of light, so the unapproachable and intelligible light came into the world through her. She is the door of life since the Life Christ entered into the world through her. She is the locked door through which no one passed except the Lord, as prophet Ezekiel said."

3. He also said, "The Theotokos is the ladder and bridge to heaven; the dove that stopped the flood of sin, as Noah's dove testified to the end of the flood. She is the divine censer since she received the fire of divinity and she is the Church of the Most-Holy Spirit. The Theotokos is the Bride of the Father, the Mother of the Word, and the Church of the Holy Spirit."

4. Again, he would say, "When you see an icon of the Theotokos with the infant Christ in arms, do you know what you see there? Heaven and earth! Christ is heaven, the One higher than heavens, the Creator of heaven and earth. And the Theotokos represents the earth, that is all the peoples on the face of the earth since she is one of our nations. She is from the royal and high priestly tribe."

5. The Elder would also say, "The arms of the Theotokos are stronger than the shoulders of Cherubim and of the Most-Holy Thrones. So, whom does Virgin Mary hold in her arms? Do you know whom? The One that made heaven and earth and everything seen and unseen."

6. Again, he said, "Do you know who the Theotokos is and how much honor, how much power and how much mercy she has? She is our mother, so she has mercy on the poor, the widows, and all Christians. She is always praying to the Savior Christ for all of us."

7. In nearly every sermon Father Cleopa asked the Christians, "Do you have an icon of the Theotokos at home?", and "Do you have a little vigil lamp in front of the icon of the Theotokos?" He would advise, "Take protection and help from the Theotokos, our Mother in heaven and on earth! The Queen of heaven and earth!

If you take her as your protectress, reading an Akathist hymn to her in the morning with a little lit candle and in the evening a Paraklesis, you will have helped all your life, and at the hour of your death, and on the Day of Judgment… Do you know what the Lord's Mother can do before the Throne of the Most-Holy Trinity? If it hadn't been for her, I think this world would have been lost much earlier!"

8. To those who paid for church services he would say, "I have established great services here, but if one does not do anything at home, what it says in the Holy Scriptures is fulfilled: when one prays and another does not, one builds and the other one tears down! I'll give you just this advice: after the Morning Prayers, read the Annunciation Akathist with a lit candle. You will see that the Theotokos is quick to hear!"

9. A disciple of his said, "When I came to Father Cleopa, I told him that I would like to stay in the monastery. Then his holiness said to me, 'If you are determined to endure three beatings per day and one meal every three days, then stay in the monastery!' These words strengthened me and made me more determined. I understood that I had to have more will and that God would help me."

10. Many times, Father Cleopa said, "What are we? A handful of dirt on the bottom of a grave! We were made from good earth, but we defiled it and we will go down in the earth and defile the earth! What are we? Filthiness and food for worms."

11. Father Cleopa always repeated, "Tomorrow, the day after, I will go to Christ! Tomorrow the Old Rot Man leaves! Tomorrow you will see nothing but a cross in the cemetery! Tomorrow, or the next day, memory eternal for Old Rot Man! Take it, take a broken piece tied up with wire! Tomorrow, I go to my brothers. They are calling me, 'Come on, brother! Stop talking with people!'"

12. On his name's day, when the Fathers gathered in his cell and wanted to chant "Happy name's day" for him, the Elder stopped them and said, "Not like that but, 'Memory Eternal, Memory Eternal, May his Memory be Eternal!'" Or he would say, "Happy Name's Day, Old Rot Man!"

13. To those tormented by the passion of fornication, the Elder would often say, "Death, death, death! Coffin, shovel, spade, and pick…. Saint Basil the Great said, 'When you see the most beautiful woman in the world, take your mind to her grave a few days after she died. Such a terrible smell and putrid moisture exudes from her body, that all the bathrooms in the world don't smell worse.' Look at what you lust after!"

14. When someone wanted to photograph Father Cleopa, he would say, "Look for a donkey, take its picture and write 'Cleopa' on it!"

15. Father Cleopa said, "Saint Basil the Great said that the greatest wisdom that preserves man from all sin and leads him to heaven, to eternal blessedness, is death. Death and thinking of death. And having the 'Lord Jesus…' prayer in their mind and heart."

16. Another time he said, "This body drags us to the ground, as Saint John Damascene said, 'Earth comes from earth!' But we cannot let it, we cannot follow this carrion."

17. Father Cleopa advised women who argued that they had bad husbands not to divorce but rather to pray for them, "It is not me, but the Holy Apostle Paul tells you, how do you know woman, that you won't save your husband? Don't you know that the husband who is not a practicing Christian is sanctified by the wife who is, and the other way round?" And he had the same advice for men, and many rejoiced seeing miracles in their homes.

18. Many Christians today fear charms and curses. Father Cleopa advised them, "Don't be afraid of curses! Fear God and take care not to upset Him through sins, and charms will have no power on you! Repent, confess your sins, fast, and attend the Holy Unction service!"

19. When sick persons came to him, he put their names on the prayer list and told them, "The greatest service for the sick is the Holy Unction. But it is of no use if a person has not confessed. So, first of all, go and confess all your sins, and then do a Holy Unction service."

20. In the case of young people who wanted to get married, he counseled and blessed them, wrote their names on the prayer list for the holy services and told them, "Pray to the Theotokos with fasting and prostrations, and read the Annunciation Akathist!"

21. When someone was worried about the times we live in and asked, "What is going to happen, Father?", Elder Cleopa answered, "The years and the times have been set by the Father in His lordship. As the Father wants it, so will He do!" And if someone would say, "There's bad weather outside," the Elder answered, "Everything that God gives is good!"

22. To the monks and brothers who wanted to leave for the wilderness, he would say, "Do you have 20 years in the monastery in the lowest forms of obedience? Only then can you go to live alone. Whoever wants to go to the wilderness, says Saint Basil the Great, should have the Starets' blessing, and should take another one or two fellow monastics with him, and have experience in obedience and cutting off one's will in the monastery". Do you think that the wilderness is a joke? If you were to be tied to a tree there, the first night you would come to the monastery with the tree on your back—such great temptations you would have from the devil.

23. Again, he said, "A spiritual father for nuns should be at least 50 years old and have 20 years of obedience in a monastery."

24. Even when he was just drinking water, Father Cleopa would ask for a blessing from his cell attendant or from one of the novices.

25. Sometimes, when it happened that he entered his cell and could not pray because of all the Christians following him, he would say, "I've entered the cell and I haven't done my prayers. I've entered like a thief and a robber!" And he would get up and make three semi-prostrations to the ground, saying, "Most-Holy Trinity, our God, glory to You!" Then he would make a semi-prostration to the Theotokos and to Saint John the Baptist, and sometimes he also commemorated the saints of the day.

26. One disciple would say, "When I asked for a blessing to eat, Father Cleopa would say, 'Eat, drink, sleep!' And I asked him, 'What does this mean?' And he said, 'Eat when you're hungry, drink when you're thirsty and sleep when you're tired!'"

27. The Elder spoke many times about his infirmities and illnesses, saying about himself, "Old Man Rot, 86 years old, six operations, a broken arm and broken ribs…" He would have his disciple say these words to whoever came to him. Some would say to his disciple, "Why are you saying this? We come to Father Cleopa as to a saint! Why are you listing so many illnesses and infirmities to us?"

28. One time a disciple asked Father Cleopa if he could go outside the monastery without his eksorasson. He replied, "The day that you go someplace and leave this monastery without your rasso, you will do 1,000 prostrations! Even if you don't wear it you should have it with you."

29. His disciple also testified, "I never saw the Elder without his belt or cassock. He sometimes even wore a woolen or sheepskin leather vest over his cassock."

30. Many times, Father Cleopa said, "The Church is our mother! Don't leave the Church because we unite with Christ here. Mary and Martha are reconciled here. Keep the order of services and meals according to the typikon. The Church holds us all!"

31. Again, his disciple would say, "While I was Father Cleopa's disciple, he had the habit of doing this rule: Morning Prayers, the Akathist to the Savior with the Canon and the Akathist to the Theotokos, especially the Annunciation Akathist. And on the feast day of a saint, he would read the Akathist of that saint. Then he read a few kathismata from the Psalter and three or four canons to the Theotokos. Afterwards he would speak to the faithful who came to him.

"Around 3:00 or 4:00 p.m., he started his evening prayer rule: he would finish the mode of the day from the book of Canons to the Theotokos (he would read a mode a day, that is seven canons), the Canon of Repentance, the Canon to the Guardian Angel, the Canon to all saints, and he would read from the Psalter. Afterwards he would speak to the faithful and sit at the table, then say the Evening Prayers.

"When he stayed in the evening with the faithful until he was too tired to continue, he went back to his cell, made three semi-prostrations, then he went to sleep. But even though he was so tired, he did not sleep much. He would awaken after an hour at the most, read the Evening Prayers and say the Jesus Prayer. He always had his hand on the prayer rope, to the extent that his thumbnail that he used to move the knots on the rope was deformed. He also read from the Holy Scriptures and the Holy Fathers."

32. He went outside every night and prayed, especially after midnight. Even during winter, he would stay outside for at least one hour. He recited the Jesus Prayer, listened to the night birds, gazed at the starry sky and rejoiced in the stillness. He sought to be in the open air, to be alone and undisturbed. Yet many times he would be interrupted by brothers or lay people. Then, after he told them to leave, seeing that he could not escape them, he would speak to them a little or withdraw to his cell.

Other times, being very tired, he would wake up around three or four in the morning and do his entire prayer rule. During this time, he enjoyed more silence and solitude.

33. When the faithful asked him if it was good to read the Psalter, Father Cleopa answered, "Saint Basil the Great said that 'it is better for the sun to stand still than for the Psalter to remain unread in Christian houses. And as the sun is the greatest among the luminaries, so is the Psalter among the other books inspired by the Holy Spirit.' Keep the Psalter like tasty Easter cake. When you are hungry, cut another slice, eat some more, do some more work, then read another kathisma, or two, or three, as many as you can."

34. Sometimes, when he was doing his prayer rule, the Elder was sought out insistently by the faithful. He came out and spoke a while with them, then said, "God will tell me, 'Well, monk, you worked in other people's fields but in your own field thorns, thistle and weeds have grown.' Do you work my field? That is why I must work my own land." Then he would return to his cell and continue his prayer rule.

Sometimes he would not come out at all, telling them, "I must still work my own field, because God will tell me, 'You worked other people's fields, but look at your own.' Come back after an hour!" But sometimes the waiting time went down to ten minutes or a quarter of an hour, depending on how the Elder felt.

35. Father Cleopa would also sometimes say, "What can I do, since the Holy Fathers said, 'Flee the world! Flee the world!?' And the Savior said the same, '*Woe to you when all men speak well of you, for so did their fathers to the false prophets*'" (Luke 6:26).

36. The Elder would ask the monastics who came for advice what monastery they were from, if the monastery was in a remote and quiet place, if it had a communal life, one money bag, one table and one church. Then he asked them if they ate meat at the monastery.

If they said that they ate meat, Father Cleopa would feel sad, "Well, if I were there! Look, do you see Saint Calinic? He is watching us!" And he would point to the saint's icon: "Saint Calinic made a testament in which it is written, 'When a monk or nun eats meat in the monastery or in the world, when visiting relatives, then all the monastery's assembly should gather, curse the one that ate meat and lash them 39 times on their back! One more, again, and again! And if they do not stop, they should be separated from the monastery's community.'"

37. A monk once asked Father Cleopa what the Savior was referring to in the parable of the great banquet (Mt. 22:1-14) when He said that a man entered the feast hall and was not clothed in a wedding garment. How could that person have entered? To which the Elder answered that the reference is to those who receive Holy Communion unworthily.

38. During communist persecution, Father Cleopa stayed in the wilderness for many years, and the asceticism and temptations that he endured have remained unknown. However, a few of them were found out. While the Elder was still alive, he told us that we would find out the rest of them after his death.

39. "Father Cleopa," one disciple said, "tell us what it was like during those 10 years in the wilderness. What kind of temptations did you have? I heard that you fought with the enemy! How and what did he tempt you with?"

"If you want to know what's like to live in the wilderness, you go and stay there for a year and you'll see!"

40. One brother asked Father Cleopa, "What should I do, Reverend Father, to be saved?

"Have the fear of God on your right and remembrance of death on your left, and in your mind and heart the prayer, "Lord, Jesus Christ…", and you'll become a saint, brother!"

41. Once Father Cleopa said to one of his disciples, "If you knew how much I pray for you at night with tears, so that you should have love between you all!"

"May Heaven Consume You."

42. One brother said to the Elder, "Father, pray for me, too, the sinner, and if you go to the Lord, don't forget me."

"Yes! You, brother, eat and sleep until you've had enough, and I'll pray for you!"

43. One day a brother went up to Father Cleopa's cell downtrodden. One of the Elder's disciples saw him and asked, "What's wrong, brother, why are you sad?"

"I'm going to Father Cleopa, because I have some weighty temptations and I cannot bear them anymore."

After a little while, the brother, now with a luminous face, descended from the Elder's cell. The disciple saw him and asked, "Well, did you find him?"

"Yes, with the help of God, and now I feel like I'm soaring out of joy." This was Father Cleopa's gift: to deliver us from temptations.

44. One Father asked him how to pray. The Elder told him, "Pray at first audibly—from the mouth prayer passes to the mind, and then to the heart. But for this we need great effort, many tears, and the grace of the Holy Spirit!

45. "Father Cleopa, give me a useful counsel," one Father said to him.

"Remember death. Death, death, death! Fear of death preserves us from every sin!"

46. He said to one of his disciples, "Prepare to have patience, to receive blows, to be hungry and thirsty. And if they cast you out of here, don't leave! Stay at the monastery's gate and if the police take you, come back and die inside the monastery!"

47. One faithful person asked, "How should I prepare for the monastery?"

"When you come to the monastery, this is how you should come: determined to patiently endure death from all!"

48. The Elder would also say, "We should never say that we have made a good start. We don't even know what that person who makes a good start looks like. We should pray, 'Lord, help me to make a good start!'"

49. One brother said to the Elder: "Father, I can't pray enough! What should I do?"

"Haven't you heard what the Apostle says? Pray without ceasing! So, pray as much as possible day and night and you will feel the grace of the Holy Spirit in your heart!"

50. Another brother said to the Elder: "Father, if we are going to be in prison for our faith and if they change our thoughts through hypnosis, will we be guilty?"

"No one can change you if you have 'Lord Jesus…' in your heart. When you say 'Lord Jesus…' all of hell quakes, only say it from your heart!"

51. One disciple asked the Elder how he could be saved. The Elder answered: "Patience, patience, patience. And when it seems to you that you've run out of it, start again: patience, patience, patience, patience. And not just till spring time, but till death time!"

Then he asked, "What should I endure?"

"Endure all accusations and dishonor for the love of Christ!"

52. "How many clothes should a monk have?" someone asked him.

"Two changes of clothes! Why? Do you want to become a hermit with a wagon of clothes? And when they tear, put one yellow patch, a red one and a green one…!"

53. To lazy people, the Elder said: "Set the cadaver to work and the mind at the Lord's feet, that is to pray…"

*Father Cleopa
in the winter
of 1996.*

54. Once a brother came to Father Cleopa after he had listened to him many times and asked him, "Father, what must I do to be saved?" And the Elder, who knew his heart, answered him, "Do what you know and you will be saved." Then he examined himself and realized that it wasn't knowledge that he lacked but spiritual living.

55. Again, the Elder said to one of his disciples, "When you havestayed nine years in a monastery and taken seven beatings a day and food once every three days, then you'll be a good monk!"

56. One Father asked him again, "When can you become a fool for Christ?"

And the Elder replied, "After 40 years of monasticism!"

57. The brothers asked him again, "Father Cleopa, your brothers practiced harsh asceticism, but we cannot do that."

"Well, you don't want to, you don't want to, you don't want to! Ask the Theotokos for help! Say the Annunciation Akathist in the morning with an oil lamp lit and the Paraklesis in the evening and you will be able to endure to the end!"

58. When one brother revealed his desire to suffer for the Lord, the Elder told him, "I'll see what you do when they put you in cars and take you to the valley!"[80]

59. One Christian said to him: "Father, I don't believe devils exist!"

The Elder, after teaching him much from the Holy Scriptures, told him, "If you still don't believe devils exist, go to the wilderness, start to fast and pray, and they will scratch you!"

60. One of the monks in Sihăstria Monastery said to the Elder:

"What should I do, Father Cleopa, to be saved?"

"You should have death continually before you and 'Lord Jesus…' in your mind and heart, and don't be afraid of anything! Have the repentance of the thief on the cross!"

61. Again, he would say to the brothers: "Everything is transient! Take care of your soul, confess, receive communion, lead a pure life, give alms, do everything you can, and live in love with one other, because love never dies!"

62. To other Fathers he would say: "No one can pull you out of hell, only the mercy of God and good deeds."

---

[80] Elder Cleopa was referring to the experience of being taken away by the Securitate secret police forces *(t.n.)*.

63. He also said this: "Have the heart of a son towards God, the heart of a mother towards others, and the mind of a judge towards yourself."

64. Older Fathers testify to a miracle that took place at the reliquary of Saint Parascheva of Iași on October 14, 1951. On the feast day, when people were waiting in line to venerate her, two old women from Focșani came, too. Seeing the swarm of people, they said to the priest standing guard, who happened to be Archimandrite Cleopa, "Father, give us permission to venerate Saint Parascheva without standing in line because we are sick, and place this pillow under her head which we brought from home as a thanksgiving for the help she gave us!"

"May the Lord bless you," Father Cleopa said. "Go and venerate!"

After the Christian ladies venerated, they came with the pillow to place it under the saint's head. In that moment the priests and the faithful witnessed a miracle. The saint lifted her head by herself, and after the women set the pillow, Saint Parascheva laid her head on it.

65. Father Cleopa had a great devotion to the saints. Sometimes he commemorated hundreds of saints during the Holy Unction service. He also knew most of the saints in the calendar and synaxarion by heart.

66. A disciple once asked Father Cleopa if it is good to work during the feast days of certain saints that were listed by the typikon as non-working days. To which the Elder told the following incident: "Once we had been sent to scythe by the Starets on the day of Saint Panteleimon, in the afternoon. We began to have some great pain in our legs, and not just me, but all of us who were swinging the scythe. And the pain did not subside before evening. Since then, we have never worked on such days."

67. Father Cleopa told us that, being called by Patriarch Justinian, at the time when he was confessing the latter, he urged him to complete the canonization process of a few Romanian saints, which happened in 1955.

68. One disciple asked him: "What is pure prayer?"

"To say it with your mouth, to understand it with your mind and to feel in your heart."

69. Another time he said, "During prayer don't receive thoughts or imaginings. The gate of the heart has two toll houses: the toll house of imagination, and the toll house of reasoning.

The toll house of imagination is the first station. The shortest rule for prayer is not to imagine anything when you pray. Because if you stop at imagination, then your mind can't enter your heart at the time of prayer. So, during prayer you are not permitted to imagine anything. Not even holy imaginings, not Christ on the Holy Cross, not the Throne of Judgment. Nothing. Because all imaginings are outside the heart, and if you remain and worship these, you are not worshiping Christ.

"And at the toll house of reasoning, which is at the gate of the heart, our mind encounters other evil spirits, '*theologians of darkness* and *philosophers of hell*,' and they give the mind spiritual reasonings. In the moment of prayer, what you see is what appears in the words of the Holy Scriptures, how the Savior was tempted on the mountain of Quarantania, since their role is to tempt you from Scriptures. And all kinds of true and lofty reasonings come to us during prayer! But the devil isn't upset by this, when he sees that you reason. He rejoices. Right, great that you are theologizing[81] when you pray! Brothers, such things are not appropriate at the time of prayer!

"The devil's purpose is to give our mind over to theologizing and to bring to mind all Scriptures, if you wish, only so that you don't pray! He knows that prayer burns him. And you obtain spiritual conceit. 'That is why such lofty words as these come to me when I pray to God!' And he laughs, his mouth wide open, from ear to ear! You are not praying then, but theologizing. The Savior tells you to pray: '*Do not speak with many words like the hypocrites since it seems to them that because of their many words the Lord will hear them!*'

"And during prayer, especially during the prayer of the heart, when we want to lower the mind into the heart, we should pray with a single thought, that is, thinking only of the name of our Lord Jesus Christ. For this reason, we descend into the heart saying, 'Lord, Jesus Christ, Son of God, have mercy on me a sinner.' A different reason than this should not be sought for. If you abandon this theology during prayer, with the help of the Lord, your mind will enter the heart immediately."

70. Another time he said: "As soon as the mind enters the heart, you have a natural sign. It starts like a nail of fire and your heart gets warmed up from its center. Then all the heart gets warm, then your chest, your shoulders, your spinal cord, your whole body and powerful sweat begins to flow and your eyes begin to pour hot tears of repentance with great fire. This is prayer of fire!

"Now as the Groom encountered the bride, Christ does so with our soul. This spiritual union makes man one spirit with God. It is what the Apostle says, '*The one who unites with a harlot becomes*

---

[81] That is, you are thinking of the words of the Scriptures.

one body with her...and the one who cleaves to God is one spirit with Him.' This union and cleaving to God in the heart through Jesus Christ brings a great spiritual sweetness and great warmth."

71. He also said about the prayer of the heart: "But it is not the foundation of the work, nor sweetness or the warmth in the heart. The foundation of the work is breaking the heart, pain of heart for sins, and tears of repentance that flow at that time. In this state our soul has such joy, such lightness, such warmth and spiritual sweetness that after one awakens from this union with Jesus Christ in the heart, such a one cannot say even three words.

"What joyous moments, what sweetness, what joy such a one has in his heart! And if a worker of prayer stays in this condition for one hour or two, with the mind descended into the heart, that is the mind united to the heart, after he comes back to his senses, for a week or two not one thought from this world can enter his heart! The heaven of his heart is purified to such an extent that the climate of the heart is full of the work of the Holy Spirit. Oh, joyous heart, that has drunk the tears of repentance and great love from the union with Jesus Christ—spiritual love which no language can describe!"

72. Again, he would say: "Obedience without prayer is just slavery, but he who does obedience with prayer serves the liturgy."

73. He would also say: "Humility is born of obedience without complaint."

74. Again, he said: "Prayer is not conditioned by time or place. It is the food for the soul, as the Holy Apostle Paul says: *'Pray without ceasing!'*"

75. One close disciple of Elder Cleopa told us: "During the last years of his life, the Elder, being overly tired, had me speak with the people until he came. I would tell them spiritual things which they were interested in.

"But when Elder Cleopa came, he would just say, 'May heaven consume you! My dear children, look, I am a pot tied together by wire, a putrid old man. I am 86 years old, six operations, two broken arms, I am sick, I can no longer continue...' and the people would begin to weep. Then he would say a little story or some useful counsel, and when it was over, the people would tell me, 'Father made an impression on us, he moved our souls. We have never seen a man like that in our lives.' And so I understood that it wasn't words that moved people, but the grace of the Holy Spirit that rested in Father Cleopa, which touched the hearts of the faithful, comforting them, changing them, and warming them with his love."

76. One brother from the monastery was troubled since children sometimes came and made noise and ran around on the hills. He came to the Elder and asked what to do. Father Cleopa told him: "Well, remember, weren't you a child once? I love children very much because they are like angels! And I am worried one of them might fall and break an arm or leg. Christ also loves them and says: *Let the children come to Me and do not stop them, since the Kingdom of Heaven belongs to such as these.*"

77. Father Cleopa said: "Don't give advice to anyone until you yourself have lived it! The one who gives advice but not from his own experience is like a spring of water painted on a wall. But the one who speaks from experience is like a spring of living water!"

78. One faithful person asked, "What should I do to be saved, Father Cleopa?"

And the Elder replied, "Listen, brother. You know how to pray, you know to go to Church, you know to fast, you know to give alms, you know all of God's commandments. Only, you should want to fulfil them, otherwise you can't be saved!"

79. Father Cleopa was asked one time by a Father from the monastery: "Reverend Father, what will happen to Sihăstria Monastery if Your Holiness departs for the Lord?

And the Elder looked down and said: "Walls, walls, walls…!"

80. Another time a Father from the monastery told him: "Your Reverend Father, tell us a word about holy prayer."

And the Elder said: "Prayer is the food and life of the soul. Just like the body dies without food and drink, so does the soul without prayer."

81. Father Cleopa told his disciples: "The body is Martha and the soul is Maria! Martha labors for the earthy things, and Maria, who is a symbol of the soul, stays at the Lord's feet and prays. That is why the Lord said that *Mary has chosen the good part.* We are obliged to make peace between Martha and Maria, that is first to pray and then to do obedience with love and with prayer in the mind and the heart."

82. One Father went often to the Elder, kneeled and asked him to bless him. His Holiness would put his hand on his head and made the sign of the Holy Cross saying, "May the Lord bless you!" And this Father bore witness that he would leave the Elder with great peace and quiet and would feel, for more than half an hour, some warmth like fire and his soul filled with humility and tears.

83. A different Father, when Elder Cleopa was still alive, said, "When I leave after confessing to His Holiness, I go to my cell and say only this, 'Lord Jesus Christ, through the prayers of Your Most Pure Theotokos and of Father Cleopa, have mercy on me a sinner!' And humility and tears would come to me to the point I could not stop weeping."

84. An older Father asked Father Cleopa: "Your Reverence, what would you do if you get sick and cannot read your prayer rule? Will you have one of the brothers read it for you?"

"No, I will pray, 'Lord have mercy...'"

85. Once when someone showed him the new church in the monastery's orchard, admiring its beauty, Elder Cleopa said: "Yes, brother, but it is more difficult to make a true monk than a cathedral!"

86. The Elder also said: "Hey, boy, don't wait around and waste time. Take a book in your bag wherever you go, to shepherd the sheep or the cows, or where you are sent, and read the word of God!"

87. Sometimes he would say: "If I read a book two or three times, I almost know it by heart."

88. Father Cleopa also told his disciples some of the troubles and temptations he had that came from people. But about temptations that came from the devil when he was in the wilderness, he wouldn't talk much, mostly because he was discrete and because there wasn't anyone who could understand him.

89. Sometimes he told us: "The Holy Fathers stop me from speaking more, since they say, 'Don't speak of your own things.' But I will say this much: if you had been there in the wilderness tied to a tree and had seen a devil, you would have pulled out the tree by its roots and run with it on your back!"

90. Some monastics from Pucioasa[82] wrote to him a few times and Father Cleopa gave them an answer in a well-thought-out letter that said: "It stinks at Pucioasa and the stench won't leave until you obey the Holy Synod!"

91. He also said that around the year 2000, divine signs would be shown, quoting Saint Agathangelus, who foresaw this.

92. The Elder's close disciple told us: "Many letters came, addressed to Father Cleopa, with all kinds of troubles and problems, and his holiness told me to answer them. Many Christians also came and the Elder had me speak to them and write their prayer lists. Since I was very busy, I did not succeed in doing all of my prayer rule and monastic canon, and I asked him what I should do. He told me: 'Do obedience, write letters, speak to people, and say, "Lord have mercy..." because, 'the benefit of your brother is your fruit,' as the Holy Fathers say.'"

93. Again, his disciple said: "In the last years, when I was writing letters to the faithful, if I fell upon a more difficult problem, I would ask Father Cleopa and he would answer in brief, and then would tell me to write to them that he is old, sick and cannot write anymore. Then he would send me to tell the people that he is weak and that they should no longer come to 'Old Rot Man; that Old Rot Man has died! He is no more! He's departed...!'"

94. In 1996, when the head of Saint Andrew the Apostle was brought from Greece to Iași, one brother wanted to go and venerate it. A driver offered to take him to Iași. But the brother wanted to go without the Starets' knowledge. He went to get Father Cleopa's blessing only, since he was a spiritual son of his.

---

[82] Literally "brimstone," the name of a famous monastery that became schismatic, not following the new calendar *(t.n.)*.

When the Elder heard what it was all about, he said with a loud voice, "Well, brother, you have one Starets and one God!" "But what should I do, then? Go to the Starets and ask him?" —said the disciple. "Yes! Go and ask for his blessing," Father Cleopa answered.

95. Once a Christian asked the Elder: "Father Cleopa, what should I do because I can't find a spiritual father."

"You should find him? He should find you," the Elder answered.

96. One brother asked Father Cleopa to commemorate him at prayer. The Elder answered, pointing his finger to an imaginary trail, curving around on the ground: "My Prayer is like Cain's smoke! It crawls on the ground like this…"

97. Once, sitting on the porch, he looked directly at his disciple and said, sincerely and purely: "I don't know what so many people are looking for, coming to me, a putrid old man!"

98. Another time, after he confessed to the Elder, a brother said, "Father, don't forget me in your prayers, because I'm very sinful."

"May the Lord help you!" said the Elder. Then he said quietly to himself, "I am worse than all."

99. One disciple recounted that sometimes, the Elder would do the following during confession. Knowing that his disciple loved praises, he showed that he himself was more sinful, more greedy and worse than all, insulting himself in order to teach his disciple the work of humility.

100. One day a faithful person came to Elder Cleopa and said to him: "Father, I think that you are a saint!" Then Elder Cleopa answered him: "And I think that the devil spoke through your mouth."

101. Once a reporter came to interview the Elder saying, "People want light, they want living water…"

"Yes!… People have the light from the Holy Gospel, from the Prophets, from the Apostles, from the Holy Fathers, from the great holy hesychasts and millions of martyrs… So, they have many places to get light from!

"Someone can only get darkness from me. I am a son of darkness, not of light. A sinful person, full of malice, full of weaknesses, sleepy… I don't have the love of God, I don't have self-control, I don't have discernment, I don't have anything! Everything, I lost everything through my laziness and I don't have anything good in this world!

"The Apostle Paul said in his Epistle to Saint Timothy, *Christ Jesus came into the world to save the sinners of whom I am the first.* If the one that had been lifted into the third heaven says that he is the first among sinners, what can I say? That I have done something good? Never, in the ages of ages!

102. In the last years of his life, his right eye teared. Even when he spoke with people, from time to time, one tear drops or two flowed from his eye, a sign that his heart prayed ceaselessly.

103. When he was in the wilderness, he had a terrible temptation of fornication. The devil of fornication appeared to him and asked, "Are you going to fall into fornication now?" And the Elder replied, "Anyone can fall, for what is man and woman? They are rot and stench."

Another time when he had a similar temptation, he stepped on coals with his feet in order to cast out the demon of fornication.

104. Sometimes people came to him who were troubled and they asked him about wars and the signs of the end of the world.

And Father Cleopa told them in a loud voice, "The Father is at the helm!" and he read verse 10 from Psalm 32, *The Lord brings the counsel of the nations to nothing. He makes the plans of the peoples of no effect. The counsel of the Lord stands forever, the plans of His heart to all generations.* Then he encouraged them, "Don't be troubled and don't be afraid because it won't happen like they want. Well, they want to do so much! Fear not! Pray and make the sign of the Holy Cross with faith, and all the devils will flee!"

105. Father Cleopa also said: "Don't do any work until you make the sign of the Holy Cross! When you go on a journey, when you begin work, when you go to study books, when you are by yourself and when you are with many, seal yourself with the Holy Cross on your forehead, your body, your chest, your heart, your lips, your eyes, your ears, and let all of you be sealed with the sign of Christ's victory over hell. Then you won't be afraid of sorcery, spells, and witchcraft. They melt away through the power of the Cross, like wax before fire, like dust in the wind."

106. Another time he said: "Faith is concentrated in the Creed."

107. Once a woman came to Elder Cleopa with her grandson who had been accused of murder, being innocent. The grandson told the Elder that he was in a court case for murder and he did not tell him he was innocent. The Elder interrupted him and said: "You are not guilty and you won't go to prison!" And truly, shortly after, the young man was acquitted.

108. When the Elder had withdrawn to the monastery's apiary,[83] he was visited by a faithful person who told him,

---

[83] Father Cleopa used to withdraw here. He would come to the apiary on Monday morning and go down to his community cell on Thursday evening or Friday morning. When he was at the apiary, he did his rule of prayer in the morning and at about ten

weeping, that he was sought after by the Securitate. After he give the Elder an account of his situation and gave him a list of names for his prayers, Elder Cleopa told him: "From now on don't be afraid anymore!" And truly, from that point on, he was no longer followed.

109. One brother who came to the monastery thinking that he would be staying for two or three months went to confess to Father Cleopa. But the Elder said, with an innocent and determined voice, "Well, you've come to Uncle Costache![84] Now, you're not going to leave from here!" And that's how it was, since through the mercy of God, he remained in the monastery.

110. One brother had undertaken some ascetical work that was beyond his strength. He did not sleep on a bed, read a lot from the Psalter, and did many prostrations—not for a good cause, however, but in order to quiet the bodily passions, without cutting off the spiritual ones. Because of this he was angry, he would judge, condemn and have temptations.

Once he went to Father Cleopa to get a blessing. The Elder, seeing the brother approaching him, pointed to a text written in large font, placed under the icons, and said, "Look at what's written here, 'Good is not good when it is not done well.' I had them write this there!"

Then the brother, recognizing that the Elder had said that after being illumined by the Holy Spirit, realized that he had started down a wrong path.

---

o'clock, he left for the mountains. He would come down at noon and ate a little, then he would rest. After that he would do his evening rule of prayer and leave again for a quiet place. Towards the evening, he would come back for dinner, then spoke with his disciples on the verandah. Very rarely did he receive faithful here, as this was his cell for a solitary retreat. It was here that he put together his last books of spiritual teachings.
[84] Father Cleopa's civil name was Constantine and Costache is a diminutive of that name. Here, he was referring to himself before taking the monastic veil *(t.n.)*.

The apiary house for the Sihăstria Monastery.

111. One brother asked the Elder: "Father Cleopa, what should I think about when I read the Psalter?"

"You should think that you are sinful."

112. One hieromonk went for the first time to Father Cleopa to ask for spiritual guidance. "Bless me, Reverend Father Cleopa!" The Elder looked at him and said, "Who is this priest?" After Father Cleopa counseled him, the hieromonk withdrew amazed that, without having met him, the Elder knew that he was a priest.

113. One Father from the monastery told us:

"Coming frequently to the monastery and listening to Father Cleopa, I thought I should take up Christ's yoke, too. But I wasn't decided. Then I thought about asking him, since he was the one who prompted my zeal for Christ. 'Whatever he tells me, that's what I'll do!'

"When I asked him, Father Cleopa, seemingly knowing my heart, said to me, 'Don't come! Stay in the world and do your mission!' At that time, I was more zealous and was distributing holy books.

"After about two years, when my heart was totally inclined towards monasticism, I decided to go to the monastery, but with a certain fear, thinking about the Elder's words. And praying to God, I came to him and declared, 'Father, I want to come to the monastery!' 'Come!' Father Cleopa said, filling me with joy."

114. A few months before the Elder's death, a hierarch from Greece came and did not leave the Elder alone until he agreed to give him his prayer rope. Many years before, Elder Cleopa, inspired by the Holy Spirit, had told him that in advance that he would become a hierarch.

115. One brother told the Elder: "Father, at the monastery, there is a lot of work and not enough time for church. What should I do?"

"Brother, when one's hands are working, the mind should be praying, saying, "Lord Jesus…" permanently!

Father Cleopa together with the Greek bishop whom he foresaw would become a hierarch.

116. Another brother asked Elder Cleopa, "How many times should I say, 'Lord Jesus…' in a day? And the Elder replied, "One million times!"

117. One disciple, seeing Elder Cleopa sitting on the verandah, drew near to him, kissed his hand, and asked for a blessing. But he did not reveal that he was being attacked greatly in his heart by evil thoughts. The Elder, looking at his face, said, "Brother, go to your spiritual father, make a clean confession and ask for a canon that can deliver you from the unclean thoughts that control you."

118. When he was speaking with people, Father Cleopa often told them, "The angels of God brought you to the holy monasteries, my dear children! You don't see them, but each one of you has his guardian angel near him." And the Elder looked gently at the people, as if he had seen their angels.

119. Once a faithful man came to the Elder with one of his relatives that had been drawn into the sect of the Jehovah's Witnesses. The faithful person had tried, through many discussions and arguments, to bring him back to the right faith. Even though the sectarian had been proven wrong by various questions, he wouldn't acknowledge that he had strayed. Finally, the faithful man convinced him to go to Elder Cleopa.

At Elder Cleopa's cell there were a lot of people, as usual. The Elder was giving a sermon on the topic "How the devil deceives man." Awaiting the sermon to end and finding a fitting moment, the faithful man wanted to challenge the Elder to discuss with the sectarian, so that he could be clarified concerning the right faith.

But at that moment, he saw that his friend's face was completely transformed. His face was now exceedingly cheerful, radiating an indescribable joy. Listening to Father Cleopa's homily, he had been profoundly moved in his heart so that he had no more questions. When the faithful man wanted to begin a discussion with the Elder, the sectarian said, "I no longer have any questions. I have never seen such a person in my life!"

This is one of the many cases when Elder Cleopa's simple presence was sufficient to change a man's heart. Then the Elder clarified the one who had strayed, and the latter became a good Christian.

120. A faithful woman from an intellectual family in Piatra Neamţ came to Elder Cleopa many times, complaining of her husband's lack of faith. He was a professor of physics who had declared himself a complete atheist. At Elder Cleopa's proposal, the woman succeeded in convincing her husband to come to the Elder even though the professor said, "I have nothing to speak with a priest![85] No one can convince me of anything!"

When they arrived at Sihăstria, Father Cleopa was speaking to the people. After he finished speaking with the faithful, the Elder, tired after a full day, did not spare himself at all. He stayed with the professor, reciting to him astronomical information about interstellar distances, physics, natural laws, the laws of creation, and many other things.

At the end of the discussion, which had extended until midnight, the professor pulled out a little notepad and wrote, "Father, in all the schools where I studied, I have never heard such things! How do you know so much?" "Is there anyone who's stopping me from knowing?" asked Father Cleopa. In the end, the professor asked to confess.

---

[85] The professor used the word "popa," a derogatory term for priest *(t.n.)*.

After a while, his wife came joyfully to Sihăstria, saying, "Father Cleopa, since my husband had that discussion with you, he has completely changed. He goes to church; he prays and tries to convince others of God's existence!"

121. In general, Father Cleopa was not in favor of extreme asceticism, even though he practiced great asceticism. But the saints are always harsh with themselves and full of love towards others.

He used to say that the forest is not frightened of the one who takes a lot of wood all at once and overloads the wagon. It knows that the wagon will break down farther on, since it is overloaded. Instead, the forest is frightened of the one who takes a piece of wood, a small load. The forest is afraid of such a one because it knows that little by little, he will cut the whole forest down.

122. Once a novice came to visit the Elder after only a few months in the monastery, saying, "Father, I have great spite for the devils. Let me read Saint Basil the Great's Exorcisms!" Father Cleopa said to him, "You, buddy?! Woe is you! You have spite for the devils? You should see how much spite they have for you! Get out of here, don't do such a thing… Hear this, he joined the monastery the other day and wants to curse the devils and read Saint Basil the Great's Exorcisms. Great hero!"

123. Once a Starets from a large Russian monastery came to ask Father Cleopa for advice. After he told the Elder that they didn't have much time for prayer and that they scatter their efforts greatly, he asked, being determined to do as the Elder said, "What should I do, Father Cleopa? Limit works and labor to the minimum?" The Elder answered, "Follow the Royal Path!" That is, without exaggeration, neither to one side nor to the other. Everything should be with good discernment.

124. Elder Cleopa said, "We should have the conviction that we err toward God in every moment. Without this humility in the heart, we cannot be saved"

125. To a group of seminar students, the Elder said, "When you become priests, you can give a canon to people to do alms. But not to those who are rich. They have money in their pockets galore, they come and put a stack of money on the table and say, 'Done! I am saved.' But the Kingdom of Heaven cannot be purchased with money!

"Have them fast, do prostrations and keep vigils… Because then they strain themselves, and they have a reward from God. Have the poorer ones give alms. They have to strain themselves to find money, and so they have a reward from God."

126. Elder Cleopa, when he spoke and gave advice, always remembered the Elders whom he had known, saying, "Father Ioanichie Moroi said that… Father Paisie Olaru used to say… Father Vichentie Mălău said…" For the Christ-loving Elders always bore great spiritual wisdom.

127. Elder Cleopa, when he was still brother Constantin, spent many years in obedience tending Sihăstria's sheep. His sister, Ecaterina, who lived in obedience in the community of Agapia Monastery, visited him sometimes. Always seeing him with the sheep, she told him, "Well, brother, are you always with the sheep, always with the sheep? Ask for obedience at the Church! You were tending sheep at home, you're tending sheep here, too!" And brother Constantin, like a true man of obedience, answered her, "Get that kind of talk away from me!"

128. While still with the sheep, Father Cleopa met many hermit monks and nuns in the forests around Sihăstria and he brought food from the pen to many of them. One nun, Cleomida, the daughter of a minister in the Romanian government, asked brother Constantine once, "Tell me, brother Constantin, have you memorized the Psalter yet?" "I have only learned about 40 psalms," he answered. "Learn it all by heart, because that is what is required of a monk!"

129. From 1930 to 1944, a chanter named Neculai Dumitriu lived in the village of Borleşti, Neamţ. He was faithful and pious and came often to Sihăstria Monastery.

In 1934, he got sick and died. But when they were taking him to the cemetery, he rose from the dead and lived many more years. When he would come to the monastery, he would recount with tears how he witnessed the torments of hell and those burning in flames.

When he chanted at the stand, all the people wept. Countless people were helped by him during his life. He was asked once, "Why do all the people weep when you chant?" He answered, "When you chant from the heart, it reaches the heart!"

When Father Cleopa was young, and had joined the monastery for a few months only, chanter Neculai told the other monks, "You're laughing at him, but you should know Father Cleopa will be your Starets!"

This prophecy was fulfilled in 1945.

Chanter Niculai Dumitriu.

130. While Elder Cleopa was a Starets at Sihăstria, it happened that the shepherds lost the sheep. They looked for them for a while, but did not find them and were afraid to tell the Starets. In the end, they had no other option but to go to Elder Cleopa. He listened to them and then took them to the church, where they all got on their knees before the icon of the Mother of God and began to pray. After they prayed, the Elder told them, "Come on, let's go together towards Sihla and Coroi's Gorge!"

On the way, they took many stops, praying to discover the sheep. Finally, with the help of God and of the Theotokos, they reached a small clearing where they found the sheep, which were peacefully resting. Then Father Cleopa said, "We have great joy that we have found the sheep, but a thousand times more that God guided us. Listen to what I say, don't begin anything in life without praying to God and to the Theotokos!" Heading back with the sheep towards the valley, they made just as many stops as when they came, thanking God for all His help.

131. When he came as Starets to Slatina, Father Cleopa began by visiting the monastery. The first time he was brought to the chancellery, but he asked to continue farther. So, he passed through many cells which he blessed until he arrived at a more secluded storage room where carpentry and building tools and materials were kept. The Elder stopped here joyfully and said, "This will be my cell!"

The brothers, who were joyous that God sent them a Starets for the salvation of their souls, decided to clean up the room, but the Elder stopped them saying, "Brothers, I don't need help, I will do everything necessary with my own hands!" And he began to work. For furniture, he put a table and a bed with simple sheets on which he laid out his sheepskin coat. He also kept his books and the letters he received from throughout the country on the bed.

Father Cleopa together with his beloved disciple, Protosyngel Varsanufie, who followed him for nearly half a century.

132. Father Cleopa remained for many years in the wilderness with his disciple, Protosyngel Varsanufie, who had come to the monastery by the Elder's advice and prayer. And here's how he met Father Cleopa.

He was married and was working in the forest. One day his cant hook was stolen; being poor, he had no other and was not able to work.

Varsanufie came to Sihăstria to pay for a prayer request so that the thief would be found. Then, Father Cleopa told to him spiritually edifying words, which made him forget about the cant hook and yearn for the monastic life instead.

He told Father Cleopa his thoughts, and the Elder said he could only come to the monastery if he could live in abstinence with his wife for a year, otherwise he could not come. Father Varsanufie and his wife decided to do as the Elder advised.

He had great temptations from the devil not to serve Christ but to remain at home. One night the evil one came to them in

The spiritual teacher with his disciple.

the form of an ugly man, black and hairless, and he roared so wildly that the house shook and the windows cracked, saying, "You wretches, what are you doing to me!" Then the demon disappeared. After a year, they both left for the monastery, the husband for Sihăstria, and the wife for Agapia Veche.

133. In 1953, Father Varsanufie was tonsured into monasticism and in 1956 he was ordained a hierodeacon and a priest in Sihăstria Monastery. He was one of Father Cleopa's most faithful disciples.

In 1997, when old Varsanufie was ill on his deathbed, Elder Cleopa began to read the prayers for the departure of the soul. While the Elder was reading the prayers, Father Varsanufie peacefully gave up his soul into the hands of Christ.

134. One Saturday morning, in 1992-1993, around 8 or 9 a.m., after Father Cleopa finished his prayer rule, seeing there were no faithful at his cell, he called out to Varsanufie, who was now his spiritual father, in a loud voice, "Varsanufie, bless me to go to the apiary!" "No, because people will come, looking for you here," Father Varsanufie said. "Varsanufie, bless me to go to the apiary," Father Cleopa said once more in a louder voice." "No, because people will be asking for you," came Father Varsanufie's answer.

Father Cleopa did not say anything more, but he slowly left for the apiary. When he arrived, he found the apiary locked. The Elder had the key in his pocket. He tried to open the door but did not succeed. Then he began to knock from door to door and to call out. Nothing. Everyone had left for the church. He tried again to open the door but to no avail.

It was a bit chilly outside and his hands began to freeze, so he thought about going back. When he arrived, he went to Father Varsanufie, made a prostration and said to him, "Father Varsanufie, bless and forgive me!" To which he answered, "May the Lord forgive you, and don't do it again!" A little later you could hear Father Cleopa saying in his cell, "Well, well, look what gift Father Varsanufie has! I couldn't get into the apiary without his blessing!"

135. Birds comforted Father Cleopa greatly. He often spoke of the "lads of the woods," the owl, the pelican and other birds, even showing us how they sing and what their voice was like, rejoicing our hearts.

The Elder told us, "What great joy I had when I received Holy Communion the first time in the wilderness, when a flock of birds came and sang to me so beautifully…!" The Elder fed the birds of the sky with love, when he could.

And this love was never interrupted. Two fathers told us how a few years before the end of Father Cleopa's life, after the Elder took communion in the Church, while he was heading back to his cell, a flock of small birds came chirping and landed on his shoulders, head and arms, and pecked his beard and cassock without, however, touching the disciples.

Then they flew into a tree and began to sing. Then the Elder uttered, sighing, "How much I would like to live again with the birds in the forest!"

136. The Elder said, "Once I was arrested by the Securitate at Slatina Monastery and then brought to Fălticeni. I was beaten there and thrown into a cellar where a few hundred bulbs were lit. Everyone who went in there came out almost mad. I was taken in there to lose my mind. I couldn't see with my eyes and I couldn't bear the heat. Then I lowered my mind into my heart with the Jesus Prayer. After an hour they pulled me out and all of them were amazed that I could still talk and walk without anyone holding me."

137. Father Cleopa would often remind us of sins that spring from self-love and urge all to repentance, saying, "Self-love is the spring and root of all evil and of all sin! Self-love is the irrational love of the body and it is the most grievous and subtle of all the passions that enslave human nature."

"From self-love are born pride, conceit, haughtiness, hatred, jealousy, spite, envy, cruelty, duplicity, rivalry, remembering wrong-doings, desiring vengeance, gluttony and many others. Also, from self-love are born self-pity, self-preservation, self-justification, self-satisfaction, self-praise, self-glorification, self-pleasure, thinking highly of oneself, and all of the known and unknown sins." Sometimes the Elder would say by heart hundreds and hundreds of sins that spring from self-love.

138. You could not grow weary of listening to Father Cleopa. Whatever he said was interesting. He would talk about his childhood, about life in the monastery, how he had been persecuted and arrested, fled to the woods, then about how he was in service to the people, about his pilgrimages to Jerusalem

and to Mount Athos, and many other little stories. Often those who listened to him wept, and sometimes the Elder wept, too. Everyone was moved spiritually, not only because of what he said but because of God's gift that was inside him; his simple presence—through the work of the Grace of the Holy Spirit of which the Elder was full—changed the hearts of people.

139. When the Elder spoke, he spoke by the inspiration of the Holy Spirit. Once, when the hall was full of faithful, the Elder began to say something disconnected from what had been discussed up until then, something which seemed not to interest anyone. But at the end a lady, who had been staying in the back, came forward weeping and said to him: "Forgive me, Father, I am a sinner!" The Elder had been speaking to that woman.

140. His cell attendant bore witness about Elder Cleopa: "I think that Father Cleopa was clairvoyant. Since he told me many things while he was alive that I did not believe, but they came to pass just how the Elder said. He saw my heart and would tell me what was good for me. At the time, I didn't understand him. But it would have been better to have been obedient with greater attention. Yet, he loved me and gave me what was good for my salvation. I am certain that Father Cleopa was a saint! I feel his help. I feel that he is with me! Remembering the Elder gives me peace, quiet, joy, and hope that he is praying for me!"

141. One of his disciples said: "Father Cleopa always spoke for the fortification of the soul. No idle word could be found in his mouth. He knew how to multiply this talent. On the days there were no pilgrims, he would take his prayer rope and go to the mountains. Many times, I saw him under a tree, kneeling, or on a stump completely absorbed in prayer. I had to yell several times for him to hear me. If I brought him news that a group of people had come, at first he seemed disappointed because he lost his peace, but being overcome with love and the faith of those who came, he received them and spoke to them, strengthening their faith and comforting them in their disappointments and troubles. Then again, he would withdraw, praying for them that the Good God would give them a 'corner of heaven.' He would also say, 'If I had a big knapsack, I would put you all in it and take you all to heaven.'"

142. In the last years of his life, the Elder had moments of great fatigue to the extent that he could no longer receive people. So, he would say to his disciple, "Close the door twice and don't bother me even if the Emperor of Japan comes!" But while the Elder would not have gotten up for the Emperor of Japan, for the love of the Emperor Christ and of the faithful, he would always get up when he was called and would comfort the people, giving teachings and blessings to them all.

143. Father Cleopa also told this story:

When I was in Iași for an operation, they had to do a urography on my kidneys. It was Great Lent. They did a medical test on me, but it failed to yield a clear result. Then a doctor came to me and said,

"Father, in order to have a clear result of how your kindeys function, from the urography, you must eat three eggs!"

"Listen, lady. Even if you give me mountains of gold, as high as the distance from Nicolina to Copou,[86] I won't eat three eggs for you during Great Lent!"

"Look, that's why you monastics come to the hospital, and that is why you die!"

""Look, that's why you come to the hospital, and that's why you're dying!"

---

[86] There are about five miles between the Nicolina district and the Copou district *(t.n.)*.

"So, what if I'm dying? Is it some king who's dying? Old Rot Man is! What? Am I the only one who's dying? Doesn't everyone die?"

"And why won't you eat eggs?"

"I don't believe in eggs!"

"What do you believe in, then?"

"I believe in the Father, in the Son, and in the Holy Spirit!"

She left and told the director of the hospital about me. "We have a Father who won't eat eggs for the test!"

But the director knew me and told the doctor, "Well, do you know who this Father is? It is Father Cleopa! He lived nearly 10 years in the wilderness on one potato a day and some weeds…"

When she heard this, she came to me in the hospital room with fasting food that she herself prepared and asked for forgiveness. and then I went again for the test.

She did the urography test without eggs. Then she came with the image after the investigation, saying,

"Look, Father, how beautiful it came out!"

"Well, lady, did you get it without three eggs?"

Everyone laughed. The left kidney was visibly swollen, but the right one was normal.

"Do you see it came out without the eggs?"

"Forgive us, Father! We haven't seen such a thing since we've been here!"

When he was discharged, the hospital's guardian told me, "Father Cleopa, if you had stayed a little longer in the hospital, I would have finished building my house with what I received from the visitors who came to you!"[87]

---

[87] In Romania, the hospitals often do not have long "official" visiting hours, but it used to be that if you slipped some cash to the guardian, he or she would let you in. Here, the guardian is referring precisely to the money that he received by letting people in to go and visit Elder Cleopa *(t.n.)*.

144. Father Cleopa often talked about this time of his life:

"After the operation they brought me to the recovery room. I slept on a folding chair there for three days and three nights. When I woke up, they said,

"Father, did you know that you slept for three days and three nights and you kept talking the whole time?"

"I had no idea! What did I say?"

Father Cleopa in 1997, after his operation in the courtyard of the Holy Three Hierarchs Monastery, Iași.

"Father, do you know how many sermons we recorded? Look here at what we recorded!"

They showed me whole cassettes. There were sermons which I had given 30 or 40 years before. Yet I didn't know anything!"

145. During the time the Elder spent in Parhon Hospital in Iași, he amazed everyone. Even the doctors had made room in their agenda to go and listen to Father Cleopa.

Many people, hearing that the Elder had been admitted in the hospital, came and brought him all kinds of food. He called the nurses to take what he received to the kitchen and to the other patients. Upon his departure from the hospital the doctors told him, "Father, as long as you stayed in our hospital you helped us a lot with supplies. What you received here sufficed for all the ill people!"

146. From 1996 on, he endured great pain for two years in his right kidney which no longer functioned. From the beginning of the illness, he did not want to go to the doctor and did not take any medicine. Then, with great difficulty, he went to the doctors in Iaşi, out of obedience to his Eminence Metropolitan Daniel and to the Starets. But it was hard for him to accept pills or to have injections.

147. Likewise, the Elder had a weakened heart, to the point that the doctors told him to only speak to people for one hour at most per day. But Elder Cleopa could not keep the advice since hundreds of people came to his cell from all over the country and wanted to hear him and to rejoice in the Elder's presence. And the reverend Elder spoke to them for hours on end. At night, many times he could not even sleep, breathing with difficulty and groaning because of fatigue.

Elder Cleopa did not forget what the Holy Fathers say, that joy comes from sacrifice. And the All-Good God, seeing the love of His pleasing son, Cleopa, comforted him here with heavenly joy, and after his repose He hosted him in the heavenly dwellings, where there is eternal joy which, *eye has not seen and ear has not heard nor have entered into the heart of man.*

148. The Elder had the divine gift of spiritual vision. Out of the multitude of people who came to him, the Elder knew through the Holy Spirit which ones had good deeds, even if they had not spoken a word, and he would look at them with special joy and bless them.

149. Once a tour bus of faithful people came from Serbia. After the Elder spoke with them for about 30 minutes, they began to ask questions regarding their pains and troubles. Among them were a few ill people and they began to ask him,

"Father, I have been sick for so many years. I have gone to doctors, what else should I do?"

"Go to the doctor and see what you have. Get an operation," the Elder said.

"Father, I have a daughter at home, sick for a few years. I have troubles with her. What should I do? Should I go to the doctor with her or not?"

"Go to the doctor," the Elder answered.

"Father, I am sick, too. What should I do?"

"You should do a Holy Unction!"

"Shouldn't I go to the doctor?"

"No, no! You go to Holy Unction!"

Then someone else said to him,

"Father, I am sick, too. What should I do?"

"Go to the doctor and see what you have."

That would happen time and time again. For each one, he had a special answer, fitting to their problems.

150. An ascetic brother came to the Elder once, saying: "Father, will you bless me to eat once a day after sunset?" "You, brother?" said the Elder. "Can't you see how skinny you are? Eat twice a day and may heaven consume you!"

151. Having been asked by the brothers how he spent his time in the wilderness and what he ate, Elder Cleopa told them, "Learn how to fast! I ate one potato a day, but there will come a time when you will be glad to have one potato per week, if you're going to have even that!"

152. Two women possessed by the devil came to Father Cleopa and he blessed them saying, "After three Holy Unction services you will be healed." And that is how it was by the mercy of God.

153. Just a little before Father Cleopa's departure to the Lord, two Christian ladies from Poiana Teiului commune came to receive a blessing. In response to their request for guidance, the Elder told them, "I am going to the Lord now, but difficult times await you!"

154. Father Cleopa knew beforehand of the end that awaited him and spoke of it in parables. Once he said, "Well, what a large and beautiful cross I will have at my head!" In the days just before Father Cleopa's death, the large cross was finished, which now stands in the middle of the monastery's cemetery. The Elder's grave is found at its feet. Another time, even though the cross had not been started yet, the Elder revealed what would be written on it. But no one at the time knew what he was speaking of.

155. One of Father Cleopa's disciples said about him, "Much could be said about our reverend Father Cleopa. But the greatest thing is that the holy Elder had God in his heart! He lived in God and God lived in him!"

156. Before Father Cleopa's death one brother found an apple tree in the monastery whose fruit had a unique flavor. That is why he named it "the apple from the garden of heaven." He wanted to bring some to Father Cleopa, but he was embarrassed. Yet, the Elder knew his thoughts and told him, "Go and bring some now, because next year you won't be able to bring for me."

157. A faithful woman who had great esteem for Elder Cleopa and who often came to visit him told us the following, "I was with Father Cleopa two months before his end. When I arrived at his cell, it was as if Father Cleopa was waiting for me. He received me with great love, to the point that I was amazed at how much attention he gave me, a sinner. He invited me inside and told me to sit on a chair. I did not want to sit before him and I got on my knees and kissed his shoes.

"After that I told him about my troubles and he told me what to do, and at the end he said, 'We're not going to see each other again after this day. We'll see each other in heaven!' And I said, 'But I'll still come by, how can it be that we won't see each other? And then, me, going to heaven? I'm a sinner.' But the Elder told me, 'Yes, to heaven! And even if you come again here, we won't see each other any more.'"

"Then I left and I completely forgot what Father Cleopa had said until I found out about the holy Elder's death."

158. A faithful woman from Constanţa came to visit Sihăstria one month before Father Cleopa departed to the Lord. This woman used to come frequently to the Elder. Later, she told us the following, "On October 29, 1998, I came to Father Cleopa's cell to seek counsel and he told me, 'Sister, when you come again to Sihăstria, go up there to the cross in the cemetery and tell me everything you have to say, and if God permits it, I'll hear you and help you.'"

159. On November 3, 1998, Father Cleopa told his disciples, "My days can be counted on your fingers! Soon you will chant Memory Eternal for me! Please commemorate me in your holy prayers!"

160. Father Father Cleopa's disciple told us these things, too: "On Thursday towards Friday, and Friday night towards Saturday, a few days before he was to go to the Lord, I slept in the same cell with the Elder. He was preparing for Holy Communion. I was amazed at his asceticism. He barely slept all night long, and he strove to read the prayers but could not since he was exhausted and weak. He prayed with his mind and his hand worked the prayer rope, but he could not keep his eyes open to read the prayers in the book. He slept a bit, then again would awaken and strive to pray!"

Part Five

Further Sayings and Spiritual Advice

1. The greatest wisdom for man is the fear of God, fear of death, and to have "Lord Jesus…" in mind.

2. We should have patience until death time, not just until spring time! May heaven consume you! As I see you all here, may I see you all like this in heaven!

3. A spiritual father strengthens souls with his words, writes with his hand, and counsels with deeds and way of living.

4. The core of a monastery is its spiritual fathers.

The great Spiritual Father, Archimandrite Cleopa Ilie.

5. Reading and watchfulness of mind keep you close to God.

6. We should have this conviction, that there is no moment when we are not erring before God and for this reason, there is no moment when we have no need of Him.

7. Prayer strengthens faith.

8. In all things, humble yourself.

9. It is better to give a little less and then to be sorry that you did not give more. Two virtues meet here: alms and humility.

10. A full stomach does not help to know God.

11. Read any useful counsel, but do not become proud.

12. One brother asked Father Cleopa, "Father, it seems that I am on vacation in the monastery! What should I ask for in prayer?"

"I have nothing. I am nothing. I can do nothing. That's what you should say," Father Cleopa answered.

13. From the sheep and the apiary, if you give alms, you see how you'll get prosperity.

14. Filling up the stomach puts on hold the working of a refined mind.

15. One Father told a brother, "Eat more so that you can work!" But Father Cleopa did not agree to this.

16. Humility is salvation's gate.

17. A Christian man asked Father Cleopa if he would be saved. The reverend Elder answered him, "Yes, you will be saved, but don't do what the world does."

18. Thoughts will battle you until death. I am now nearly 90 years old and I cannot escape thoughts.

19. One brother asked Elder Cleopa if it is better to stay in the monastery or to return to the world. The Elder answered him, "Stay here, don't go back to the world. It is Sodom and Gomorrah there!"

20. If you take care of the Church, God takes care of you!

21. Let us have a watchful mind so that we do not sin in thought, with the mind or with the imagination.

22. Sometimes, when the people would press and push around him, the Elder would say, "Hey, don't kill the old man!"

23. One brother who was troubled asked Father Cleopa what to do. And the reverend Father told him, "Go to the church, and when you can't go to the church, pray in your cell."

"Father, how about only staying in my cell?"

"No, because you can't do what the Church does."

24. When I was a brother in the monastery, the Elders had me read from the Egyptian *Paterikon*. One of them said, "Come, read again from Abba Arsenius." And it said there that Abba Arsenius only slept one hour a night. "Woe unto us," the old Fathers said, "That's a monk, not us!"

25. Once the Elder was in the cemetery and he said to one of the brothers, "Well, boys, you are as tall as fir-trees, but you could also fall like fir-trees in a storm, because you don't thrust your roots into the Holy Scriptures and in the lives of the Holy Fathers, who are like a book for us."

26. Elder Cleopa also said, "The Holy Fathers say not to condemn and even if you see something, not to believe it; but if you believe without having seen, you have erred before God all the more."

27. One brother asked the Elder,

"What should I do when I condemn others? It seems to me that a certain brother does not do obedience, another one doesn't come on time to help me, and I complain and condemn."

"Death, death, death!"

28. The Elder urged everyone to forgive and make peace. But sometimes he spoke of Adam's fall.

"Adam, why did you err?" God asked Adam.

"The woman you gave me urged me to!"

"Why did you do that?" God asked the woman.

"The serpent tricked me and I ate."

"Not one of them said, 'Forgive me.' If they had, God would have forgiven them both. See what not asking forgiveness when we err means?"

29. Temptations from the devil are much worse than those from people.

30. Measure makes man a man.

31. Sometimes he told the faithful that the devil deceives us the most through delaying repentance. So, he says everything is good and true, "but let it be, don't repent now, later, tomorrow, next year, in your old age…" And that's how the devil wins over most people.

32. Once a brother came back tired from his obedience and the Elder told him, "Say 'Our Father' once and go to bed. Then, after you rest, do your prayer rule."

33. A young hieromonk went to Father Cleopa and asked, "Father, who should I receive at holy confession?" And the reverend Elder said, "Receive everyone with love. The young, the old, the sick, and the monastics. Don't push anyone away."

34. Father Cleopa said to a priest, "Well, Father, you read Saint John Chrysostom's Exorcisms, but if you read them without fasting and prayer, the devil will slam you and the one you are praying for."

35. Man, doing God's will, becomes His son by grace. According to essence, only One is the Son of God, our Lord Jesus Christ.

36. A doubtful man is unstable in everything he does.

37. Sometimes, when Elder Cleopa was tired, he told his disciples, "I am going to sleep at least till tomorrow morning!" But after two or three hours the Elder would wake up for prayer, urged by the Holy Spirit.

Under a hornbeam tree, where he often spoke to the faithful.

38. Elder Cleopa insisted very much on blessings. For example, when he was in the apiary and had to speak to the faithful or had other work to do, he would say, "Your blessing and forgive me, Father Marcu, because I am going to speak to the faithful!" "May the Lord bless you!" Father Marcu would answer and Elder Cleopa would leave immediately.

39. When you cannot do something, say you cannot.

40. When you are ill, get behind the illness.

41. When man repents, God wants to be a liar rather than to be unmerciful.

42. Toiling the body shortens the years of repentance.

43. We should bring a pure sacrifice to God, as the Holy Fathers say.

44. The homes of the ones who bring gifts from their own work to churches and monasteries are blessed.

45. One brother said to Elder Cleopa, "I lifted up my hands, Father, being alone, in order to pray with raised hands." And the Elder told him, "Beware, the devil might raise you up even when he slams you…"

46. Another brother was attempting to avoid ever getting angry, to have no vainglory, to remember death etc. But Elder Cleopa told him, "When you see a young one rising to heaven, pull him down by one of his legs."

47. The Elder would say to the faithful, "Pray for at least one hour in the morning and one hour in the evening. Do not skip Morning Prayers and the Annunciation Akathist and in the evening the Paraklesis of the Theotokos and the Evening Prayers."

48. Once Father Cleopa said, "Don't be afraid, brother, because no one leaves this world without paying his debts."

49. Another time he advised a brother, "Do not spend time in the place where you erred against the Lord."

50. One day a disciple came to Elder Cleopa and said, "Father, can I hit myself and slap myself when I have unclean thoughts?"

"If someone hits you seven times a day, endure it."

"But if I hit myself?"

"This thought is from the devil. Be ready to receive!"

51. Elder Cleopa would say, "Don't turn too widely when you're ploughing, 'cause much soil won't be good for sowing." In other words, we should do everything with measure.

52. A faithful woman from Galați County asked for some counsel of spiritual benefit from Elder Cleopa, and he answered, "I have read your letter and I advise you that, if you have a mind to join the monastery, do so. Do not look back like Lot's wife who was lost. It is good to also take the girl with you. May the good Lord lead you to heaven!"

53. A Christian asked Father Cleopa, "Father, my wife committed suicide while she was alone in her room. I found her dead. Can I commemorate her with the dead in the Church?"

Then the Elder said categorically, "No! We are not permitted to commemorate anyone who committed suicide, even if they are close relatives. Everything remains to the mercy of God. Only those who were psychologically ill can be commemorated during services."

54. A woman who had given birth to four children and had aborted another four came to Elder Cleopa and told him her pain. And the Elder said to her, "Sister, you built four churches and you demolished four and you've got down to zero! But repent and God will forgive you."

55. Two young people got married and had children, without knowing that they were blood relatives. Their spiritual father advised them to confess to a Hierarch and to follow his advice. Meanwhile the husband was encouraged to ask for Archimandrite Cleopa Ilie's advice too, whom he did not know yet.

When he went to see him, he couldn't get close to him, since Elder Cleopa was surrounded by many faithful. So, he waited his turn. All at once, the Elder called him and said, "Antonie, come over here!" He thought the Elder was calling someone else and did not go. After a short while he called him again, "Antonie, come over here!" But, not knowing that he was being called, again he did not go. So, the Elder, looking at him, made a sign with his finger and said to him, "You, over there, Antonie, come to me!"

Overcome with fear, Antonie said to himself, "How can this Father know me, when he's never seen me?" Then, having gone to the Elder, the latter consulted with him for a long time and let him go in peace.

56. A faithful woman from Greece heard that her problems could only be resolved by Elder Cleopa. So, she went to the Elder and told him that her daughter wanted to have a child. After 40 days her wish was fulfilled.

57. One woman told Elder Cleopa that her husband was beating her. He asked her what his reason was. Then she said that her husband was working in the forest and when he was coming home, he did not find any food ready. And the Elder said to her, "But do you know what working in the forest is like? Wait for him with food and a glass of wine!"

58. Once a woman came to Father Cleopa saying that her daughter had got pregnant, being unmarried. And the Elder told her, "Let her give birth, and God will arrange a man for her!" After a little while she was married and gave glory to God.

59. Father Cleopa told a future mother, "Don't be afraid, whatever might happen, for God is with you. And if a mother dies during childbirth and is a good Christian, she passes into the ranks of the martyrs."

60. The Elder also said that pregnant women have to confess and receive communion before giving birth.

61. One young family that had children and wanted to raise them according to God's will wanted to stop having children. Elder Cleopa told them, "Each one should stay in their own place. Sleep in separate rooms and live in purity. You won't be the first, nor the last. And if it happens that you make a mistake, start it all over again from the beginning, until you succeed."

62. A faithful woman left home with her mother against her husband's will and took the car to go to the memorial service of a relative. Returning home late, they first passed by Elder Cleopa's cell and asked him to pray for her so she would not have any problems with her husband upon her arrival at home. Elder Cleopa answered her peacefully, "Go in peace, without fear, since when you arrive home, you'll find him on his knees before the icons and he won't ever say anything to you." Truly, at home she found her husband exactly as Father Cleopa had foreseen.

Another time he told her, "Don't ever be afraid of anyone or anything, just pray! God and His Mother see you and hear you!"

63. One Christian man retired and then went to the monastery where he ate only fasting food. His children became sad and brought him to Elder Cleopa in order to convince him to at least drink milk on Saturdays and Sundays, but the Elder told them, "The man wants to go to heaven and you're pulling him down!"

64. The child of a female doctor was very spoiled, but when he would be taken to Elder Cleopa, the latter's kindness and gentleness made him behave very well and listen attentively, then he would sleep with his head on the Elder's knees.

65. A mother went to ask for advice from Elder Cleopa and to share with him her pain that her only son, who graduated the university with the highest average grade, left for the monastery. The Elder admonished her saying, "It's not you who supported him throughout his school years; it's not thanks to you that he got only good grades, but thanks to God. He bore him through everything, and now if he is in a holy monastery, rejoice, don't weep, because it will be good for you too in heavens." In this way the mother was comforted and went home with peace in her soul.

66. Once a group of children came in a tour bus and Elder Cleopa blessed all of them and said gently, "Innocent children, look how innocent they are!"

67. A few years before Elder Cleopa departed for the Lord, a man from Giurgiu County came to the monastery and told us the following:

My father was very ill, to the point that he was bed-ridden. One day, when I got up, I saw my father doing work in the yard. I was very amazed and I asked him, "Father, what's with you? What happened?" Since only a miracle could have done this.

He said to me, "What can you know?"

"What, father? Tell me!"

"Last night Father Cleopa came to me from the Holy Monastery of Sihăstria, he blessed me and I became well."

I asked him, "Father, what does that Father look like?" He described him to me, and now I have come to the monastery to see what Father Cleopa looks like. And to my surprise, Father Cleopa is exactly how my father described him to me!"

68. A faithful woman told us how her father was healed by Father Cleopa's prayers.

"It was the end of the year 1995. I had been a few times to Sihăstria and I had already met Father Cleopa. My father was very sick and for about 40 years, he had been tormented by the passion of drinking. After many attempts, one day I arrived with him to Elder Cleopa. He was sitting in a clearing under a hornbeam tree with a few other Christians. We sat on a bench exactly in front of Father Cleopa, who was speaking to those present.

"All of a sudden, he stopped for a moment, looked above our heads and began to speak about the passion of drinking. It seemed like my father had become dumbfounded on the bench. Father Cleopa's talks lasted for a while, then he dismissed us and gave each of us a blessing, as he usually did. I drew close with my father and when he bowed his head, Father Cleopa took his head with both hands, made a big sign of the cross above it and told him, 'So, beloved, make a clean confession and the Mother of God will help you. May we see each other in heaven!'

"We left in peace. What happened then, I don't know. For nearly 30 years I had not seen my father make any sign of the Holy Cross, but now when we got home, he entered the living room and made three great prostrations. I looked at my mother and she looked at me, and we were amazed. Since then, my father has been delivered from the passion of drinking. He confesses and goes to church."

69. In 1997, a Christian lady from Bârlad, the mother of seven children, two of whom were in monasteries, asked Elder Cleopa for a blessing and he said to her, "Sister Ștefana, may your end be in a monastery! May you not be taken from the world at harvest time!"

Then he told them, "May Heaven consume you! You don't know how many little flowers the angels are gathering up behind you! May we see each other in a little corner of heaven!"

70. To an unmarried woman who was in doubt, Elder Cleopa declared, "You do not want to weary yourself! You don't want to climb the ladder! You're just standing there on the fourth rung! Pray more and you will come to the monastery!"

71. A Christian lady wanted to see Elder Cleopa since she had never seen him. Passing in front of his cell she made a small bow and said in her mind, "I kiss your hand, Father!" And immediately she heard in her thought the Elder's voice saying, "May God's peace be with you, daughter!" Then with her heart full of joy and peace, she moved on.

72. One Christian man from Soroca, Bessarabia, came with a group of faithful and with their priest to venerate the monasteries in Moldavia. After they venerated at the church, they all went to Father Cleopa's cell and asked him for spiritual guidance. At the end, the faithful man from Soroca told Father Cleopa that a wrongdoer had stolen his horse one month before and he had not been able to find it.

Father Cleopa encouraged him and said, "Brother, go home, no problem, and you'll find the horse in your yard!"

As soon as the man got home, he saw the horse grazing in his yard, and he gave glory to God!

73. After he finished his homilies, Father Cleopa would say, "Dear ones, I feel so sorry for you! If I had the strength, I would put you all in a sack and take you to heaven! May there always be a vigil lamp burning in your house day and night before an icon of the Theotokos!"

74. Once a group of faithful came to the Elder, and he asked, "Where are you from, dear?"

"From Bârlad."

"Well, from so far away! Do you know that since you've set your mind on coming to the monastery, your angels count your footsteps, money, and toil? With all of these, your angels will present themselves at the Final Judgment, with this money that you did not spend in a dance club, in a pub or at weddings with musicians, but gave to Christ!

"Well! If you could see your guardian angels near you as they are, you would die of joy!"

75. "Hey, tell me, folks, how many hours a day do you pray?"

Some would say five minutes, a quarter of an hour, etc.

"I feel sorry for you, dear ones. If I were to go to the Theotokos, she would ask me, 'What did you do there, monk? Did you teach people about prayer?' Since Saint John Chrysostom says that a good Christian should pray at least four hours a day. I don't tell you to pray that much, but at least one hour in the morning and one at night. I'm not scolding you; I'm giving you advice. Look here, when you get up in the morning, make three signs of the cross and say, 'Glory to you our God, glory to You, for not taking me this night, but You've awoken me!'

"Throw cold water over your eyes and begin the Morning Prayers and the Annunciation Akathist of the Theotokos, and don't let a day go by without doing that.

"Let us take the Theotokos as our assistant throughout our lives, on Judgment Day and in the afterlife. Again, in the evening, you should do the Evening Prayers and the Paraklesis to the Theotokos. And whoever can, should do the Midnight Hours! Prayer in the middle of the night is like gold before the Savior."

76. "Let's see, how you make the Sign of the Holy Cross. Do you do it correctly and does it look big? In the name of the Father on the forehead, of the Son on the chest, and of the Holy Spirit on the shoulders! This is the Cross of Christ. He was crucified on the Holy Cross, and the two thieves were tied with ropes on the lower crosses.

"Take care of the Cross of Christ! Don't do it as a small sign, since then it looks like you're playing the kobza, and you make all the devils sick with laughter and put them in a hospital!"

77. "Go to the Holy Church every Sunday, don't ever be absent. If you are absent for three Holy Days in a row from the Holy Liturgy, you take your soul directly to hell!"

78. "Do you know what you should do if you want to be wise? Go to the cemetery with a little candle and put it on your grave, on your brothers', at least once a week, on Sundays or Saturdays.

"Listen to what the divine Father John Chrysostom says, 'Go frequently to the graves, oh Christians, to the cemetery. Because if you go there often, you'll get more wisdom than all the philosophical schools of the world could teach you!'

"The cemetery brings us so much use. Because we see that what those who lie there are today, we'll be tomorrow. Don't you see that they are silent? But they always speak, 'Well, brothers! What we are today, you will be tomorrow! And what you are today, we were yesterday. Look, you are coming here. It's you who are coming to us, not us going over to you.'

"All of us are going towards eternity. If not today, it's tomorrow, or the day after, but we're going to the grave. Moment by moment. I had a clock, somewhere, where I used to live. It had an alarm that sounded like this: 'the grave, the grave, the grave—the grave, the grave, the grave, the grave—the grave, the grave the grave, the grave'... That's what its alarm was. And it always reminded me of the grave. I had a different clock, I don't know how many years later, that didn't say 'grave' but something different: 'soon-soon, soon-soon, soon-soon...' And that clock taught me that I'll be leaving soon. If you could make yourselves such a clock and keep it in your home, a clock that would say, 'the grave, the grave, the grave, the grave - the grave, the grave, the grave, the grave…', you would not need another philosopher.

"Because if we did not forget the grave, there would be great joy. We would not be afraid of the grave. Not at all. If we know that we put in our sack what we need, let's go to the grave! Because life is beyond the tomb; it is not here. Here is deception. Haven't you seen? *His days pass as a shadow.*"

79. "Make your Holy Confession pure, according to the church order! Take a little notebook, go inside a room and begin to write all your sins, since you were little. Do you know when children begin to sin? When they understand things. Then they also understand what sin is!

"We should note down everything we have done since childhood. We shouldn't expect the priest to ask us questions, but we should tell our sins. And we should go to our spiritual father when he is not so busy. Do you know what a correct confession means? It is like a second baptism. It feels like we have been born again!"

Elder Cleopa advising a group of faithful from Serbia (1998).

80. A Christian lady from Baia Mare heard about Elder Cleopa's departure to the Lord. While she was preparing to come to the funeral, her daughter said to her, "Mom, I dreamt about Father Cleopa this night, that he was going up to heaven and was clothed in white vestments!"

81. A woman named Vasilica, who was ill from an unclean spirit, came to Elder Cleopa to find ease in her pain. Once she asked him what to do about her illness, being very much tormented by demons. The Elder told her, "Sister, have patience, because you will become healthy!"

After Elder Cleopa departed to the Lord, that sick lady came to his tomb at Sihăstria and prayed in tears for God to save her from her illness. But the devils cried out in anger against her saying, "Go away from here, because this is a saint and he is burning us!"

82. Elder Cleopa said, "Any sick person who believes in Christ and has the true faith, needs to say just this, "Thank You, Lord, that You have given me suffering and scolding! Thank You Lord, that You love me and scold me!'"

83. A woman from the village of Flămânzi commune, Botoşani county, had heard about Elder Cleopa through books and from people. She had a husband who was a drunkard, and a very bad mother-in-law.

One day they both reviled her and she no longer knew what more she could do. She locked herself inside the house and began to pray to Father Cleopa, even though she had never seen him, saying in her desperation, "Father Cleopa, don't leave me! Father Cleopa, don't leave me!"

As she was lying in bed, she felt a special spiritual peace and joy. She lived this joy for about one week and peace was made in her house.

In the summer of 1999, the woman came to Sihăstria Monastery, venerating Father Cleopa's tomb in tears. She gave thanks to God for the help she received and felt the same joy and peace in her soul that she had when she was in her trial.

84. A woman from Bârlad said, "I was here many times, at the monastery, with one grandson of mine, since he was 3 ½ years old. Each time we came to Father Cleopa, he asked about my grandson, Alin, whom he loved very much. The Elder loved everyone the same, but it is not possible to say how much he overwhelmed the children with his love.

"One of these days, my grandson was wearing thin clothing since it was hot when we had left home. Father Cleopa seeing that the weather had changed and become cold, told him to go and put on something warmer. But the child said, 'Father, I don't have anything else to wear except what I have on now!'

"Then Father Cleopa called his disciple, 'Brother Ioan, fetch that thick woolen sweater and give it to this child so he doesn't catch a cold!' And the disciple gave the sweater to the child."

And so, Father Cleopa's sweater remained with the faithful people in Bârlad, his disciples, and whenever one of them is sick, has a cold or another disease, they go to Alin's grandmother in Bârlad, put Father Cleopa's sweater on for a minute or two, and feel relieved from their illness.

That is why the faithful in Bârlad say, "Just as the Holy Prophet Ilias left his coat to Elisha, so Father Cleopa Ilie has left his sweater for us to find comfort in our troubles!"

85. Many Christians have been writing to us since Elder Cleopa's departure to the Lord and they say that they feel helped by his prayers. One Christian woman wrote that one of her

relatives, being very sick, fell into despair. But by saying, "Father Cleopa, help me..." she was overcome with such peace and joy that she no longer wanted health or anything else, and she carried her cross with joy.

86. The Elder's cell attendant testifies, "Many who remember Father Cleopa obtain courage and zeal to proceed on the Lord's path. Peace, joy, and the spirit of holiness are felt by many that enter the Elder's Cell. This was felt even when the cell was empty, with no icons and nothing inside. Until not long ago, the Elder was sharing words, but now he's sharing spirit to the hearts of the faithful."

87. A few months after Elder Cleopa's translation to the heavenly realms, a Christian lady who was close to him came to Sihăstria for Holy Pascha, but did not go to the Elder's cell, thinking there was no point in going there since he had died. But while she was resting in the arhondariki[88] before the Resurrection Service, she had a dream. She was in front of Elder Cleopa's cell, thinking that he had died, and he immediately appeared at the door's threshold and said to her,

"Come inside, why don't you enter?"

"But aren't you dead, Father?" she asked.

"Don't you see that I am alive?" said the Elder.

The second day, the day of the Resurrection, the woman went to Father Cleopa's cell and venerated the Holy Icons, strongly believing that he was alive and praying for those who ask for his help.

*

---

[88] Guest house in a monastery *(t.n.)*.

Many people venerate in Father Cleopa's cell and grave, and they take earth and flowers for a blessing, affirming they feel help through the holy Elder's prayers. Thinking about the testimonies contained in this book and many others that have not been written here, we are certain that the Good God has placed him in the host of the Holy Fathers. For this reason, we, too, dare to pray saying, "Our pious Father Cleopa, who have obtained great grace from God, pray to the Savior Christ for us sinners!"

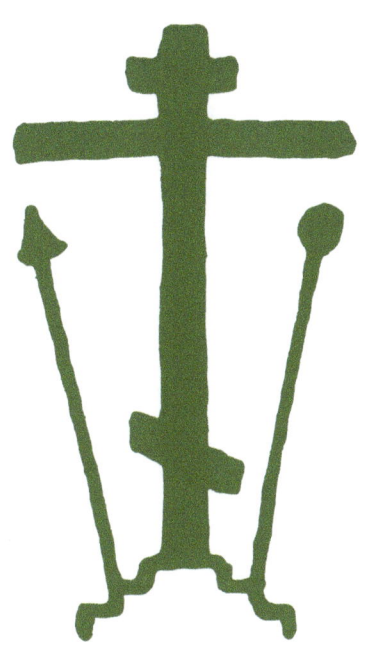

www.ingramcontent.com/pod-product-compliance
Lightning Source LLC
Chambersburg PA
CBHW051259120626
46547CB00015B/2009